AF316626

WHY BLACK WEALTH MATTERS IN WHITE AMERICA

TURNING BLACK SPENDING POWER INTO GENERATIONAL WEALTH

SOLOMON RC ALI

STAR84 MEDIA, LLC

By Solomon RC Ali

Published by Star84 Media, LLC

Visit the author's website at www.solomonrcali.com

LIBRARY OF CONGRESS CATALOGING-IN-PUBLICATION DATA

Names: Ali, Solomon RC, author. Title: Why Black Wealth Matters in White America : Turning Black Spending Power into Generational Wealth / Solomon RC Ali.

Description: Georgia : Star84 Media, [2022] | Identifiers: LCCN 2022914444 (print)

ISBN: 9798218039820 (hardcover) | ISBN: 9798218039837 (ebook)

Cover design by Tariq Bey

Contents

ACKNOWLEDGEMENTS

I would like to start off by thanking God, my creator, through whom all things are possible. He has allowed me to endure and persevere. He has been patient with me to give me understanding and allowed me the gift of wisdom.

I would like to thank my parents for the love and nurturing they have provided, through their guidance and support. Every time I have needed help throughout my life, my parents have always shown up, even when they have been disappointed in my actions.

I would also like to thank the United States military for providing me with important leadership and management skills. My time served in the military showed me how to lead, manage, and respect diverse cultures and backgrounds.

I need to acknowledge my athletic coaches who taught me to keep going one step at a time while pushing forward and sticking to the basics.

I would like to thank my family and friends for their ongoing love, support, and nurturing; especially those who listened to me when I was down and out and had trouble picking myself back up. They did their best to provide words of encouragement to keep me motivated and moving forward.

Lastly, I would like to thank my team starting with my best friend and business partner Ms. Nicole Singletary, my business associate Ms. Bethiel Tesfasillasie, and my trustee and counsel Mr. Ernest "Woody" DeLong. Thank you to my other advisors, all of whom have ridden this rocky roller coaster with me for the past four years. They have assisted me to get my story out into the right hands so that it may help develop young minds as well as old, to contribute toward people fulfilling their dreams and goals.

For every individual who has loved me and encouraged me along the way, given me a kind word or scripture that I read to encourage myself when there were no others around, to them, I say thank you and I love you.

Finally, I did not think or believe that I could write this book, even with the support and assistance of my team and others. Never had I believed that I could do such a thing and thought completing a book was an accomplishment for other people. With that being said, I need to thank myself for finding the faith and the courage to take the leap and complete this project.

Lastly, I want to give a special thank you to all of you who are reading this book. My hope is that these pages will bless your life and enrich you and your family. Just as there have been mentors along my path who empowered me to make the right decisions for my future, even when it wasn't convenient or comfortable, I hope that within these pages you find some of the mentorship, tools, and inspiration to start on your journey toward building generational wealth.

—·—

FOREWORD
LES BROWN, WORLD RENOWNED MOTIVATIONAL SPEAKER

I have a tremendous respect for those who recognize their greatness and work to hone it and share it with the world. Solomon RC Ali has been preparing his greatness for decades. From an early age, Solomon identified his adept entrepreneurial skills. He has been cultivating them ever since, and he generously presents his rare wisdom in this special book.

Indeed, Solomon RC Ali is an entrepreneur extraordinaire. He has started businesses and facilitated mergers and acquisitions, as well as major investments that have aided the progression of industries and innovation. His unique insight is needed in the times we are living in. Solomon is the right voice at the right time. The skills he shares in these pages will help equip you, the reader, with the practical and actionable skillset you need to live your dreams and take your life to the next level.

In this book, Solomon illustrates possibilities and proven methods to bring out the greatness in you, regardless of your life situation. Each chapter is designed to give you the keys to a new future. He provides, not just inspiration, but a blueprint that will help you to finance your dreams and implement effective strategies toward your financial freedom, through an achievement-driven system.

Additionally, Solomon will show you how to ignite a success mindset, sharpen your skillset, and monetize your ideas. This book is a groundbreaking read! Get ready to experience an incredible journey that will open a new realm of enrichment as you apply these outstanding principles.

Les

INTRODUCTION

The general population, otherwise known as the 99%, have a love/hate relationship with wealth. They resent those who have it but spend their lives attempting to get it for themselves, all the while self-sabotaging that effort in ways that are avoidable if they knew the rules and established the right money habits. Yes, the wealthy have rules. The reason most individuals never accumulate any substantial savings is because they do not understand the nature of money and how it works.

Unfortunately, much of this lack of understanding and lack of access to financial education comes down to systemic racism that has been passed down from generation to generation within the Black community, *my* community. Beyond that, a good portion of financial inequity comes down to destructive money habits passed down through the generations by Americans across all races and ethnicities. But make no mistake, there is an emotional pathology that has taken root among Black Americans, in particular, that has caused us to relinquish much of our collective wealth to other communities. We will unpack this Black American financial conundrum and how to correct course throughout these pages.

Somewhere along the line, many of us got confused as to what it means to be an American and to live the American Dream. The way our media has promoted glitz, glamour, hyper-consumerism, and the notion of getting what you want *now* and paying for it later has all contributed to our collective financial downfall. I am here to tell you that the American Dream is built with discipline, elbow grease, and delayed gratification. I will be dishing out a lot of tough love in these pages, but I promise you that by the time you reach the end of this book, you will *want* to change your money habits. We will work together to shift the reward centers of your brain so that you feel empowered and excited by saving money and investing in your future, and downright bored with the notion of the work/borrow/spend/debtor lifestyle you may currently be living.

You won't want to go back.

Most Black Americans, Hispanics, LatinX, Immigrant Americans, and many women throughout American history, had been shut out of the American financial system they have helped to build. Yes, that is a lot of Americans who have been denied access to the American Dream of financial independence and generational wealth. Many of us have historically had to operate on the financial fringes. That meant we couldn't accumulate wealth in large enough numbers to make significant political inroads, keep ourselves safe, and improve our own communities. But much of that is now changing. and it is time for us to change with the times we are living in. Our very survival depends upon it.

If I didn't mention you in the above list, please do not be offended or feel dismissed by my words. If you picked up this book and you have had enough of working, borrowing, spending, and working some more to pay off accumulated debt, this book is also for you.

Yes, I will be writing this book from the perspective of a Black man in America, because that is what I am and that is the point of view I have experienced since my birth. However, if read thoughtfully, these rules about money and how to accumulate wealth apply to everyone regardless of race, gender, age, and even income tier.

Let's get into it.

CHAPTER 1

—·—

BLACK CONSUMERISM: A SHADY DEAL

"There are few things more dishonorable than misleading the young." – Thomas Sowell

Wealth responds to a sound set of rules and principles. People who know the rules build wealth. Everyone else will work, borrow, spend, accumulate debt, and work some more.

To understand how I, a Black man born into a working-class family, learned the game of wealth and how to play it to my advantage as a minority in the United States of America, you need to know where I started. Until the age of twelve, I was born and raised in a section of Los Angeles, California that is better known by some as South Central LA. I spent the early part of my childhood surrounded by people who worked hard for a living, mostly on assembly lines and in factories. They struggled to make ends meet and many were what we now refer to as "working class" or "working poor." At some point, my parents started paying attention to money and knew they could do better. My grandmother owned several rental properties. As my grandmother's health deteriorated, she gave my mother her rental properties. My parents saw the value in owning rental properties. This gave them the desire of wanting more. They then exercised deferred gratification until they were able to purchase additional rental properties. This additional income was a blessing to our family.

My astute mother listened to some of the people she knew from around the neighborhood speak about pooling their money together to invest in purchasing existing businesses that yielded decent returns on investment. In order to invest some of their money into investment properties and into the business that ran those properties, we had to find creative ways to preserve what we had in order to save money. Oftentimes our furniture, as nice as it was, was covered in plastic to keep it from wearing out, and we went without some of the small things that other families took for granted. My parents were playing the long game, which for them was getting my brother and me out of the South Central district of Los Angeles.

By the time I was in middle school, my parents wanted to give me a suburban upbringing and they scraped together enough money to move us to a middle-class Los Angeles suburb called West Covina. Unfortunately, it was not my idea of Shangri La. As the only Black family in our neighborhood, I was relentlessly picked on, bullied, and scapegoated. I understood what my parents were trying to accomplish, but I also realized that there had to be more than one way to achieve the American Dream; one where people didn't make fun of your hair texture and call you a "gorilla." I just knew I wanted to get the hell out of there, get to work, and start making money.

When I look back now, I believe it was that combination of seeing my parents' disciplined sacrifice and their commitment to upward financial mobility, along with my utter disdain for being the only Black kid in my new neighborhood, that ultimately drove my relentless ambition for success. You see, I never felt completely at ease, and so complacency never had the opportunity to set into my spirit.

I went from high school right into the military. Upon earning my honorable discharge in 1986 at the age of twenty-two I returned home and began looking for a job and couldn't find one. Frustrated but not discouraged, I assessed my accumulated skills and remembered everything I had learned about maintaining investment properties under my parents' watchful eye and work ethic. I decided to go into the maintenance business, where I began cleaning residential apartments to prepare each unit for incoming tenants. I ran this business for five years and made a pretty good living at it. In 1987, at the age of twenty-three, I became a single father to my daughter, Rashell, which made life more joyous but a lot more complicated. Suddenly, I was balancing single fatherhood and a new business as I coordinated school drop-offs and pick-ups with managing the task of cleaning and maintaining apartments. It was a juggling act and a test of my time management skills, and there were last-minute emergencies and other hiccups along the way, but I continued to thrive.

In fact, business was going so well that I began to hire a staff to work under me as I continued to feverishly build my book of business and plan out my next moves.

By 1996, at the age of thirty-two, I married my wife Anne, and as we were building our life together, her mother's health began to fail. We knew that Anne's mother needed more hands-on help and expertise than we could offer her on our own, and we began to interview assisted living facilities. After many interviews, we were sorely disappointed with the level of care we had witnessed and my wife and I decided that in order to get my mother-in-law proper care, we would have to take matters into our own hands.

I took money from our maintenance business and invested it into a building which I then converted into an assisted living facility. After getting all of the proper certifications, I elected to run every aspect of the assisted living facility on my own for a while. From caring for every aspect of our residents' needs to handling the business side of things, I wanted to learn the entire business from the inside out. I worked 24/7 for those first eighteen months to ensure the quality of care we provided at our facility and to learn and adhere to industry standards. My wife came to visit and help out on weekends and eventually we onboarded a full staff. As our success grew, we then invested that money into nursing homes around the Los Angeles metropolitan area and made even more money. My engine was firing on all cylinders. Work, work, work and earn a pile of money. That's all there is to it, right? Wrong. Working for money *exclusively* is not sustainable in the long run, certainly not in the autumn of one's life, and it is not how you build long-term generational wealth.

I went broke just as fast as I got rich. I lost it all because I didn't understand money. Anyone can make money, but you've got to understand what money is, what it's not, how to use it, and how to have your money go to work for you in the long run.

I know what you are thinking. "This is the typical story of 'man makes his fortune, loses that fortune, and regains his fortune.' There are a million books about people just like you, Solomon."

You may be right, I did make a fortune. I also lost it all due to financial ignorance and then regained it. But the specific circumstances surrounding my story, what I learned, and everything I am about to teach you is your key to an exclusive club that is growing more exclusive and elusive by the minute, particularly in these times of economic volatility. As the middle class continues to shrink while the rich get richer and the poor keep getting poorer, you will develop a skillset to help circumvent this disturbing paradigm.

I will be teaching you the rules that I learned the hard way about earning, saving, investing, and leveraging your way to financial freedom. I am also going to teach you why *Black Wealth Matters in White America*, more now than ever before, and the inside information that is often shared in affluent families and exclusive social circles, that is passed down through the generations.

Before we get started, some people hold tight to a belief system that caring too much about money or gaining wealth makes them materialistic, greedy, shallow, or of less integrity.

Let's dispel this myth right up front and get it out of the way. The average American, throughout our country's history, and especially people of color, were shut out of our country's financial systems, thereby not gaining the access or opportunity to accumulate wealth. It also eclipsed our understanding of money that could have been passed down through the generations in *our* families.

Generational wealth is more than a trust fund, stock portfolio, or bank account. It is a mindset. The wealthy have a code of rules and an arsenal of inside information about money that gets passed down from parent to child. More generational wealth means more societal and political influence and less vulnerability to the ills of civil rights infringements, and other violations of your personal liberties, your safety, and your dignity. In short, wealth equals freedom and the resources to protect your God-given rights as a whole human being.

The Wealthy Have a Different Mindset

Earning a lot of money does not make you wealthy. You will never out-earn your lack of financial education or your bad money habits. It is like trying to out-exercise your lack of nutritional knowledge or your bad eating habits. It is exhausting to take two steps forward and three steps back, not to mention futile. Being wealthy is much more about your financial behaviors and your financial intelligence quotient than it is about how much income you earn. Wealth is also not an aesthetic pursuit. Driving an expensive car, buying a house you cannot afford, and wearing high-end fashion labels do not make you wealthy. In fact, for most folks who have not yet attained enough wealth to afford those things comfortably, it can surely make you go broke.

Let's take a look at a well-known billionaire. Sir Richard Branson has a current estimated net worth of $4.3 billion, accumulated from his Virgin brand and an additional portfolio of assets. As with many wealthy people, the wealth they have accumulated is not an accident. If you took all that money away from him, he would still retain the same knowledge and behavioral patterns that made him wealthy in the first place. He would still understand how to raise capital, develop and scale businesses, and invest his money with wisdom. If he had to begin today, I am quite sure he would have a large net worth, once again, in less than five years' time.

Here is another thing I am certain of: If need be, he would not be above manual labor, grunt work, or any other type of hard work. Believe it or not, many wealthy people are not snobs when it comes to hard work. It is just the opposite.

Conversely, an individual who has poor money habits and wins the lottery still does not understand how money works or the behaviors needed to grow and sustain long-term wealth. There is a good chance they will be flat broke in less than five years. Although they were gifted a giant windfall, they were not wealthy, because they did not know the rules of wealth. Ever wonder why so many professional athletes and recording artists have gained enormous riches only to then lose it all?

To bring this lesson home, a person who earns $100,000 per year and spends $100,000 per year will prosper far less than a person who earns $40,000 per year and spends only $20,000 per year. The latter person is on the path toward building wealth, whereas the former person is spinning their wheels and making no progress toward achieving long-term wealth. In fact, bankruptcy could be in his or her future if there is an abrupt loss of income. You now have the idea. Wealth is the result of a specific thought process, applied knowledge, discipline, a set of behavioral patterns, and time, more than it is about a specific income. The higher the income, the more opportunities to save and invest; but behavior, values, and discipline are the ultimate deciding factors in your financial fate.

Flash Does <u>Not</u> Equal Cash – It Mostly Equals Broke

Let's take a snapshot of Black American money habits and the value we have brought to this country's economy. In recent decades, the Black Americans' value to corporations has largely been in the volume of consumer goods we consume, which is greater than the average American. With a handful of exceptions, we have traditionally been consumers rather than creators, savers, lenders, and investors.

According to the Selig Center for Economic Growth at the University of Georgia, "Black buying power [rose] from $1.3 trillion in 2017 up to $1.54 trillion in 2022. The 108% increase in black buying power between 2000 and 2017 outperformed the 87% rise in white buying power and the 97% increase in total buying power (all races combined) during the same time period." Based on anecdotal evidence, Black Americans are the largest consumers. We have been emotionally conditioned to believe that acquiring and displaying material things gives us value, rather than producing, saving, investing, and ultimately lending. As it stands now, every time a Black baby is born in America, you can almost hear Madison Avenue rubbing its hands together and rejoicing, "Another future consumer!" Great for corporations, bad for Black wealth. If you are a hyper-consumer who has bought into the notion that expensive and flashy material things give you more self-esteem, make you important, and add to your value as a human being, your spending habits are also great for corporations, but not so great for you or your familial descendants.

If you look at money as energy and the exchange of energy, that is a lot of energy that is being freely handed over by Black people in this country. Black people have been all too eager to relinquish their resources, aka their wealth-building tools, in exchange for the next, newest, greatest thing being marketed to us. Things like shoes, clothes, leased luxury cars, rims, handbags, and other flashy accoutrements will never make you wealthy because they are not income-producing assets, and they surely are not money in the bank. Less money spent equals more money in the bank.

The wealthy are not consumers. Yes, we all consume to some degree, but the wealthy are measured and strategic with how, when, and why they make a purchase. Their bank accounts' bottom line is far more important to them than the visual appearance of wealth. Once they have obtained some wealth and they do decide to make purchases within the luxury market, it typically amounts to a small percentage of their total net worth. The *ultra*-wealthy *(think multi-millionaires and billionaires)* do have the ability to purchase the highest-end luxury items that amount to a small percentage of their total net worth.

If Aesthetics Do Not Equal Wealth, How is Wealth Defined?

The longer you can go without working and still have the ability to meet your financial obligations and retain your current lifestyle, the wealthier you are. Could you go one month, three months, six months, or a year without working? Or do you need that next paycheck to make ends meet and keep your creditors at bay? The wealthy always save and invest a portion of their income, because they know that money equals freedom. Money also equals the ability to make *more* money. This is when your money starts to work for *you*, rather than the other way around. I have made my money my best employee. I give it a dollar and come away with $1.25, $1.50, or maybe even $2.00 depending upon market variations and the dividends I receive through my portfolio of business investments.

Wealthy and Poor People Focus Their Attention on Different Types of Money

There are three types of money. Earned money is the result of performing a job. You are exchanging your time and labor aka your energy output for money. Portfolio money is the result of money generated from income already earned that is now gaining value from individual stocks or bonds, or a diversified investment portfolio. Passive money is income that is earned from real estate, intellectual property, or multi-level marketing businesses with a workforce actively selling underneath you. With the last two types of income, portfolio income and passive income, you are essentially getting paid over and over for work that has already been done, or income that has already been earned. You have income-producing assets. Most Americans are sorely lacking in the second and third types of money.

Work/Borrow/Spend/Debt is a paradigm that is no longer sustainable for people of color, nor is it for anyone who wants to grow financially. First, you only get compensated when you work, and there are a fixed number of hours in the day and a fixed amount of energy you can output to perform that work. That means there is a cap on how much money you can make through earned income. We exchange our energy for money. You only have so much energy. Earned W2 income through an employer is also heavily taxed. Your salary or wages are taxed by the federal government, your state's government *(with a handful of exceptions)*, your city's government in places like New York City, and by the Social Security Administration. When all is said and done, you are lucky if you hold onto 50% to 60% of the money you have worked for. Then, if you overspend what you do bring home in a misguided effort to obtain the aesthetics of the wealthy, you are forfeiting any real power and keeping yourself on a hamster wheel. This disparity in how money is seen and utilized is why poor and middle-class individuals attempt to get rich by working more and working harder, and ultimately burn themselves out.

Wealthy individuals, on the other hand, focus on the other two types of money: portfolio money and passive money. These forms of income are not dependent upon the number of hours in a day or your personal energy output, so they grow indefinitely and are taxed less. According to Forbes, the current long-term capital gains tax rate ranges from 0% - 20%. Short-term capital gains tax is a bit higher, though short-term investment losses can be deducted from your total tax liability for the year, thereby offsetting the gains you earn.

The point being, a person who is solely dependent upon a W2 salaried income and who makes at least $50,000 per year is in the 22% tax bracket, higher than a wealthy person's capital gains income tax bracket. If you earn $100,000 in exchange for your work, you find yourself in the 25% tax bracket. You are earning less than the wealthy and paying more of a percentage of your income to Uncle Sam.

It is important to understand that if you invest some money for thirteen months you will pay less on that investment income in the form of capital gains tax than you will on your earned salaried income. The more that pyramid flips in favor of investment income or passive income, the less tax you will ultimately pay.

"The Borrower is Slave to the Lender" - Proverbs 22:7

As Black Americans, we are a spiritual people and always have been. It is ironic that one of the most repeated and taught Bible verses about the borrower being a slave to the lender has largely fallen on deaf ears within our community. Proverbs 22:7 clearly states that "the borrower is slave to the lender."

Yet, many of us have chosen to continue to enslave ourselves in the form of credit card debt, government assistance, and subprime interest loans that prevent us from building any real wealth and keep us beholden to a system that has marginalized us. As a Black American man, I have made the conscious choice to structure my finances to be a lender and not a borrower.

You will want to set a goal of building strong credit that you use sparingly, and only for the purpose of generating income-producing assets.

Let me repeat that: You will want to use your credit sparingly, and only for the purpose of generating income-producing assets.

For example, you can purchase a car with financing once you have saved enough money to put a minimum of 20% down on the car at signing. The car's purchase price should be no more than 15% of your total household income. Endless payments at high interest rates will leave you spinning your wheels *(literally)* and are to be avoided. If you currently make $100,000 per year or less, then we are most likely talking about a certified pre-owned or used car with a transparent warranty that covers a minimum of engine and transmission repair or replacement up to 100,000 miles. This car should be purchased with a solid down payment, paid off within one year, and then driven for at least 5 years with no monthly car payment. As you make your monthly payments over the course of one year you will also watch your credit score increase.

At the end of that year, you now own an asset, free and clear. The car payment that no longer exists can now be invested into a high interest yielding Roth IRA mutual fund, or, if you lack a liquid emergency fund, you can start applying it toward that.

Now you are working toward building wealth. Although a car is a depreciating asset, not having a monthly car payment is a wealth-building tool. That $300 monthly car payment can now be invested or saved, your monthly car insurance payment will lessen on a car that is owned outright as well.

Add that saved money to be bundled with the car payment that no longer exists, and before you do another thing, you are already likely socking away anywhere between $350-$550 per month. You can then eventually apply the trade-in value or sale value of that car toward your eventual next car purchase. Here's another thought: if you have a child who will be of driving age within the next five years, allow that child to inherit the car you own free and clear. You are giving them the gift of starting out in life with no car payment.

A home is another potential wealth-producing asset since homeownership allows you to bypass rent payments that do not build equity and continually go up based on rental market fluctuations. If held onto until the market is favorable for sellers, you can likely sell this asset for a profit. You can also rent it out to a qualified tenant at a modest monthly profit to earn yourself some passive rental income. If you are not yet able to purchase a home, your rent should be no more than 25% of your total gross household income, so that you can save toward home ownership or invest in another income-producing asset, like a business.

A strong credit score *(typically 740 or higher)* can also be used to leverage borrowed money into profit so that you are not servicing the interest on that borrowed money, but rather capitalizing on it and profiting from it. The gross profits generated through leveraging borrowed money is servicing the debt's interest, while you pocket the net profits leveraged from that "debt."

The beautiful thing about earning asset-based income is that it does not require your physical presence like a job does. Employment is trading time for money with little leverage. Borrowing at high interest rates and making indefinite payments on debt also offers no financial leverage. When you strategically borrow money to acquire income-producing assets, rather than for the sake of consumerism, you make money off of the difference between the borrowed line of credit and the profit you earn by leveraging that borrowed line of credit.

If I get a $10 million credit line from the bank and they are charging me $1 million in interest per year, but I can leverage that $10 million to earn myself $3 million per year, I am earning a net profit of $2 million per year, while my income-producing asset is servicing the interest debt for me.

To bring this example more down to earth, if you borrowed $30,000 from the bank to either invest in an existing business, improve upon a piece of property you plan to sell or rent out, or to start a business, and your interest rate is 5%, you are paying $1,500 in yearly interest on that loan. If you clear a profit of $3,000 in your first year, you have achieved a net profit of $1,500. This is much better than you could get from a traditional savings account. The other half of your gross profit is servicing the debt for you until that debt is paid off. You have now leveraged debt into passive or portfolio income, or equity income if you are actively working that business.

Leverage is described in the dictionary as "the mechanical advantage or power gained by using a lever, or the power of action." Leverage merely compounds one's strength and effectiveness. The ability to be paid for work that you do not do is the result of leverage. It engages a multiplier effect as an asset develops in value.

The most important thing you will ever hear about building wealth is this: Getting wealthy is not easy, but it *is* simple. It is not easy, because it requires the ability to delay gratification. However, the rules are quite simple. The second most important thing you will hear about building wealth is: There is no excuse to not save and invest. The third thing is not as readily known, but also important: Just like casinos, banks always win.

The strategy I have adopted with my own finances is that I always prefer to position myself as a "bank." In other words, whether I am investing my own money, or I borrow money to invest, I position myself as the lender/creditor in some capacity because the lender always wins.

How Do I Borrow or Lend Money as a Banker or Creditor, If I Am Not Yet Wealthy?

If you are not wealthy *(yet)*, the best approach is to leverage your creativity, intelligence, and your network. Pool your resources and partner with people to accomplish the same end and hire someone to help you form your own company and structure your group deal. A pool of people in your network would put in what they can afford and get their pro rata share based on the amount of their investment; whether real estate, small business, stock portfolio, or into a currently undervalued asset with a high potential for growth. My personal belief is to position yourself as the creditor in whatever you invest your money into. You are still considered to be an investor, but you are not investing in equity, you are loaning out money as a creditor so that you stay in first position to collect, no matter the outcome.

In my opinion, like it or not, the fate of your finances, your retirement, and ultimately your ability to establish generational wealth for your descendants comes down to your commitment to the concepts laid out above.

Purchase less than you can afford *(and definitely not more than you can afford)*, shun consumerism for its own sake, avoid unsecured/credit card debt, save and invest in a portfolio and/or passive streams of income, and only borrow money to leverage into income-producing assets.

Financial freedom doesn't just belong to a select few. It is time for us all to win with money.

CHAPTER 2

—·—

BLACK LIVES (DON'T) MATTER

"If you are neutral in situations of injustice, you have chosen the side of the oppressor." – Desmond Tutu

Historically speaking, Black Lives Don't Matter. That has been proven since African Americans first arrived on American shores in Jamestown, Virginia in 1619. Though we are "free" and some of us have financially flourished in recent times, we are still getting shot and incarcerated at alarming rates. Just as the only way up and out of poverty is through education, mentorship, hard work, and goal setting; from my studied perspective, the only way out of our circumstances as a hunted subset of Americans who are continually in danger of becoming an endangered species is through financial empowerment and the building of community infrastructure and generational wealth.

If we really tear this American capitalist system down to the studs, No Lives Matter. It isn't individual lives that matter at all. It is a sad fact that power matters, money matters, influence matters, corporations matter, and, yes, Wall Street matters. Although there are indeed exceptions to this rule, generally speaking, each white life is worth more money, more political influence, and has more overall economic value, and therefore, more consequences to our structure of government and our American way of life.

Your life has enormous intrinsic value to your friends, family, and local community, but to the political industrial complex, your one human life has no intrinsic value, nor does mine or anyone else's for that matter. As long as our economy keeps humming along, each individual is of little consequence to the whole of America.

So where does that leave us as human beings? The picture isn't as grim as you think. Regardless of how you view politics or who you or I have previously voted for *(and even if you do not vote)*, our most recent 2020 presidential election proved that when voters, particularly voters of color, turn out in record numbers, mountains can be moved. When less of us show up, we are not considered and will continue to be marginalized. As a man of means, I will keep it one hundred percent real with you and acknowledge that I am a Republican. But whatever your political affiliation or leanings, you have to understand that complacency is the enemy of freedom, dignity, safety, and prosperity for our people.

Political complacency, financial complacency, and social complacency will keep you locked into a fate you may not be in favor of.

When I was struggling financially, I was treated one way. Now people treat me differently because I am worth a lot of money. This begs the statement, "But Solomon, as people of color, we should be treated equally regardless of what we have or do not have." I agree with you. However, that is not how our current socio-political American construct works. If you want your kids to stop getting shot in the streets, then you need to stop thinking and behaving like a consumer, and start thinking and behaving like an investor in your family's financial future and in your own community.

We cannot just keep marching for our rights. If marches worked, we would not still be getting incarcerated and shot at alarming rates. Are we beginning to see those who infringe on our civil and human rights be held accountable? Yes, but it is too little too late, and it has not and will not stop the genocide of African Americans right on these shores. It will continue until you take the proverbial red pill of financial knowledge, accountability, legacy building, and community building outlined throughout these pages.

Many of us are familiar with the bible verse Proverbs 22:7 (NIV), which states, "The rich rule over the poor, and the borrower is slave to the lender." Being that we are a spiritual people, many of us can recite this scripture when called upon to do so. But do we, as a people, live by its tenets and truly understand what it means?

How much of your weekly and monthly income is owed to a lender? Let's look at History.com's definition of sharecropping, another phrase we are all too familiar with. "Sharecropping is a type of farming in which families rent small plots of land from a landowner in return for a portion of their crop, to be given to the landowner at the end of each year."

How many of you reading this book are unwitting modern-day sharecroppers? Are you paying large sums of money to access your own income? Are you paying a landlord *(without a strategy toward ownership)*? Are you paying large amounts of fees and interest to payday advance companies and credit card companies? Do other people or entities control how and when you earn money and where the bulk of that money goes each month?

Now ask yourself, how would your ancestors feel about you being content to live your life as a 21st century sharecropper? If you are enslaved to Visa, Amex, MasterCard, and the like, because you had to have those rims, that handbag, those shoes, that bottle service at the club; you, my friend, are a sharecropper. You are paying the bank a premium for the so-called privilege of keeping up with the Jones, for the so-called privilege of looking "successful," and for the so-called privilege of looking like someone whose life is worth a damn.

I know this sounds harsh, but I am not writing this to make friends. I am writing this to wake you up to the fact that many of you out there are headed straight toward an iceberg, and we, as people of color, are headed toward that iceberg if we do not work together. I need you to become part of the solution.

The importance of becoming a lender as opposed to a borrower can sometimes take years, even generations, to sink in, but we do not have that kind of time. We are being called to a higher order for the sake of our own lives and those of future generations.

As Black folks, we have been called Negro, Colored, Black and African American. I have omitted another word that I do not wish to give ink to. These identifiers have been accepted by American institutions and have permeated public opinion and conversations throughout the ages. For the most part, although we have tried to adopt some of the vernacular as our own, Black and brown people have not been the originators of any of these identifying labels. The institutional and societal devaluing of Black lives has been consistent, and it has been accepted as a "non-issue" in the interest of watering down and disassembling the fight for our human rights by "Any Means Necessary."

This present-day Black Lives Matter movement is, indeed, a watered-down agenda-based movement initiated and financially backed by organizers to not have the American public be held accountable for not having a real discussion about the "color" problems in America. This problem is not a white issue or an American issue, but a problem based on the color of one's skin that is a different hue from this country's founding fathers.

The murder of George Floyd on May 25, 2020, during the height of the COVID-19 pandemic benefitted from a tremendous captive audience of homebound quarantined Americans, many of whom were out of work. It shone a light on an injustice that many Americans, as well as those around the world, had previously turned a blind eye to. With little else to do and pent-up frustration at the state of our world, masses of people could not turn off what they saw on their televisions and mobile devices and carry on as usual.

The death of this human being who was held down with a knee pressed into his neck by a police officer for eight minutes and forty-six seconds, while other police officers watched on and were complicit, was and still is indescribable to anyone who values human life. This cowardly pathetic excuse for a public servant and his fellow so-called public servants revealed in the harsh light of day what Black lives meant to them.

If Black lives mattered to the founding fathers of this country they would not have called another human being "3/5 of a man (or woman)." If Black lives mattered, the original thirteen colonies would not have subjected the native people to such cruelty and the stealing of their land and exploitation of their hospitality. After all, they left Great Britain's rule due to unfair treatment by the British government, including taxation without representation. If Black lives mattered, the Fourteenth Amendment, Civil Rights movement, Jim Crow laws, public lynching, police brutality, and redlining would not have occurred. If Black Lives Mattered, every aspect of human decency would be shared and enjoyed by every American, regardless of the color of their skin. Every day America goes out of its way to uphold the Dred Scott v. Sanford court ruling *(Dred Scott v. Sandford of 1857 was a landmark decision of the U.S. Supreme Court in which the Court held that the U.S. Constitution was not meant to include American citizenship for Black people, regardless of whether they were enslaved or free, and so the rights and privileges that the Constitution confers upon American citizens could not apply to them)* by not holding perpetrators of many unacceptable hate crimes toward Black and brown people accountable.

Until and unless this narrative completely changes, Black and brown people should always look at our government and our communities with reservation and suspicion. Most importantly, we should extricate ourselves from continued "sharecropping," behavior, stop letting our valuable dollars leave our own communities, and start holding ourselves and each other accountable for our financial habits.

The "Black Lives Matter" movement should be talking about the African American individuals throughout American history whose creativity, ingenuity, intellect, and perseverance have contributed tremendously to our modern-day lives; the unsung heroes who, throughout history, have been denied their due and financial compensation for their undeniable contributions, either because of their gender, the color of their skin, or both. Our movement should assert these facts rather than simply begging for our lives to matter to white or non-Black America.

A Brief History of Black American Contributions *(sourced through Wikipedia)*:

Garrett Augustus Morgan, Sr. was an African-American inventor, businessman, and community leader who invented the three-position traffic signal as well as a smoke hood, a predecessor to the gas mask, most notably used in a 1916 tunnel construction disaster rescue.

Lewis Howard Latimer was an American inventor and patent draftsman for the patents of the incandescent light bulb.

George Washington Carver was an American agricultural scientist and inventor who promoted alternative crops to cotton, and methods to prevent soil depletion *(a prevalent modern-day problem)*.

Madam C.J. Walker was an African American entrepreneur, philanthropist, and political and social activist; and the first recorded African American female self-made millionaire. Walker made her fortune by developing and marketing a line of cosmetics and hair care products for Black women.

Elijah J. McCoy was a Canadian-born, African American inventor with 57 US patents, most having to do with the lubrication of steam engines.

Dr. Patricia Era Bath was an American ophthalmologist, inventor, humanitarian, and academic. She was the inventor of laser cataract surgery.

Thomas L. Jennings was an African American inventor, tradesman, entrepreneur, and abolitionist with the distinction of being the first African-American patent-holder in history; he was granted a patent in 1821 for this method of dry cleaning.

Lyda D. Newman was a patented African American inventor and involved activist for women's suffrage. She is known for the invention of a durable hairbrush.

Ellen Eglin was an American inventor who invented a clothes wringer for washing machines.

Lonnie George Johnson is an African American inventor, aerospace engineer, and entrepreneur, whose work includes a U.S. Air Force term of service and a twelve-year stint at NASA, where he worked at the Jet Propulsion Laboratory. He also invented the Super Soaker water gun in 1990, which has been among the world's bestselling toys.

From haircare and dry cleaning to cataract surgery, aerospace engineering, our national traffic light infrastructure, soil and irrigation improvement, and even wildly popular toys, African Americans throughout history have made remarkable strides and contributed enormous value to American lives. What makes this more impressive is the fact that so many of these innovations were achieved under oppressive, discriminatory conditions.

Rather than begging and marching for our right to live, love, prosper and be free in the United States of America; we should be claiming and owning our collective value as we continue to lift that message through a seismic shift in our financial values and behaviors.

Community Wealth-Building in Black Communities

According to the website Community-Wealth.org, "In Richmond, Virginia, the Mayor recently established the first City-government Office of Community Wealth Building. Community wealth initiatives have also been launched in cities as varied as Cleveland, OH, Washington, DC, Atlanta, GA, and Amarillo, TX."

The article goes on to elaborate, *"When families possess assets — valuable skills, social networks, a home, some savings, an ownership stake in a business — they enjoy greater resilience, and are better able to withstand occasional shocks like unemployment or illness. They can plan for their future, send a child to college, feel secure in retirement. A job may start or stop. It is assets, of various kinds, that yield greater stability and security. As this is true of families, it is also true of communities.*"

Please dial in to that last passage. Put down the phone, turn off the television, and read it again.

"These strategies reverse the focus on 'chasing companies to relocate to my city/my neighborhood.' All too often this includes greater tax breaks and lower wages for companies that may well relocate again for a better offer in another community/city. Community wealth, on the other hand, is tied to place. <u>The people who own and control the businesses live there</u>."

Community wealth aims at improving the ability of communities and individuals to:

1. Increase asset ownership

2. Create anchor jobs locally by broadening ownership over capital

3. Help achieve key environmental goals (including decreasing carbon emissions)

4. Expand the provision of public services by strengthening the municipal tax base

5. Ensure local economic stability

Investing Locally

Significantly strengthening and growing local capital is critical. Strategies include:

1. Building new, and strengthening existing,

community-based financial institutions

2. Preventing local financial resources from "leaking out" of the community

3. Leveraging the use of procurement and investment from existing local anchor institutions such as hospitals, universities, foundations, cultural institutions, and city government

4. Finally, working aligned impact investors and financial institutions to grow affordable capital committed to building local wealth

I am now going to ask you to re-read the above once again, because I really want it to resonate. I want you to take pause. This, my friends, is the undisputed roadmap to Black financial empowerment, Black freedom, Black generational wealth, and yes, Black Lives Mattering.

Starting today, and for one full week, I want you to take on the daily task of recording in a notebook where you spend your money each day for seven days. Start this journal the same week you pay your rent or mortgage and utility bills to make it simple. I also want you to record every gallon of milk, every box of cereal, every piece of produce, every box of cookies, your gasoline, clothing, shoes, cosmetics, alcohol, pencils, books, credit card bills, grooming/beauty products... everything. It is an arduous task, but it is important for you to know where, when, why, and how you are spending each dollar and to whom you are giving your money.

Next, at the end of one week, I want you to itemize each of the consumer products you have purchased, all of the debt you have paid, and all of the living expenses you have paid. I want you to then Google each of these companies and create a ledger of which of these companies, if any, are A. local to your community, B. benefiting your direct community and C. Black-owned.

You may come to find that all of your money is leaving your family line and leaving your community, and lament that you are late to this party. Fear not. Remember, you are awakening to a new way of thinking about the correlation between money, community building, wealth building, and Black lives.

What You Can Do Right Now

Seek out Black-owned businesses to purchase from, and if they are local Black-owned businesses that have ties to your community, even better. If you have a favorite brand that is not Black-owned but that derives a large portion of its revenue from Black consumer dollars, consider writing them a letter, sending them an email, and contacting them through social media to ask how they are re-investing all of their Black-contributed revenue back into the Black community to help uplift and support a large portion of their customer base. Encourage your friends, family, and colleagues to do the same.

Ask these companies how they vote on public policy, specifying the issues that you care about and that affect your community.

Remember that shopping locally keeps money in your immediate community. You can also start a fund within your local community, pooling together money and resources to invest back into your community in a cooperative manner. Everything from fresh produce garden co-ops to clothing to beauty supplies to your local butcher, baker, or candlestick maker (if you will) should support your community in one way or another.

Look for banks that have Black employees and other employees of color and investigate if the institution where you bank has any Black board members.

As we have spoken about in previous chapters, if you are of African American descent, one of the best ways you can start investing back into the Black community is by paying yourself 30% of your monthly income each month toward an emergency fund, long term liquid savings, passive investment income, and long-term retirement investments.

Start being more discerning where, when, how, and why you spend your money, and with whom, and start saving and investing a percentage of your money each month. If you need to start with as little as 5 or 10% and build up to 30% over time, that is fine. If you need to close your debt gap and supplement your income to create room for saving and investing, do it.

According to USHistory.org, "Influence refers to the outcome of an attempt to change someone's behavior or attitude. Power refers to the means by which the influence is accomplished, and Politics is the pursuit of self-interest in an organization to protect or further either individual or organizational goals."

Let's break down how Black America needs to play a larger role in influence, power, and politics, and how this ties together with Black wealth and Black lives. Yes, we have our leaders' putting boots on the ground to fight for justice every time a Black life is egregiously taken out of fear and ignorance. But up until now, we have operated on a reactionary basis, rallying in the streets upon the latest infringement on our human rights and our lives, but what are we doing that is proactive?

The George Floyd Justice in Policing Act of 2020 promises "to hold law enforcement accountable for misconduct in court, improve transparency through data collection, and reform police training and policies." This is a commendable stride in getting our police departments and our politicians to recognize that there is a problem that needs to be addressed, and in taking a step toward trying to right some wrongs, but unfortunately, the wrongs continue to pile up.

A September 10, 2020, CBS News article titled, *It's Been Over 3 Months Since George Floyd Was Killed by Police. Police Are Still Killing Black People at Disproportionate Rates* states, "Over the following three months, from May 26 to August 31, police in the U.S. killed 288 people, according to data from both The Washington Post and Mapping Police Violence, two organizations that have kept comprehensive lists of people who have been killed by police. Of the 288 people listed by either the Post or Mapping Police Violence's database, 59 were Black, 102 were White, 42 were Hispanic or Latino, 5 were Asian, 2 were Native American, and the race of 78 people was unknown."

102 white people and 59 black people, yet black people only comprise 12% of the United States population, as opposed to the white population, which comprises 73% of the United States population. How are we insulating our communities against such acts *before* they occur?

Getting out to vote has helped in the past, but in today's climate, it is not moving the needle enough for my liking. In generations past, voting helped to place officials in office that looked after your best interests or, at the very least, aligned with your interests. Today that is not the case. Politicians seek only to solicit your vote and they get it through a lot of empty promises, that do not come to fruition. I know many of you will strongly disagree and that is okay but think of this book as our contingency plan.

Wealth makes a difference in how you are treated, full stop. People, in their prejudice, will think you are smarter, and that you, perhaps, even know something they don't. With wealth comes reverence.

Having been on both sides of this fence, I have seen how people treat those with no money and how they treat those with money. What if a community of people who look like me *(and possibly like you if you are a Black or brown-skinned American)* all had the means to place the right people in office who would authentically align with our values, see our lives as valuable, and carry out the act of proactively changing the laws to ensure that every human being would enjoy a better quality of life?

This is where wealth comes in because it is not just about getting out to vote. It is being able to support the right candidates and get them on the ballot so that you can have the opportunity to actually vote for the right people. Aren't you tired of having to vote for bad, worse, or downright deplorable? I don't know about you, but I am sick and tired of being sick and tired of this old routine. Placing the right people on the ballot to vote for takes money and it takes influence.

Let's stop being okay with getting out and voting for leftovers, for candidates who do not necessarily serve us, but whom we vote for as our only option. Let's begin building wealth so that we can put our money behind people who truly represent our cause and our lives. This is not about building wealth to purchase a luxury car, a larger house, another pair of designer shoes, and the like. That may be an eventual byproduct of managing your money in a productive way, but people, our lives are on the line. We have bigger fish to fry.

When you have wealth in your communities your local businesses participate in funding your chosen candidate to change policies and laws. This is what is going to stop people from being shot on the street and discriminated against.

It has recently been stated by billionaire Warren Buffett, "A nice car, house and a degree are the old status symbols. The ultimate flex is freedom. Time freedom, location freedom, and financial freedom. Freedom and health are the new status symbols."

Freedom, what a concept. Not being shackled to debt and borrower's interest, not being shackled to a particular paycheck for the rest of your life, not being shackled to a specific geographic location if that location does not serve you or your family, shackled to poor health, and shackled to a system of government that is harming you. Wealth changes the picture of who you can help get into office to change how companies do business, and what they expect from their politicians. It's the community that hires the police department. With wealth, you can say, "We are the group with money who can hire you, and if you do not protect and serve with integrity, we can also fire you."

An Issue of Proximity and Access

Because African Americans comprise only 12% of the United States population and an overwhelming amount of us live in and around larger urban areas, the average American in the so-called "fly-over states" across Middle America often has little to no interaction with any Black or Brown people apart from the occasional surface interaction in a store or restaurant. They do not know us as human beings and oftentimes they do not care to know us. They are not looking at us as their sister, brother, next-door neighbor, or fellow parishioner from their house of worship. This presents a significant problem and seems to be a bridge too far for many of these folks to cross.

Naturally, you are going to have more compassion and empathy for people you know more intimately and socially, because you feel that you understand and can identify with them. People throughout these United States are not interacting with each other enough. They don't live together, work together, break bread together, laugh and cry together.

Until we get to know one another, we cannot champion each other's causes. This foible is not a Black or white thing. It is a human thing. Travel is the enemy of bigotry. Communication is the enemy of bigotry, and wealth and political influence are the enemy of politics as usual and infringement upon our basic human rights as citizens of the United States of America.

Chapter 3

The "African American" Experience

"I love America more than any other country in this world, and exactly for this reason, I insist on the right to criticize her perpetually." – James Baldwin

I have spoken to many non-Americans from all corners of the globe, and of all skin tones, who have moved to the United States of America. Aside from bringing their own cultural norms and expectations to the conversation, they bring with them an "outside looking in" perspective of the Black American or "African American," much of it shaped by the news media. I am going to intentionally use the term "African American" throughout this chapter, because for the purpose of this part of the book, the term perfectly and succinctly describes who and what we are: people of African heritage and lineage, who are not directly connected to our African heritage, and who are designated as Americans by natural born citizenship.

As African Americans, we are thought to be a strange folk. Not fully African in our inability to trace our true and holistic lineage back generations, that which gives most Americans a sense of grounding, self-esteem, and cultural validity. And yet, we are not fully American in our inability to enjoy the institutional financial stability, safety, and liberty of non-Black Americans. Yet here we are.

I see African Americans as the ultimate survival story. Sadly, most of my non-American colleagues, friends, and acquaintances who have shared their unvarnished opinions with me have confided that, to them, the average African American's temperament and work ethic leaves much to be desired. With a lump in my throat and all the restraint I can muster, I methodically and dispassionately try to educate them on the history of African Americans in the United States of America, and the systemic racist discrimination that has permeated every area of our lives and our ancestors' lives, and how it continues to impact our communities today.

Though we, African Americans, have arguably played the largest role in building this nation's prosperity and infrastructure, we have been shut out of and disenfranchised from the spoils of our centuries-long contributions. Sadly, we paid the price of building this country, not just through centuries of forced free labor, but through being subjected to torture, beatings, hangings, rape, and our families being broken up and sold as chattel. It left our communities with a bruised collective psyche that will take another few centuries to heal.

Our modern marches, demonstrations, and the constant fight for African Americans to be treated as wholly equal in the United States of America exist on the bloodied and blistered backs of our ancestors who were stripped of everything and paid the ultimate price. They deserve, and we deserve, to see African American wealth, freedom, and safety come to full fruition in this country.

Three modern-day examples of financial disenfranchisement would be how millions of working-class African Americans contribute to this country with our tax dollars, paying the salaries of everyone from politicians to police officers, while our neighborhoods and public schools languish, and many of us are harassed and killed at the hands of trigger-happy police officers who feel threatened by our brown and black-hued skin tones. Secondly, African Americans are the largest overall consumers in the United States, contributing more to our national GDP than any other American population. Yet too many of us have been systematically shut out of any clear path toward participating in this country's vast wealth, due to a lack of access to key financial and investment markets. Third, currently, about 30% of men serving on active military duty are African Americans, and close to 17% of women serving on active military duty are African Americans.

That is more than Native Americans, Asians, and Hispanics, and more than white men and women on current active military duty as proportionate to their population. We are sending our children into battle to defend and fight for this country and its allies' freedom and the privilege to live the American way of life, but those freedoms are rarely extended to us as citizens of this country. Ours is a country that has failed to adequately fight for us.

However, too many people I know do not see this picture. Instead, they see a group of people who are not motivated enough to take advantage of the opportunities afforded to most Americans. Well, we have not been most Americans, not by a long shot. At best, African Americans have been treated as America's guilty embarrassment; something to be handled and dealt with so the situation doesn't create a political and financial backlash that threatens our country's very power structure.

At worst, we have been treated as America's illegitimate child from a scandalous affair that never should have happened in the first place. Think about the story of Ishmael and Isaac in the Bible. Abraham's aged wife Sarah, believing she could not provide her husband Abraham with a natural son, encourages her husband to engage in sexual relations with their domestic employee, Hagar. Abraham and Hagar's union produces Ishmael. Ishmael is innocent. He did not ask to be born, and yet, he finds himself in the crosshairs of a resentful Sarah, who ultimately banishes Ishmael and his mother Hagar from their home.

As African Americans, we didn't ask to come here, and in many ways, we have been punished for it ever since. We were brought here as products, not as people. We had to fight to be recognized as people. Let that sink in for a moment. At one point in America's history, according to the law of the land, each African American was thought of as 3/5 of a human being. From three-fifths of a human being to swearing in our first African American president in 2009, there is no doubt we have come a long way. But we must not grow complacent in the fight, as we have a long road still ahead before financial equality and racial equity can be achieved.

But I digress...

African American history paints a portrait of us being the unwitting builders of and victims of capitalism, rather than the beneficiaries of it. We can break this cycle and prosper greatly in America, but as long as systemic and institutionalized racism exists, we will be running that marathon with a handicap that appears to people from foreign shores as "laziness," while everyone else in the race appears to be enthusiastically sprinting full speed ahead. The truth is, they've got bionic legs and we're working with two sprained ankles.

Alas, an overwhelmingly common perspective about African Americans upon a foreigner's arrival to the United States is that of "lazy" or "trifling." Some even label African Americans as fast talkers, not very smart, shifty characters, and ill-equipped to take advantage of the opportunities offered in this great country.

These friends, acquaintances, and colleagues of mine consist of people of African, Hispanic, Caribbean, and European ethnicities. What do they all have in common? They weren't born in the United States and their opinion of most African Americans leaves a lot to be desired.

What they all fail to understand is that the complex journey of African Americans benefits them as well as white America. African Americans have been stripped of their original heritage, lied about, lied to, placed in slavery, killed *(the word "murder" comes to mind)*, and discriminated against. What we, as African

Americans, have endured and continue to endure is absurd. The complex, painful and resilient journey made by African Americans is who I am, and who I am proud to be a part of. I believe we are a strong people; survivors in the truest sense of the meaning, and perhaps some of the most forgiving people in America.

We aren't perfect, but we have continuously demonstrated the greatest ingenuity to overcome and achieve against insurmountable odds and adversity. Although many of the people from foreign lands that I have spoken with had undo bias against African Americans, some of them have reflected and reassessed their perspective as they have spent more considerable amounts of time in this country. Some have expressed to me that their early biases were wrong and were based on lies and deceits shared throughout the media and other platforms. It becomes apparent to them that our sullied media reputation as African Americans continues to translate to systemic racism and vice versa. White Americans with particular racial bias who are placed in key positions of authority have consciously or unwittingly helped to create a national infrastructure of this systemic racism, not only in America, but around the globe. It is one geared toward the disdain and dismissal of African Americans as a people. This is why African Americans from all walks of American life have to fight and overcome, even to this day.

Many white Americans have expressed remorse over the history of their ancestors, although there are some who believe that it was in the past and does not exist in today's society. As you read these words, you might be reflecting on your own experiences and interactions with family members, friends, colleagues, work associates, and even the random social acquaintance you spoke to at a cocktail party. Whatever the detailed circumstances, each and every one of us can pretty well gauge what most white Americans think and feel about the Black American experience and how Black Americans have lived their daily lives.

I have found that these conversations have taken place at weddings, holiday gatherings, around the proverbial water cooler, or maybe even at a company Christmas party. One of my own personal experiences includes a friend of mine who happens to be white, and with whom I have discussed this topic over many a dinner or casual outing. Feeling comfortable with me, they have also stated the same views as the foreigners I am friends with. At first blush, their overriding belief is that African Americans have the same opportunities as white Americans, and perhaps have simply not risen to the occasion. Their views are that African Americans lack ambition or direction, especially when it comes to education. In addition, they have stated that African Americans *(and they always let me know they are excluding me)* are angry and defensive all the time. They don't take into consideration the hardships that we have gone through as individuals and as a community, trying to survive and make it in America; a place that has repeatedly, throughout history, let us know that we are not full-fledged human beings. Perhaps this is where the saying, "walk a mile in another man's shoes" proves relevant. If you haven't lived it, you can't really know it, and the empathy quotient just isn't there.

I am sharing my point of view in the spirit of bridging the gap to help people understand what is really happening to people that look like me.

In recent studies, many African Americans have proved to be the opposite of lazy. Statistics have shown that African American women continue to graduate from college at a higher rate than their white counterparts. They are also starting more businesses than any other race, including white Americans. However, lack of access to capital remains an issue. African Americans are still reaching success in the face of systemic racism. If you are white in America, you cannot fully understand the impact of our challenges as Black Americans, because it does not directly affect you. The perspective of some of my white friends is that racism is not a reality, but an imaginary bogeyman; a figment of the Black man's (and woman's) imagination. They are privileged in that they have not had to worry about living our struggles. They don't have to worry about their kids being senselessly murdered because of their appearance, or just simply trying to survive on a daily basis.

We can go round and round in circles over whether or not systemic racism exists in the United States, or to what degree it exists. What came first, the chicken or the egg, and whether or not African Americans should "just move on and get over it." In my opinion the term "move on," is hurtful. You are telling a traumatized people to move on while our centuries' long wounds continue to be ripped open every time another Black person is senselessly killed in this country. Imagine telling a rape victim to just "move on" while that victim is under constant threat of possibly being raped again.

If someone hears your story and tells you to "move on," they are listening but not taking the time to hear or acknowledge the deep-seated pain and trauma you have experienced. From a philosophical standpoint, we can engage in bottomless conversation, but that won't solve these problems. And by the way, neither will more constitutional amendments, more government programs, or more white liberal apologists. So, what will level the playing field for African Americans? The answer is financial equity in the American dream in the form of access to capital.

I believe the solution is to provide African Americans with access to capital and the entrepreneurial skills and information which can lead to financial freedom and decrease, if not eliminate, Black people being killed and denied access to jobs.

As you continue to read these pages, I hope to illustrate this issue from all points of view. I think we can all agree that if everyone in our society, no matter what their gender or skin color, can be presented with equal access to working and growth capital and better job opportunities, this will create safer communities for all.

To help illustrate some of these different outside perspectives on African Americans, I have gathered stories told to me by people of all races and genders who have moved to the United States from another country. You will see them scattered throughout this book. The names have been changed to preserve anonymity, but the stories are rich with context.

Meet *Betami, Age 41 – An East African Immigrant

I came to America more than thirty years ago at the age of eleven. Coming from the country of *Eritrea* in *Eastern Africa* as a young child, I struggled to understand and adapt. As I was busy learning the language and the culture of my new land and acclimating to the school system, I observed a tremendous gap between African Americans ("Black people") and foreigners who were descending on this great America.

I remember being placed in the local middle school. I wasn't up to par education-wise due to the massive shift in language and educational requirements, so I had to work twice as hard. As a result, I spent a lot of time at school before school, after school, and even during summers, doing anything I could to catch up. Since they couldn't place an eleven-year-old in elementary school, I had no choice but to adjust quickly. With the help of my parents and the school, I ultimately thrived. In fact, I did so well that I eventually skipped a grade. Socially, things were a little strange, to say the least. Although I shared the same skin color as my African American classmates, I did not receive the warm and fuzzy welcome I had hoped for. I looked like them, but I didn't speak like them, and they saw me as a strange sort of outlier, someone who was not part of them. As a result, I was largely ignored by the African American students.

Conversely, the white kids were exceptionally drawn to me and wanted to know all about my African culture. I was like a walking, talking social studies project for them. They were endlessly curious about me and seemed to genuinely want to help me gain the lay of my new land. I appreciated their overtures but couldn't help but feel hurt and confused about being ostracized by the "Black" kids. It took a lot of time, years really, for me to piece together this whole African American puzzle, and to really understand where these American Black kids were coming from.

It didn't help that I came to the United States in the mid-eighties, right around the time of Quincy Jones and Michael Jackson's *We Are the World* effort to raise money for Africa with the brand banner of "U.S.A. for Africa." All those television commercials depicting all Africans as impoverished, backwoods people desperately in need of "just 50 cents a day" to survive were baffling. Boy did Africans have an image problem in the eighties.

It might surprise some people to learn that the part of Eastern Africa where I grew up, *Eritrea, was a relatively affluent region. My family and I lived in a six-bedroom home, my brother and I were cared for by a nanny, and my father was a successful professional golf player.*

But the African American kids didn't seem to want to be associated in any way with me, the African girl. Perhaps they felt somehow superior because they were American, whereas I was from a place that, in their uninformed minds, was the lowly continent of Africa. I had no idea at the time that there was also some resentment at play. After all, I was an African girl whose family emigrated to America of our own free will and I arrived with my cultural heritage intact, something they did not have.

The white kids, on the other hand, saw me as somewhat exotic, coming from the land of wild safaris and rainforests, and a place where wealthy people are inclined to vacation as part of their bucket list experiences.

Yes, I came from a wealth of heritage. My parents were upper middle class. There is a caste system in my home country, but the majority of the population lived quite well. My brother and I spent our days with our full-time nanny and my dad played pro golf back home. He was preparing to compete in the Sami-PGA. During our time in Africa, we were blissfully unaware of how Africans were viewed in America, by both black people and white people. As an Eastern African, I was not aware of American slavery. I arrived on these shores at age eleven under the impression that all Africans who lived in the United States came here of their own free will, the way that I did.

Let me also be clear that we were busy dealing with and fighting political differences within our country, and some people were fleeing the country for safety and to escape this widening political division. Many countries at that time, including the United States, were allowing immigrants from my country to enter with a clear path to citizenship. I believed, and still believe, that it was a kind act of the United States government. Therefore, from my perspective, and especially at such a young age, it was hard to fathom that the same country that offered my family political asylum and the opportunity for my father to flourish in his career, would be so unkind and so inhumane to some of its own people, my people.

It wasn't until my high school years that my eyes opened when I took an African American studies class. I was gob-smacked when taught about the slave trade and the history of Africans in America. A revelation washed over me like a tidal wave. "This is why they don't like me," I thought to myself. Many African Americans also operate under the impression that Africans played a large part in selling their own people into slavery. While some of that did occur, what many people may not realize is that the majority of the slave trade was cultivated and took place throughout Western Africa, because of its closer proximity to America.

I want to be clear that I do not speak for all foreigners coming to America, but generally speaking, there is a big misunderstanding between African Americans and people of African origin who emigrate to the United States. The foreigners' perspective is this: "If one can come from a different country, overcome cultural and language barriers, and become successful in America, why can't the African American who has lived here their entire life?"

I soon learned that there was discrimination within the American system. African Americans know that this discrimination has been in existence for a long time, and they have been fighting it as long as they have been in this country. I will candidly tell you that this dynamic is very difficult for someone like me, who came from another country, to fully understand. It is hard to understand and process the traumatizing circumstances that occurred as a result of slavery.

Most of us who came to this country are not aware, or are not fully educated, of the impact that slavery has had in America. In this respect, people of African origin who emigrate to the United States share a similar view to many white Americans. It is an outside-looking-in view of slavery being long in the past, and a notion that the American dream is equally afforded to all who claim it. Having now lived the Black American experience for thirty years, I can, through firsthand experience, unequivocally state that there is much more to this story.

There have been many times throughout my life where I was given an opportunity before an African American person because I was looked at as a foreigner, and therefore "different from the average Black person." Although I greatly appreciated these opportunities, I do have memories of being told, "But you're different..." I now acknowledge that African Americans are in a very tough situation because they are discriminated against by their fellow Americans and misunderstood by foreigners as to why they are in the situation they are in. Now, as a woman in her forties, it is abundantly clear to me that African Americans have been mistreated, unprotected, and dehumanized buy their own government and many of their fellow citizens.

The African American is a great asset to this country, and they have played a great role in building this country from its foundation. How a foreigner treats an African American is a direct result of how the American system has treated them and presented their image outwardly to the world. The outside world can only respect African Americans to the extent that they are respected by their own government and fellow citizens.

If High School roused me from my deep slumber, there was an African American girl I met in college who really woke me up. After meeting and becoming briefly acquainted, she made a pointed statement toward me. "You are lucky," she said emphatically. "Because my great, great-grandparents went through slavery, the civil rights movement, the struggles of integration, and the double-edged sword of job quotas, you guys now have an opportunity upon coming to this country."

Because African Americans paved the way, I am now able to take advantage of everything they fought for, bled for, and died for. Because my father was a successful pro-golf player who played on the PGA tour alongside many of the top players at that time, his attitude was always to push my brother and I toward excellence. My college friend's family spent generation after generation in survival mode, they were disenfranchised by an exclusionary system and worked two and three jobs just to make ends meet. Her entry into college was a win for her entire family, whereas with my parents it was simply expected as the next natural step after high school.

Because so many Black families in America were marginalized societally and financially, it created a cycle of poverty and desperation in the home, leading young people to turn to illegal activities to support families who were struggling to provide even the most essential things for their household.

There is progress being made, but it is not enough to attempt to move African Americans forward with hashtags, government programs, and quotas. The mission of Black Wealth Matters and people like Solomon RC Ali and his organization in moving this community forward through the access to and the strategic acquisition of capital is being recognized as the only practical solution for cultivating Black financial stability, upward mobility, dignity, and safety.

*Betami's story provides interesting contrast regarding what it means to not only live in America as African American versus as a Black or dark-skinned person of notable origin, but the constant struggle and fight for survival that is unique to Black people born in the United States.

The challenges of raising a family as an African American under conditions of systemic racism are plenty. Millions of white-run companies as well as foreign-run companies with ten employees or more, statistically, tend to hire people who look like them. There are currently only about 150,000 Black-owned companies in the United States with ten or more employees. This means less job prospects for African Americans, and thus, more financial hardship. When we take a closer look, we find that there are approximately 14,000 publicly traded companies that currently exist in the United States, and the vast majority of these companies are run by white Americans. The unfortunate part is that these publicly traded companies have access to millions and millions of dollars of capital each and every year, whether their company turns a profit or not.

For example, it took fourteen years for Amazon to become profitable. At one point, according to their current CEO, the company did not even know if they had a clear roadmap toward profitability. Yet, they were still able to raise capital for years, which kept them afloat and operational, and gave them the ability to scale and gain market share until they ultimately became profitable. Amazon is the quintessential example of how certain companies are granted unlimited access to growth capital.

Now let's take a look at African American owned and operated publicly traded companies, of which there are thirteen in existence that I know of. I have had the honor of being both an officer and director of three of those African American publicly traded companies in the United States. Out of the millions of companies in the United States, the 14,000 who hold the distinction of being publicly traded are part of an exclusive club, and the 13 African American publicly traded companies are in a *very* exclusive club. As an officer and director of three of these 13 publicly traded Black-owned/operated companies I was given the responsibility of raising capital. Of those three, two became leaders within their industry on my watch. One was in the energy sector, while another was in smart home and two-way communications technology, whereby we license our intellectual properties to companies including Ring, SkyBell, and Axis CPI, to name a few. Our technology has helped to transform a simple doorbell into a two-way smart home security device and is used in millions of homes today.

Although I enjoy my success, I cannot enjoy it as much as I would like. The trouble is, I don't want to be part of such an exclusive club. I want to be merely one success story in a sea of millions of African American success stories where companies are able to gain access to capital, go public, and exponentially raise more capital through the decimation of shares, with the unbounded ability to scale and bring greater technological advances to these United States.

Many African Americans throughout history have unearthed some of society's most valuable inventions only to see their intellectual property stripped from them.

According to a 2018 Black Enterprise article written by Samara Lynn, which received close to 22,000 views on their website, alone, "Shontavia Johnson, a lawyer and professor of Intellectual Property Law at Drake University, wrote an eye-opening piece on the history of African American slaves being denied *(or having outright stolen)*, patents for their inventions." The article goes on to state that "the patent system–which started officially in 1787–was not open to African Americans born into slavery as they weren't considered citizens."

Some of these major contributions included traffic light modification, providing color monitors, and impacting the medical field in the surgical room just to name of few. This fact, however, did not stop their inventions from being used and exploited by white Americans, creating generational wealth for those who profited from them.

I share this to give you an understanding of how systemic racism works and how it has impacted generations of African Americans, their morale, their financial prospects, their educational and health prospects, and their distrust of the American government. Imagine, if you will, the descendants of such prolific Black inventors who were denied their patents and rightful wealth, slogging through a daily existence of survival, while their white counterparts who did profit from said inventions, are inhabiting digs from Beverly Hills mansions to Manhattan's sky-high penthouses. It's a sickening visual that must be brought forth.

The root cause of African American insecurity in this country is the lack of financial access. It cannot be overstated. Lack of access over a period of generations creates a people that exist in survival mode where productivity and creativity cannot thrive, even when the potential is there. Police brutality, redlining, unemployment, poverty, violence... financial discrimination is at the heart of it all. Financial access means that people can get out of survival mode and focus on education, culture, family, spirituality, and building generational wealth.

Let's take Facebook stock as an example. Denying a group of people access keeps them from investing in a company like Facebook in its early stages where shares of stock can be purchased at $8 to $9 dollars a share, before that stock appreciates within sixty days of being public and begins trading at above $38 dollars per share and eventually rises to $100 dollars per share.

Whether a company is Black or white-owned, entrepreneurship is laced with many challenges. However, the Black entrepreneur is not only faced with the challenges of raising capital but navigating systemic racism that has been instituted by a government body made up of men from the past who held racial and cultural bias against people of color, and who had the power to make laws and create institutions. These laws and institutions still exist today, and our elected officials, whether Democrat or Republican, have not seen fit to change many of these laws to create racial equality.

Let's look at our Gross Domestic Product (GDP). You will find that African Americans contribute somewhere in the neighborhood of 3.5 to 7 percent of the national GDP. We contribute this amount through buying products from white companies, including many publicly traded companies where we are not represented, are underrepresented, or even publicly disparaged. We are the majority consumers in the market where goods are inflated in price, and those who hire us give us low entry-level jobs even when many of us offer qualifications for much higher-level jobs.

It is said that the U.S. is one of the largest economies in the world and I personally believe that to be true. I further believe that African Americans are still slaves to white America and its government. The American system is dependent on the African American dollar for the economy's survival, which is mainly a consumer-driven economy at this point. But it goes beyond our United States economy these days. There is a global impact of African American contribution to our world economy. Therefore, the African American dollar is critical, not just to the United States, but worldwide.

In the following chapters we will discuss how African American spending dollars can be converted into African American-driven capital, investing, and wealth-building. We will also delve into financial habits within our community that are in need of re-examination and a complete cultural overhaul. It starts with a belief in the power of our dollars to build and empower our own communities.

CHAPTER 4

THE BLACK INTELLECTUAL: AN AMERICAN OUTLIER

"Intellectual growth should commence at birth and cease only at death." – Albert Einstein

"You are so well spoken." If you are white, you have probably never heard that phrase directed toward you. If you are African American, "He's so well spoken and intelligent," might be a comment uttered *about* you within earshot of where you are standing, or perhaps when you are absent from the room. Later on, you hear about it secondhand and try to shrug it off as a matter of fact. Another popular phrase we often hear, "You are not like the others. You are different." The well-meaning, yet tone deaf, non-Black person might hurl this one in the direction of an African American, oblivious to the fact that they have just profoundly insulted you by proxy. Of course it is going to hurt, because what the person is expressing is that they are surprised that you are an intelligent, well-rounded, capable, and successful human being, because of your color.

They are also insinuating that your community and your blood line are not intelligent, and they are judging an entire race of people based on their own limited experiences and lack of exposure to their fellow human beings. Some of them have formulated these opinions from their parents and grandparents. Others have drawn these conclusions from their social peer groups. Let us not forget that the majority have, at least partly, come to these conclusions via their media consumption. Regardless of how they have arrived at their unconscious (or conscious) bias, they continue to share their narrow beliefs with others, while hurting people of color simply because we are of a different and minority race. These are the phrases you become accustomed to hearing when you are what is considered to be a rare breed of unicorn in America: The Black Intellectual.

Michael Jordan, LeBron James, the late Michael Jackson, Beyonce, Halle Berry, Eddie Murphy, Dave Chappelle, Kevin Hart, Denzel Washington, Diana Ross, Rihanna, Sydney Poitier, Quincy Jones... these men and women make sense to the average non-Black American. Entertainment and sports are generally thought to be our two main avenues for success and respectability within American culture. I am by no means denigrating these people. They are all astonishingly talented, creative, smart, and innovative, and they deserve every bit of success they have achieved.

But Black Americans have an image problem around the world, and here at home. We are often branded as either thugs or celebrities; larger than life or not worthy of existing. Many non-black people react to the site of a group of black people with fear and suspicion, and they then cover their tracks by expressing their admiration for Black celebrities. They'll hang a LeBron James poster on their wall, but wait for the next elevator when a Black man gets on.

Many people see an African American man in a Benz or a Bentley, and the immediate assumption is, "He must be famous," followed by the squinting stares as white people struggle to determine if they recognize you. The notion that you may be a successful doctor, lawyer, business owner, tech entrepreneur, architect, real estate developer, banker, or investor, is utterly foreign and unexpected to so many non-black Americans.

When I pull up to a valet in my Rolls Royce, I am often met with a mix of incredulous and resentful stares. Incredulous, because my car and my appearance are not the norm, and resentment because as a wealthy black man in America, unless I am a famous ball player, rapper, or movie star, they find it mind-boggling that a person of color is driving this type of car. Many have gone so far as to inquire if I am driving my boss's car. My very existence and the existence of those like me elicit a reaction in many people that comes down to the fact that they must now go home and look at themselves in the mirror, examine their own achievements and question the validity of their own accomplishments.

I am not insinuating that one must drive a Rolls Royce to validate their accomplishments or to be deemed successful. And not everyone has the desire to possess such an item. Success comes in many different forms, and millions of people will contribute greatly to this world while never setting foot in such a car.

However, the site of me exiting my car has created something of a cognitive dissonance in people more times than I care to remember. If I am being honest, the experience can cut deep. What is perhaps even more jarring to some is the fact that I am self-taught and self-made. I am not the product of a well-connected family, an Ivy League education, or a college degree for that matter. Envy comes in many different forms. Some wish to study how I reached my financial goals as they try to follow my steps and re-bake the cake in the exact same way, only to grow frustrated if they cannot get the recipe right.

Others still have resorted to name-calling or nitpicking. Throughout my journey I have certainly encountered the classic carrot on the stick routine, where others increasingly created more hoops for me to jump through, continuously moving the bar in terms of what is needed to be achieved for me to be acknowledged or accepted in certain circles.

I have been stonewalled, delayed, derailed, discouraged, and there are those who have attempted to crush my spirit. It is through sheer resilience and perseverance, the discipline I learned in the military, as well as my own personal faith and belief in God which my parents instilled within me, that got me to my current destination in the face of discrimination and ignorance. It is for this reason that it remains jarring to my spirit whenever a non-Black person shoots me a sideways glance or makes an unprovoked comment about the car I drive. It is not because I feel that an expensive car is the totality of one's success, but because it lets me know that, at their core, they do not believe I should have the wealth to own such a car or any material thing that symbolizes financial wealth and power.

As you now know, I am a man who grew up in modest surroundings, went through the school of hard knocks, fell down more than I care to recount, and eventually earned a seat at the table through trial and error and a great deal of personal sacrifice and hard work. My wealth did not come easily. I starved and I failed. I got back up and searched for the knowledge that I did not previously possess. This helped to strengthen my weaknesses, at least the ones I could see. Of course, things that we all need to learn in order to grow are revealed to us as we are ready to receive that knowledge and improve upon those things.

Follow me for a moment as I try to explain my perspective.

You are standing in front of a door that is closed and all you can see is that which is immediately around you. The closed door is directly in front of you. You know the mistakes you have previously made to arrive at this closed door. You have worked hard to build up your mind, swearing that you will "make it" this time. You only believe this because you know you have faced many other closed doors in the past, and you made it through. Although you have mastered all of the challenges and growth that those previously closed doors ultimately provided to you, you stand in discouraged amazement at yet another door closing in your face, this time with a whole new set of challenges.

Now you hit an emotional wall of exhaustion and think, "I cannot go through this again." Ironically, for me and for many of my colleagues who have achieved great things, this is the moment of transcendence and breakthrough. This is the precursor to your life-changing opened door moment.

I know that many of you in your own lives, whether it be a business or professional pursuit, an academic pursuit, seeking your soul mate, or trying to stay ahead of the curve while doing your best to raise a family; you have spent the better part of your life either waiting for the other shoe to drop or feeling like the zenith of your dreams is always just out of reach. Vacillating between the two, glimpses of joy and contentment arise, but don't seem to stick around for very long. This part of the human experience can be frustrating, I know. No matter the obstacles you currently face or the people or circumstances you feel have conspired against you, you cannot give up on yourself or your dreams. You are equipped to handle what comes into your path. Each so-called obstacle is preparing you to meet your life's greatest opportunities in a way that you would not be ready to be had you not come through those fires. Hang in there with me, and I will hang in there with you.

One of the most significant professional doors that opened in my life is the one that I elected to walk through when I accepted a position at a technology company called Revolutionary Concepts *(stock ticker symbol: REVO)*. It was 2010, and I was still healing from one of the biggest business and financial blunders of my life which caused me to lose millions and millions of dollars and go dead broke. It challenged me in every way you can imagine. Talk about closed doors! Years back, when I had failed in my previous business, lost all of my worldly possessions, was struggling to support my family, and contemplated taking my own life, I was still in a state of financial recovery and spiritual recovery when I crossed paths with a gentleman I was introduced to through my local Black Chamber of Commerce.

We quickly became friends and he spoke highly of the CEO of a fledgling technology company called Revolutionary Concepts. I was introduced to the CEO of the company who expressed that he could use some help in raising capital and developing a potentially game-changing technology. Upon further inspection and some due diligence, it was not hard to see that their books were not in order, they were in debt, and they were spinning their wheels in the pursuit of monetizing their technology.

Under some circumstances, this would have been my first sign that I should have walked away from this deal, but my friend and the CEO were continuously asking me for my help and input. Although there were some of what I would typically deem red flags, there was one green light I could not ignore. They had the very real potential of disrupting and revolutionizing two different industries: the doorbell industry and the home security industry. When they communicated to me that they were malleable in their approach and open to my advice, and that they would allow me to re-organize and re-package their company, I felt it would be a productive collaboration. At the time, I also felt I had little to lose, and I was, frankly, surprised that they saw something in me that I had stopped seeing in myself.

This minority-owned company brought me on board to assist in developing their two-way audio/video technology and applying that technology to a smart device. After entering this first door, it was my belief that I would raise money to help them build a smart camera. They had several other professionals on board, including a finance person who was my predecessor. Evidently, their capital-raising pursuits had stalled, because they needed me to step in and reinvigorate their fundraising efforts. Feeling like I had been given a second chance after turning this opportunity down for many months, I finally officially accepted their offer to join their team and help them raise capital for their venture.

I was still holding on to some self-defeatist thinking after losing everything and having to start from scratch. Here is the scary thing about getting back up once you have fallen down: getting back up will always involve taking some new risks. After getting burned, I know that the last thing you want to do is place your hand back near the fire. If you are embarking on your second act after a tumultuous first act, know that you can now use this book as a guidepost, based on the principles I am laying out for you, to take some educated and calculated risks that stack the deck in your favor.

I fell down, I made mistakes, I put off instant gratification, and I took some calculated financial risks going forward. Ultimately, I attained hard-won wealth, and it was not without earning my fair share of battle scars. I have earned my stripes and then some. No, I am not a celebrity. I am a man who has done his homework and due diligence, studied business and finance, put my life and livelihood on the line, and ultimately found a successful formula as one of the country's top investors and intellectual property licensors.

One of the companies I oversee as CEO owns the intellectual property for the audio/video and two-way communication technology that is licensed by the popular smart home Ring Doorbell, owned by Amazon. Yes, Amazon must license the technology from us when manufacturing their famous Ring smart home doorbells. The other company where I held the title of CEO was the largest minority-owned energy company in the United States. Additionally, the private equity company that I have founded, with its focus on intellectual property, is involved in multiple technologies, a laboratory, and human resources, to name just a few of our investments that are helping to reshape our society, as we see our way out of the COVID-19 pandemic.

As Black men, in particular, we have a crisis of image and misrepresentation in the media, in popular culture, and in circles of business and socio-political intellect around the globe. We are a group that is experiencing a true public relations crisis as our mass media continues to push the public narrative of the Black man as the pro-ball player, the hip-hop figure, the drug dealer, the hustler, or the irresponsible man child who refuses to grow up and meet his manly obligations.

But how does this manufactured media image hold up to reality in 2022? We are going to do a deep dive into the stereotype of the African American man (and woman), and why Black intellectuals are often viewed as American outliers. Let's break some of our society's most esteemed professions down by the numbers, as they pertain to African Americans of either gender.

As of 2018, of the 985,000 practicing physicians in the United States, there are 50,000 practicing physicians in the United States who identify as Black or African American. Yes, we are 13% of the population, and 128,000 Black doctors would be ideal *(as that represents 13% of 985,000)*, but 50,000 of us are medical doctors and practicing physicians in the United States, and that needs to be acknowledged and celebrated just as much as a platinum-selling album or a winning jump shot.

According to the American Bar Association, 5% of American attorneys identify as Black or African American. The American Bar Association states that there are 1,352,027 licensed attorneys in the United States. This means there are currently 67,600 practicing Black lawyers who have been admitted to the Bar Association.

A 2011 article in Black Enterprise Magazine listed the 75 Most Powerful African Americans on Wall Street. From that title, one can infer that there are many others still working their way up the food chain on Wall Street who will grace that list in the future.

Have you ever heard of Bernard Beal, CEO of the nation's oldest, continuously operating minority-owned investment bank, M.R. Beal & Co, with investments totaling more than $60 billion?

Ever heard about Edith W. Cooper, Partner, Managing Director & Global Head of Human Capital Management at Goldman Sachs? In Cooper's longstanding post, she is charged with the responsibility of recruiting, developing, and retaining Goldman

Sachs' more than 33,000-member workforce, which oversees $39.2 billion in assets.

How about T. Troy Dixon, a Managing Director for Deutsche Bank who oversees a multibillion-dollar balance sheet? Or Carla Harris, Managing Director at Morgan Stanley, who helped to structure IPOs *(initial public offerings)* for companies like UPS and Martha Stewart Living, to help these companies go public?

And what about the Food Industry? Black families are known for our extraordinary skills in the kitchen, and for our ability to bring our families and the people in our communities together with delicious food. A 2019 New York Times article, titled, *16 Black Chefs Changing Food in America*, highlights the evolution and culinary emersion of southern-style soul food as it has integrated into American foodie culture. A truly beautiful cultural contribution by Black Americans is the warmth and love that we express through cooking, preparing, and sharing our food. The article goes on to highlight Jerome Grant, the chef at Sweet Home Café in the National Museum of African American History and Culture.

Do these names and accomplishments ring any bells at all? No?

I am willing to bet you've heard about the cast of *Basketball Wives* or *Love and Hip Hop*. Why is that? Why are so many African American intellectuals hiding in plain sight? Why aren't our children and *their* children seeing and hearing about these people in the media, or in school for that matter?

Speaking of school, we need more Black teachers, people! Why aren't we teaching our own children? Did you know that according to The Journal of Blacks in Higher Education, "A new report from the U.S. Department of Education during the 2017-2018 academic year, 80% of all teachers in K-12 schools in the United States are white. Only 6.3% are black/African American. African Americans make up 11% of the teachers in city schools, but only 5.5% of the teachers in suburban schools and 3.6% in rural schools. African Americans are 11% of the teachers in the nation's charter schools. In the nation's K-12 private schools, white people make up 85.1% of all teachers. Black people are 3.2% of all teachers in K-12 private schools."

In this regard, we need to do better. Black children need more Black teachers, period. This means more Black Americans who value higher education enough to pursue their Master's Degrees and PhDs in Education, and more Black Americans who have a passion to teach and pass on wisdom to a younger generation of Black Americans.

But let's not confuse a lack of Black people going into the education field with a lack of Black people getting an education. On the contrary, according to the U.S. Census Bureau, "There are 3,215,000 Black people in this country who have a bachelor's degree. And there are an additional 1,078,000 African Americans who have both a four-year college degree and a master's degree. An additional 150,000 African Americans hold a professional degree in fields such as law, business, and medicine. Another 136,000 African Americans have obtained a doctorate. Overall, 4,579,000 African Americans possess a four-year college degree or higher." If you look at our climb, "In 2008, 19.6% of all African

Americans over the age of 25 held a college degree. This is a figure that has increased significantly from 13.8 percent in 1996 and 11.3 percent in 1990." It is apparent that we are on a steady incline with no signs of slowing down. My only concern is the ever-rising "get rich quick" mentality of Generation Z as it pertains to social media fame and fortune in lieu of an education or a more sustainable career path. Knowledge is power, and if we are to make it in this country as a collective group of people, we must not forego educational pursuits and replace them with flashy trends.

As you know, I am a dye-in-the-wool entrepreneur and would never discourage our young people from pursuing success on their own terms. My message is this: back yourself up with knowledge so that you may then pass that knowledge on to someone coming up behind you. Go to school, learn your history, read, examine, and please do not take things that come your way at face value. You are better than that.

Then there are some of our country's most inspiring and insightful cultural provocateurs. From philosopher, political activist, and bestselling author Dr. Cornel West and Georgetown University Professor, author, New York Times contributor, and activist Dr. Michael Eric Dyson, to Harvard University Professor, host of PBS's *Finding Your Roots* and founding editor of the popular blog, TheRoot.com, Dr. Henry Louis Gates, Jr.; to multi-billion dollar private equity investor Robert F. Smith and writer, actor, filmmaker, and CEO of Tyler Perry Studios, Tyler Perry.

I, myself, was the subject of a recent article, titled, *Solomon Ali: The Biggest Tech Name You've Never Heard*, in a magazine called *Innovation & Tech Today*. Why did the article have that title? It is because of my unique status as the only Black American to have become, both, an officer and director of three Black publicly traded companies at the same time. Frankly, this achievement had just not been on anyone's radar up until that point. Why? Because I am an oddity, an outlier according to our popular culture media landscape.

And let's not forget about some extraordinary Black women who are challenging society's norms and breaking down barriers with their work.

Women's rights activist and professor Angela Davis, writer and poet Alice Walker, activist, writer, and professor, Bell Hooks aka Gloria Jean Watkins, Nobel prize-winning writer Toni Morrison, *CBS This Morning* anchor Gayle King, the late poet, author, and speaker Dr. Maya Angelou, the incomparable OWN Network CEO, Oprah Winfrey, and of course, our Vice President of the United States, Kamala Harris.

It is critically important as Black Americans and people of color to understand that we stand on the shoulders of giants, and not just the kind that make free throws on the court or sell millions of albums. We are lawyers, doctors, authors, professors, inventors, philosophers, business owners, educators, investors, and so much more.

So, why are other images taking center stage in popular culture, in our minds, and in the minds of our children? Why are we content with such a shortsighted view of what can be accomplished in America as it pertains to creating generational wealth?

My theory is this. Much like with the notorious 2016 presidential race, Donald J. Trump was getting most of television's airtime, and sucking the oxygen from the room and from the other candidates. Why? Because love him or hate him, he made for great television, high ratings, and lots and lots of online clicks and ad sales for a lot of big companies. The circus will always draw more attention from the media because sensationalism makes money.

In our modern-day American culture, much like in ancient Roman times, we are tuned in to our own version of the gladiators entertaining us in the Colosseum. Easy-to-watch reality television, social media gimmicks, YouTube, gossip blogs, sports arenas...these are the things holding us captive on a 24-hour mental loop called the news cycle.

Is all popular culture bad? No, it is not. We all need some entertainment, and we all like shiny novelties from time to time, but we must not forget or undervalue education, hard work, focus, determination, and self-worth. It is the ability to learn, dream, envision, and properly execute the goals that put us on a path toward sustainable financial health and well-being.

However, as African Americans, we are victims of this desire by Hollywood and our mass media to place racial and cultural stereotypes front and center for the sake of views, sales, and clicks. Perhaps you will see a Black intellectual sprinkled in the mix here or there on your favorite cable news channel, or a few times per year chopping it up on HBO next to Bill Maher. Beyond that, we are scarcely in the spotlight unless embroiled in a scandal that acts as a form of "take down news," whereby the narrative is, "I told you he couldn't have possibly been the real deal." Yes, that is another unfortunate racial stereotype that, as you know by now, I have been negatively affected by for several years. For further clarification, that is the stereotype of the Black American as the shady wheeler-dealer; the low-level "hustler," with no real redeeming or trustworthy attributes.

Here is some statistical information that supports the polar opposite of that degenerative image.

Research reveals that there are approximately 5 million businesses in the United States of America with ten or more employees, at any given time. Of that number, there are 144,000 African American companies with ten or more employees. Do we have a majority of that pie? No, not yet. But 144,000 Black American companies with the ability to each hire ten or more employees is something to celebrate.

If this is not going to be widely celebrated by the mainstream media, then we, ourselves, must celebrate it. Only then will we encourage more of these businesses to be created by younger generations coming up.

Here is where racial discrimination has worked against us. My team and I were blown away to discover that out of roughly 14,000 publicly traded companies within the United States, only sixteen of those publicly traded companies are Black-owned and/or operated. To consider a publicly traded company "Black-owned," the management must be Black. Specifically, Black control means the majority (51%) of the shareholders must be Black.

Being part of any publicly traded company is a rare and unique financial opportunity. More than 20 million companies exist today in the United States, 5 million with ten or more employees as stated above, and roughly 14,000 are publicly traded companies. The ability to bring a company public is a magnificent and rarefied achievement; an exclusive club to be sure. And guess what? Getting into that club requires capital and *lots* of it. It also requires the backing of one or more major financial entities.

Because of the marginalization of Black Americans in our financial markets throughout the past four centuries leading up to present day, this is one glass ceiling we have yet to break through in large enough numbers, and this has to change. And it will change.

When I think of these 16 Black publicly traded companies and all they have achieved, that greatness has not been without a price. No one thinks about the fight that they must have fought, the sleepless nights, the many disappointments along the way, and how many doors must have been slammed in their face before even one door opened. Yet they persevered and endured and overcame all of the obstacles placed in their path.

Nobody cared to mention my name or my accomplishments in any context in the media until the SEC decided that allowing me to thrive as one of the country's most successful holders and licensors of technology-based intellectual property was not something they were in favor of.

I have never been one to purposefully seek out the spotlight or someone who continually needs that proverbial pat on the back. But when the first public acknowledgement you receive that mentions your name in helping to move technology forward comes attached to public declarations that you defrauded investors out of first money, it is beyond disheartening. It speaks to people's desire to push the accepted narrative.

I was falsely accused of failing to disclose pertinent financial details, of being dishonest in fundraising activities, encouraging colleagues I hold in high regard to "aid and abet" my alleged unscrupulous activities, and I was accused of creating an illegal alias in an attempt to defraud or mislead investors. None of these allegations have been proven to be true in court, because they are patently false. However, once again, no one expected a Black man in America to understand the intricacies of sophisticated tax laws that enabled me to establish an irrevocable trust, legally apart and separate from me, whereby the irrevocable trust acted independently in its investment decisions. By law, there was nothing for me to disclose, but when none of the SEC's publicly made allegations were true, when the facts brought out in court did not support these allegations, the SEC chose to press forward in their take-down campaign against me anyway.

Never mind that I put my reputation and my financial future on the line. Never mind that I made investors a whole lot of money. Never mind that I played a pivotal role in forever changing multiple industries and forever changing the doorbell and how we protect our greatest assets like our homes and families. And never mind the jobs I have created because of these inventions. The narrative was all about presenting me to the financial world and to the public as a dark and shady character. Talk about poetry and irony. I would submit that the SEC has spent the last 7 years creating and augmenting this narrative about me to support their opinion. It is my belief that this matter should have been dismissed or gone to a hearing as stated under the rule of law. But more about this in a later chapter.

The massacre that took place in the thriving Black financial district of Greenwood, Oklahoma in 1921, also known as the "Tulsa Race Massacre" will not happen again, because it is now far easier to kill someone's credibility than it is to kill the actual man or woman. This is what we are dealing with when an African American man or woman transcends acceptable forms of success like entertainment and sports and dares to break into the financial establishment or dares to educate on a mass scale.

I say all of that to say this: First we must teach each other and our children about the accomplishments and contributions of African American men and women in the United States of America, and both, widen and deepen our own understanding and vision of who we really are. We must collectively acknowledge what we have brought to this country and continue to bring to this country, and therefore, what we can continue to achieve. Secondly, we are a population of people that must prioritize the dotting of i's and crossing of t's. While non-Black Americans are often given the benefit of the doubt and are allowed a more significant learning curve, one could even say more lenience, most minorities are not afforded these considerations. Therefore, thorough due diligence, knowledge of one's industry regulations and licensures, knowledge of tax laws, knowledge of best practices, showing up on time, and doing the work are all non-negotiable if we are to successfully build, succeed, and sustain generational wealth for our descendants.

Chapter 5

You Can't Outwork Your Bad Money Habits

"It's not your salary that makes you rich. It's your spending habits." – Charles A. Jaffe

If you are like most people, along the way you have made thousands of decisions about money. In fact, you make money decisions every day of your life. Everything from going to the movies, the car you decide to buy *(or lease)*, going out to dinner *(or ordering in)*, vacations, and buying various consumer-driven items. These are all money decisions, some conscious and calculated, but most, run on autopilot. This won't do.

It is time to start running your life like a business, the business of your life.

Whether you are trying to be an entrepreneur or business owner, or if you work for someone and are simply trying to create personal generational wealth, you are subject to the laws of how money works. Contrary to popular belief, you cannot outwork or out-earn your bad money habits.

Let me say that again: contrary to popular belief, you *cannot* outwork or outearn your bad money habits.

Many have tried and many have failed. Though it seems counterintuitive, you cannot simply earn more to make up the difference for what you spend. Why? Because as human nature goes, when unchecked, the more you make, the more you spend and the more money seems to just mysteriously slip away from you because of various perceived "needs." Ask any high earner who hasn't mastered the art of frugality and long-term financial planning. They will confess that the more money they made, the more money they spent... the more money they had to *keep* making to keep the machine going and to maintain a "lifestyle." According to Patrick Campbell, one of the nation's top bankruptcy paralegals, who has been preparing and filing, both, Chapter 7 and Chapter 13 *(two types of consumer bankruptcy petitions)* bankruptcy petitions across multiple states for more than eighteen years, "The majority of bankruptcy petition filers are six-figure earners, and a lot of it comes down to poor spending habits, like going out to eat instead of paying their bills."

Another important point to stress is that a human being can only output so much time and energy, and for only so many years. With that being said, you absolutely cannot look at yourself as an indestructible workhorse who can continue to output the same energy at 50 or 60 years of age as you can at 20, 30, or 40 years of age. So, you'd better start learning how to make your money work *for* you.

Think of the person earning between $30,000 and $50,000 per year who says, "If only I could double or triple my income. Then I would be in the black and be able to save some money." As evidenced above, that is not necessarily the case. Without a clear understanding and strategy for the destination of your money, your spending habits could grow to mirror, and even surpass, your earning power.

I am here to tell you that the people who win with money avoid this common pitfall like the plague. But this knowledge doesn't grow on trees, and implementing it requires discipline and a willingness to delay gratification so that you can *earn your spend*.

What does it mean to "earn your spend?" To put it simply, you should never spend more than 10% of your total net worth on ancillary and/or luxury goods and services. We are not talking about food *(not including restaurants)*, basic clothing, transportation, healthcare, and shelter. We are talking about vacations, luxury items, prestige items, restaurants, private education, and other forms of entertainment and luxury. As an example: if you earn $80,000 per year and you currently have $30,000 in savings, and your annual cost of living is $50,000, your ancillary "fun" spending for that calendar year should not outpace 10% of $60,000 – that's your hypothetical $30,000 in savings plus the $30,000 gross profit you theoretically earned that year. This means you can allow yourself $6,000 per year for entertainment and luxury spending. If that got convoluted for you, pause for a moment, write the equation down on paper and take a look at it before you continue reading. Now, this does not include real estate equity or retirement accounts that add to your total net worth. We are keeping things simple for the sake of this example.

If you would like, you can use your own numbers and plug in your own current net worth and net income after expenses, and figure out how much you can spend on luxury goods and services for the year.

The remaining profit should be paid to you, not to indulge your immediate wants, but to save and invest for your long-term wants and, most importantly, your long-term needs.

As your total net worth grows, you can raise the amount you spend accordingly, but do not disrupt the formula. Do not get fooled into focusing solely on your income. It is your total net worth, and growing that net worth, that you should be focused on. I will be mentioning this many times throughout this book. Incomes are subject to change. I cannot overstate this. And one of the biggest differences between the wealthy and middle and working class is that the wealthy consider and continually look for ways to build their total net worth, while the middle and working classes tend to focus on yearly working income.

Unless you were fortunate enough to grow up in a household of the One Percent, and even more fortunate to have parents, grandparents, or a mentor, who instilled money skills in you from a young age, the majority of us were never really taught what to do with money, nor were we taught money's real use and its power and purpose in our lives. It is something that we learn *(or don't learn)* along the way, much of the time through trial and error – emphasis on the word "error."

Yes, through trial and a lot of early error, I have learned how to harness the power of money and how to purpose and re-purpose it for growth and prosperity. I also hope to share with you how I corrected my own bad money habits and created effective money habits in my life. Hopefully, I can be one of your mentors throughout these pages. I encourage you, not just to read this book, but to study this book. Earmark it, highlight it, read it more than once, make notes and do the written exercises.

I am not going to lie to you. I am not perfect. From time to time, like all of us, I have slid backwards into some of my old habits, but I always catch myself quickly and course correct. I ask that as you remain open to evolution and set your own course on this journey, you allow yourself grace as you stumble off course and then course correct from time to time. We are going for progress, not perfection.

Bad money moves typically begin when we lie to ourselves and rationalize why an immediate want is more important than our long-term needs. Let's face it, most bad money choices have to do with buying things we cannot afford and harming ourselves financially in the process. Much of this is caused by outside stimuli and influence. With our lives now revolving around social media, those outside stimuli that cause us to "want" something are cranked up twenty-fold. We even have a name for the people who make us feel this way: Influencers. And we have a phrase for how we feel when we don't have something that we perceive someone else to have: FOMO – *Fear of Missing Out*.

Why are we allowing ourselves to be influenced in ways that move us further away from our long-term goals? If you follow influencers, please be sure their brand and messaging is in line with your betterment and long-term goals, and not associated with feelings of insecurity, lack, envy, and emptiness. Those holes will never get filled no matter how much you try to "keep up," so don't do it.

Our immediate desires have the ability to bring us fast pleasure or the expectation and anticipation of pleasure, and even the false promise of social acceptance. Many times, they are not even expensive items, but moderately priced items that add up to a lot of money over the period of a month, six months, or a year.

Here is the tricky part about getting a handle on your money and making it behave and work *for* you, especially if you tend to be a spender rather than a saver; just like with food, we cannot swear off and disavow money. When someone is addicted to food and overeats, unlike with recreational drugs, cigarettes, alcohol, or gambling, they cannot cut food out of their lives, for they will die of starvation if they do. Therefore, they need to do the important internal work to transform their relationship with food and their internal emotional issues related to food.

You cannot cut money out of your life. We need money as a tool to trade for goods and services related to our survival, and most of all, our freedom. Yes, we live in a society where we must buy our freedom. Sounds messed up on paper but think about it. What does money really buy us? When you have money in the bank, when your credit is in top form, and when your money is working *for* you in the form of investments, you have much more freedom to choose where you live, what you eat, where you travel, how you educate your children, your quality of healthcare, and how much free time you are afforded to enjoy life with the people you love.

Yes, you could drop out of society and take up residency in a sleeping bag at your local beach or park, or in a parked camper in the mountains, and tell yourself you have freedom, but do you really? You are now at the mercy of the natural elements, and other people and government entities to help protect you. That is not freedom, so we have to work within the structure we are given.

Let's discuss inner versus outer stimuli that compel us to make the money decisions we make. Our decisions are driven by the emotional state we find ourselves in, and very often it is our higher emotional states that cause us to make better long-term decisions. Whereas our lower emotional states cause us to make poor short-term decisions. When we are feeling secure, loved, and confident we are more likely to make better decisions that serve our long-term goals. When we are in a state of lack, depression, stress, fear, envy, or insecurity, we are more likely to make decisions that "feel good" or anesthetize us in the moment and do not serve our long-term goals.

This is why the internal work we do on ourselves is so important. When we feel whole, happy, and joyful, and we have confidence in who we are, we are not so hyper-focused on what we perceive others to have, nor are we as dialed into what others think of us. Our focus tends to lie on what will serve our greatest good and our long-term goals and dreams.

Secondly, we are up against a whole lot of societal conditioning thrust upon us by everything from electronics stores to car dealerships to beauty companies, and even national holidays. Everyone is constantly inundating us with "offers" to buy now and pay later. Every retail operation now has its own credit card and insider incentive deals. Many have partnership deals with banks that offer large credit lines to consumers with misleading offers like, "no interest for six months," because they know people's eyes are bigger than their bank accounts. Most consumers are lulled into becoming content to make the minimum payments well past the first six months. Always remember that large corporations do not lose.

They have done their research and they are counting on you to buy more with credit than you would with cash, to buy more than you can afford, to pay only the minimum payments, and even to miss payments or pay late. As soon as you miss one payment or make one late payment, or you go past those "first six months of no interest," you belong to them. You are now in breach of the fine print in your contract and they have free reign to assault you with their late fees and interest. These are what I like to call "legal money schemes." It is not moral, it is not ethical, but it is legal.

Cars are a major bad money habit pitfall. Why? Because second to a house, a car is the next biggest purchase we all need to make. Car purchases can be overwhelming and emotional, and to top it off, we have been brainwashed to believe that our car is our calling card – a publicly displayed barometer for how we are doing in life. Talk about a loaded decision. Car salespeople know all of this and take full advantage of these emotional and financial triggers. When it comes to buying a car, block out all the noise and consider these ten points when making a decision:

- Check the safety and reliability ratings for the car's make, model, and year.

- Preferably, buy your car outright. If you can't or won't, only purchase a car that you could afford to buy outright if you needed to. In other words, if you want to put a healthy down payment on the car and make small monthly payments, that is okay. But if push came to shove, could you write a check and pay it off? No? Then don't buy it. It's outside of your budget. If no car fits the bill at the moment, consider taking public transportation for the time being.

- Your car payment should not make a dent in your monthly income. If you feel the pain or start to sweat each month when you send your check to the bank to make your car payment, you cannot afford the car.

- Shop around for the best deal on car insurance and consider your total monthly car payment to be the monthly payment for the car, plus the monthly payment for your car insurance.

- Purchase a car with good gas mileage, preferably one that has an "Eco" option for conserving gas while you drive.

- If pre-owned, be sure the car you purchase is certified by the dealer, or get bumper-to-bumper insurance to cover future repairs.

- Be sure your car is spacious enough to safely accommodate your family and lifestyle.

- Research interest rates to get the most favorable interest rate that your credit will allow.

- Understand that a car purchase is a business transaction, not an emotional transaction.

- Choose a car price based on your net worth and not on your current income. Incomes change, employment status changes, and you do not want to be stuck with a car you will have to try and sell at a loss, or a car payment you cannot afford.

If you do all of the above the next time you are in the market to purchase a car, you should only feel a sense of pride and confidence in knowing that your car is the result of a well thought out, long-term financial strategy. This strategy can eventually lead to an upgraded car, as your total net worth grows. For now, a well-maintained used car is more than fine.

Now, if your net worth allows for it, while following the above guidelines, a luxury car may indeed be a viable option for you. If it is, congratulations and enjoy it in good health. However, if an economy car is what you can currently comfortably afford and it meets the above criteria, know that you are setting yourself up to win in the long run and that is always something to be proud of.

When you are tempted to get the impressive car with the high payment, remind yourself that each dollar is a seed and they are seeds you are giving away each month, rather than planting them to achieve financial growth. As you give up those seeds, they cannot go out and produce for you in order to eventually replace your existing working income. Those seeds are lost forever to those who have financed you, namely the bank.

Whether you are a working person trying to climb your way into the middle class, a middle-class person striving to reach the upper middle class, or an upper-middle-class person looking to become wealthy, your goal should be to accumulate as many seeds as possible so they can go out into the world and come back with "friends," meaning additional money.

The irony of money is this: the more importance you place on appearing to have money, the less money you will ultimately have. Please remember this.

The accumulation of wealth is not a difficult task, but a task of discipline. I, myself, have learned to master the discipline of delayed gratification. Within reason, this is putting off the things you want today in order to achieve what you *really* want tomorrow. So, how do we identify what it is we want *now* versus what we want *most*?

Let's take a look at what most of us truly want. When you strip away the semantics, what we all want are the following:

Love

Acceptance

Community

Faith

Health

Energy

Freedom

Security

Not necessarily in that exact order, but the above eight things are what we all really want. How we go about getting those things is where things can sometimes go sideways for us. I would like for you to pull out a piece of paper and a pen, or better yet, a notebook. Write down each of the above eight things that we as human beings continuously crave in our lives. I am betting the above list is pretty accurate, and before you rebut with your own custom list, let's analyze one of these items.

You might say, well that list is all well and good Solomon, but Power is also on my list of things I want. Okay. What do you feel that power would ultimately provide you with? Essentially, things like prestige, power, fame, popularity, wealth, and the like, are all conduits to achieving the eight above items, are they not? You might think, whether consciously or unconsciously, "If I have power, that means I will naturally have money, people will love me, respect me, and listen to me. I'll feel confident, all of my needs will be met, and I will have the freedom to live my life as I see fit."

Someone else might shun the loud energy of the spotlight and crave peace and quiet, and solitude much of the time. Maybe their sense of community comes from surrounding themselves with animals and nature, or just a few close friends and family. Either way, we are always trying to find ways to meet those eight basic human needs.

I would like you to write each of the above eight items down, and next to each of them, write how you have gone about achieving each of these things in your life up until now. Then write, stream of consciousness, where you think the ways you have gone about achieving these things have been working or not working in your life, and for your financial bottom line.

Are you moving closer to achieving these eight essential human needs, or have your decisions and actions moved you further away from achieving these things? Have you been moving closer to or further away from your greatest good?

Now write down, according to what you have read in these pages so far, some more effective ways of achieving these top eight items that all of us human beings crave. Look at the contrast on the page. Hopefully, many of you will have an "a-ha" moment that will ultimately start you on this new path.

Put off today and sacrifice for what you truly want, and you will get it tomorrow. Put your money to work. In putting your money to work you will find that it will come back with friends *(meaning more money)*. And yes, money is your friend, not your enemy. It is the misuse of money that is the enemy.

The key to putting money to work is a simple one. You look for a safe investment to place your money where there is sufficient collateral, whether that be collateral in the form of a contract or brick and mortar collateral. Look for the ability for the borrower to pay this money back to you or simply look for an investment that has the ability to give you safe returns. No, there is no guarantee, but that is why we hedge our investments with due diligence, some form of collateral, and with people who have been vetted and who have a proven track record. This is why we also honor, respect, and give thought to each and every dollar we earn, and why we save a portion of our money each month.

Please do not misunderstand me. There is nothing wrong with wanting. Wanting helps us strive for a better future, motivates and inspires us, and ultimately helps in making us better. But I can tell you from firsthand experience, you will enjoy the things you want much more when you know that it only amounts to a small percentage of your total net worth, rather than sweating that next credit card bill, loan installment, or malnourished bank account. That actually robs you of some of the joy of getting what you want. Wouldn't it be better to get something you want when you can afford it? I'll tell you this, there is nothing, and I mean nothing, like the feeling of enjoying something you can afford. It's all of the pleasure with none of the stress. Sound like a better deal?

Small expenses that add up to a lot

Have you ever sat down and journaled how much money you spend on lunch on a typical weekday? Do you spend an average of $10, $15, $20, or more? Can you even answer that question? Do you regularly ask friends to join you and sometimes pick up the tab? Are you consciously and actively aware of your day-to-day "minor" expenditures? Do you stop each morning for that venti latte at Starbucks? If so, how much do you spend? $3, $5, $7, more?

Do you know how much money you spend per day? Most people don't.

What is your overall health looking like? Is your diet a healthy one or full of extra calories, saturated fats, and processed foods that will ultimately lead to more doctor's visits, expensive medications, and even more expensive medical tests?

Do you drive a sporty gas guzzler that eats up a lot of money in gas, and costs twice as much to insure and repair?

Do you often fall prey to impulse items strategically placed near cash registers, or find that you always walk out of a store with twice as much as you went into the store intending to buy?

Many of us spend our lives trying to outwork our current bad decisions, or our previous bad decisions, that we have made. People take on overtime hours and extra jobs to try to pay down their past bad decisions... while they are currently making the same poor decisions. It sounds good in theory when you look at it from a mathematical equation. However, the problem still exists, because the problem is *you*. My problems continued to exist no matter how hard or long I worked because the problem was me. It wasn't until I changed my thoughts about money and my behaviors that my financial life transformed. We can't change yesterday's bad decisions, but we can change what you do tomorrow.

One must keep in mind at all times that your body acts as a source of energy. When you work you are typically giving your time and your energy in exchange for someone else's money. That is the conventional medium of exchange. I would caution you to be very wise in handling your money. When you attempt to outwork your bad money decisions, you are fighting against yourself. You are not fighting against the lack of money, but against your bad habits. You are spending your seed and squandering your future seeds as you run your body into the ground to try to make up the difference.

Your monies that come in should be put aside and dispersed as follows:

10% toward an emergency fund +

10% toward a long-term savings account +

<u>10% toward retirement investments +</u>

30% paid to your future self each month

Thirty percent of your monthly income goes to you in the form of savings and investments to secure your future. This leaves 70% of your earned income with which to pay your monthly bills and put toward extras and entertainment. Although, remember that extras and entertainment should only amount to 10% of your current total net worth. As the above equation builds your net worth, your lifestyle can upgrade, and it *will* upgrade.

You should always be determining how your earned income can go to work for you, and not how you can continue to work for your money. You do not want to continue to work for money as the years and decades roll along. That is a recipe for disaster and exhaustion.

Once upon a time, there was a particular car I wanted. It was a Rolls Royce. As you can imagine, this was only after my net worth had grown exponentially to justify this purchase. I wanted this car, but I waited. Although I could have bought the car years earlier than I did, and I could have bought it for cash, I waited. I chose to loan out my money and continue to see that my money was working harder and coming back with friends, so much so that it would be an ever-endless supply coming back toward me. When I bought the car, it took a financial coach to convince me that it was okay to finally go ahead and buy this car. Here is an interesting caveat to take note of: although I was able to afford it in the truest sense of the word as I outlined earlier in this chapter, after getting this car, the gratification of owning it and having it was instantly gone. Although I do, from time to time, enjoy the compliments I receive about the car, I guess what I am really enjoying is the journey and accomplishments which enabled me to purchase it debt free, knowing that it was a small percentage of my total net worth. It is a beautiful thing to be debt free and to owe nothing to any man or woman on this earth.

It is also a beautiful thing when you know that your money is working harder than you are, and every day that you wake up your money is producing more money. This is the key.

I recently helped out a young man whom I have known for many years. It was during the height of the COVID-19 pandemic and quarantine, and he would show up to work every day, opening his place of business alongside a mutual friend of mine. Including me, we were the only ones there as the Three Amigos, showing up each and every day to keep him company as he opened up and had no customers. One day he mentioned that he was struggling and could not pay his bills. I decided to help him for several months during this difficult period of time. The government later decided to give out loans to people in business to help them. My friend received one of these loans, and rather than paying me back any portion of what I had lent him, he decided to purchase himself a Rolex watch with the money. I do not even own a Rolex watch, but I managed to find the humor in it all.

I knew what I was doing when I had given him my seed, and yes, I still believe I did the right thing because I was helping a friend in need. You can't change people's money habits. You can't even change your own money habits until you decide to focus on that which is of true importance. Discipline is hard and ongoing, consistent discipline is even harder. To do without the things that you desire or want for the foreseeable future is not without its temptations. Many of us fall prey to that great temptation for instant gratification and the notion that we can get something shiny and new that we can show off on Instagram or at a party. Do you think this man I leant money to, and that the government leant money to, will ultimately succeed or fail with money? I'll let you answer that question. What I can tell you is that a man or woman who takes the few precious seeds that have been loaned and goes out and buys a Rolex watch with those seeds, is doomed to remain a slave: a slave to his appetites, a slave to his desire for acceptance, and yes, a slave to working for money and owing money.

Why do we fall into this trap so easily? How did this happen? For me it began as a young person looking at my family struggling to make ends meet. Although they climbed from working class into the middle class, we still could not buy some of the things we wanted or go to the places I wanted to go to. I looked at others who were able to do more things than we could, and it appeared they were able to do them with such ease. It was only later that I learned the lesson of deferred gratification and how my parents managed to climb up into the middle class. "No," I was told. "You cannot go on all of these trips and go to all these football camps and other summer camps." Instead, I was told, "We will send you to one or two each year, but you will not go to all of them, because we cannot afford to continue to send you to these various camps. We have other things and other priorities that need to be taken care of."

As a young child you do not understand these things. All you hear is the word "No," or the rejection of what you so desperately want. Much of the time, what you really want is to be like the others, and sometimes it is hard to grow out of that. I will call the others the "Jones's." We learn to keep up with the Jones' from the time we are children. That is what I was doing and many of you are as well. Something that is programmed into us as children which then carries over into our adulthood is causing us to spend our seed and our future seeds. It is causing us to manifest poverty for ourselves and for our kids if we teach them the same old bad habits. This programming is what must change.

When I became a young adult and went off to the military, I began to save my money. I had lots of it saved up after a time and had nothing to do with it. I needed no shelter because the army provided shelter for me. I needed no food because they provided me with food. I didn't need clothing because I was provided with clothing in the way of my uniforms. I literally had nothing that I needed to do with my money What a great place to be. You have everyone looking after you. I had a job to do and everything else was provided. And let's not forget, I was not exposed to the disease of wanting what the other guy had, because the other guys I was surrounded with were living exactly the way I was living, eating what I was eating, and wearing exactly what I was wearing. I believe this is where I first learned how to strategically loan out money and have it come back to me with "friends."

To make additional monies I also shined shoes for people. I found this to be fun and socially enjoyable since I stayed in what we called the barracks most of the time while others went out to parties and other big social gatherings, like group movie dates and restaurant outings. No, I didn't do much of that. I felt that since the military provided meals, I might as well go eat in the mess hall, so that is what I did. I watched sports games on television and shined shoes. You would be amazed at the extra money I picked up from this seemingly menial pursuit. If I shined ten pairs of shoes, I could easily make myself an extra $200 in a weekend. This was close to forty years ago and that $200 would be equivalent to about $550 today. I didn't know it at the time, but this was entrepreneurship. When my friends would run out of money before they got their weekly army pay again, I was quick to loan them the money that they needed and charged them interest on the money. It was great to get all of my money back with interest.

Typically, I would charge them approximately 10% to 20%, depending on who it was. Some people I liked better than others, but I had no problems loaning money out, because I had no use for the money since all of my needs were met; every last one of them. I had food, clothing, and shelter. I enjoyed being in the military very much.

For anyone who was or currently is in the military and is reading this book, ideally, complete your higher education. Take advantage of the opportunity that is afforded to you, pick up a second job, and secure your future. If higher education is just not for you, save your money and work toward purchasing a business. You can also combine resources and partner with others to purchase a business. This will give you a huge head start. If you are in the military, or an alternative situation where some or all of your living expenses are covered, you should be able to save money relatively quickly.

I know that for most of you, the brass ring is to own a home and you are going to need to save up a down payment to purchase that house. Here is what I will say to that. Please wait. Please don't go out and purchase your house prematurely. A house is a liability. Many will claim it to be an asset, but it is not, at least not for the foreseeable future *(approximately a decade)*.

An asset is something that you can liquidate and something that has value at all times. This is what we have been taught to believe that a house has. However, the only equity that is in your home is the down payment that you have put up for your home. Remember you saved your hard-earned money to put down on one "asset" called a home. You would have gone out and borrowed the other 80-90% to make this purchase. That may sound like a good thing because you are comfortable in making the monthly mortgage payment. But look at it this way; if you cannot make the payments, what happens? Well, I will tell you. You will lose the home, because until your home is paid off, it is actually the bank's asset. If you default on your monthly mortgage, you will lose that house and you will lose your equity and future equity. When you look at it from that perspective you have just lost all of your seeds, and that is not a good thing.

Here is the other thing. The only way to get your money back out of the home is to either sell the property or refinance it. I will caution you, even if the interest rates have dropped, do not refinance your property. If you refinance your home you could be making your burdens heavier than what they currently are. Resist that temptation.

My personal recommendation, which I admit is a controversial one, is to be simple in your approach to building equity and buy a business first. Look at what it is you like to do.

How do you know what you like to do? What would you do for free, or even pay someone to allow you to do *(strictly hypothetically, of course!)*? What places a smile on your face? Buy *that* business and you will do well. Learn everything you can about the industry, learn about the top management teams who are doing things within that industry, enjoy what you are doing and be willing to put more money back into your business, though not all of your money. If you run your business correctly, you will be able to qualify to purchase a home. You will be able to quickly come up with a down payment to purchase that home, and you will have one solid asset and possibly a second asset. But remember, until that home loan is paid off, your home is a liability. Once it is paid for, it becomes a potentially strong asset in your wealth portfolio.

Yes, it can feel exciting and empowering to get approved for a mortgage, go to closing and get the keys to your new home. It feels empowering to no longer have to say you are a renter. That is what society tells us, and there is some truth to that, but please remember, it is not that simple and clear cut. Very few things are. When you owe money to a lender, you are a slave to that lender. You must go to work to pay that lender back or s/he has the right to take that which you "own." This is because you do not truly own it until you have paid for it in full.

At one time I had owned approximately thirteen nursing homes and a whole lot of real estate. I do mean *a whole lot* of real estate; millions and millions of dollars' worth. And then later I found myself in a predicament that stripped me of my so-called real estate equity. My real estate had an LTV (loan-to-value) ratio of somewhere between 55-60%. Most people would have said that means I have a lot of equity in my real estate holdings that I could pull out at will. Well, I also believed that whole heartedly only to find out that wasn't the case one day when my business wasn't doing so well because of regulatory issues and mismanagement by my team, when the bank came in and took over by placing a receiver in my business and redirecting all of my monies to the receiver to allocate my equity and pay off what they wanted to be paid off, leaving me completely broke.

It only took a year for me to lose all, and I do mean *all*, those millions and millions of dollars, not to mention the millions that were lost from my business. So, when I say real-estate is a burden, in that it is a debt and an obligation, I speak from firsthand experience. This is not to scare you or dissuade you, but to help you understand the gravity of the responsibility and how to position yourself on more solid ground to stack the deck in your favor. I had thought I was doing the right thing by having low LTVs, but I was not. Anything that you owe a creditor is rightfully his/hers until you pay it off in full.

The more we live, the more things happen in life. People are accustomed to saying, "That's life" or "Shit happens." Forgive my French, but the old "Shit happens," when it is happening to you, is a tough pill to swallow. But you cannot blame anyone. I cannot blame anyone but myself for what I had gone through, because I made every single decision leading up to that point, thinking that I was doing the right things, or knowing that I was avoiding doing the right things and putting off until tomorrow what could have been done today. "I'll get to those papers another time," "I'll look into that issue another time," "I'll speak with that employee later," "I'll comply with that regulation when I get around to it," and the best one of all, "This money will never stop coming in." I didn't know at the time that salaries, in fact all forms of income, are subject to change. What's not subject to change are good money habits, maintaining a healthy net worth, and taking the time to stay on top of industry regulations, infrastructure, management, taxes, and other important business matters.

Yes, I not only had a bunch of commercial properties and apartment complexes and single family homes, I also had fancy cars. Not just one fancy car. I think at one point we had as many as 7-12 fancy, luxury cars including cars we acquired through our company. I learned the hard way that all of this fancy stuff I had was nothing but a bunch of debt. When my business became severely compromised and I could not pay for it, it was all gone; poof, up in smoke. I prayed and I prayed, and asked God, "Why?" I asked where He was and why He hadn't come to help me when He had come so many times before. There was no answer, or so I thought. I felt like a living embodiment of a story I had read in the bible, The Book of Job.

Job was a man who was challenged. A man who had lost everything. That was me and I could identify with this man. At the time, I could not hear God or see God, and many people were quick to point out to me that I had been the architect of my own financial undoing.

I knew in my heart I had not intentionally done anything wrong, but I had to admit that I had mismanaged my money. I had leveraged properties that were owned free and clear to buy other properties. These were commercial properties that were attached to my nursing home business. I thought the nursing home business would be able to pay for these properties and that I would definitely come out the other end a winner. Well, that was a really hard lesson to learn. It was a lesson that almost cost me my life.

When you take a steep fall, you don't see a way up and out. You don't see how you can ever get back. I did build my way back, brick by brick, lesson by lesson, application by application, but it is far easier to maintain and build than it is to lose everything and rebuild from scratch. You must look at yourself and every decision you make, and you must justify your actions for spending money and why. You must ask yourself, "Do I need what I am about to purchase? What benefit will that have in the long run, or am I giving up my future seed for something that may turn out to be empty later?"

Many of us have bought things such as clothes or shoes only to wear them a handful of times. If you are making these kinds of purchases on credit or with credit cards, please stop. You are going to go off a cliff without a parachute. Stop. Reevaluate your life. God has given us wisdom and intuition. The greatest financial work any one of us can do, and the greatest work I did on myself, was to look at myself, figure out my emotional/financial triggers, learn to control my material desires and emotions and conquer them so that my money worked for me instead of sentencing myself to a lifetime of working for my money. You cannot continue to borrow against your future earnings and expect a positive outcome, because life will happen.

Whether you or a loved one gets sick, someone loses a job, a business goes under or slows, or some other emergency arises, living life means something will happen and you will not be prepared for it if you have spent all of your seed. All those people you enjoyed impressing suddenly won't mean a thing when your survival is compromised. Sadly, for some people it takes hitting this bottom to realize how little people's opinions matter in your life.

I do not want you to make the same financial mistakes I have made, and therefore, throughout this book, I will be giving you inside access to some of my favorite financial and business experts who will share their wisdom and expertise with you.

Meet Dr. Rolanda "Ro" Schmidt, International Finance Ph.D.

To second these important sentiments, I am letting my friend and colleague, Dr. Rolanda "Ro" Schmidt, Ph.D. () weigh in on financial habits and wealth building. "Dr. Ro" as people call her, is a former Tax Accountant with seventeen years of experience, a Ph.D. in International Finance and Professor of Business and Finance, where she has taught at Cardinal Stritch University and Northwestern University.

Having seen many of the mistakes families and business owners have made with their money over the past two decades, which she chronicles in her own book, *Don't Live Like Caviar on a Hot Dog Budget*, she leads with some homespun financial advice that adds up to good sense. "If it's not broken, don't pay to fix it and don't buy a new one." As for Dr. Ro's financial upbringing, she says, "Although my dad gave me some financial tidbits, like the importance of having insurance and not accumulating debt, it wasn't a strategy for creating generational wealth." She admits that in her early adulthood she often justified expensive purchases with the need for "quality, regardless of price." Although it's nice to have nicer things, she recalls, "I didn't look at how these items would affect me, financially, and my future." It was a neighbor in her community that gave her that a-ha moment, changing the course of her financial destiny at the age of twenty-two. "What rocked me was a client of mine who lived next door and she had cancer. Her husband knocked on my door one day and said his wife refused to expire until I completed her taxes. Once she got word that her taxes were squared away, within 45 minutes she was gone."

The tragedy of this story, she says, is that within six months of the woman's passing, her financial astuteness and savings were squandered by irresponsible and disrespectful family choices. "I watched this woman's hard earned generational wealth dissipate with her husband's irresponsible financial choices. No trust or educational funds had been created for their children, the man went back to using drugs because of his grief, and his children went to live with their grandmother. The family had nothing after years of this woman working and being so diligent with her finances. That was when I said, 'What am *I* doing? If something happens to me, how are my children going to be taken care of?'"

"It is 'I' disease that does so many people in," she says. "Not *eye* disease but *I* disease. *I* want this and *I* want that, rather than, 'Do I really need this right now?' Sometimes you have to sacrifice and not get that five dollar coffee, or not get your nails done that week, if it means working toward a worthy long term goal."

Dr. Ro's Greatest Tips

You don't have to go broke to live like you are rich. Wealth is a state of mind, not a material item, and feelings create things. However, if a wish item is nonnegotiable, you can swap out overpriced retail for scouring upscale thrift stores. Bonus: You get to have the experience of "thrifting" while pouring over gently loved luxury items, each with a rich story attached to it; and make yourself look like a million without spending it.

For all negotiable cravings and "wants," keep that money you would have spent and instead invest it in your children's college fund, a high yielding mutual fund, or well researched stock. You'll get the thrill of the "spend," knowing you are actually spending that money on an investment in your own future.

Have contingency plans in place in the form of a liquid fund for life's little (and big) emergencies.

Asking yourself if you can afford something before you go ahead and purchase it. This simple, yet powerful, question will stop you in your tracks, make you think twice, and wake you out of your impulse buy trance. You may go ahead with the purchase, you may not, but make it a conscious purchase rather than an impulse buy.

Do I really need this car? Do I really need a house this size? Or am I trying to impress neighbors, acquaintances, frenemies, or judgmental family members?

Take care of your family and your well-being, and trust the people around you that have done the things you want to do to help guide you.

Find a financial mentor and be willing to sacrifice. Stop, think, and listen to a mentor. Don't try to put your hand in every pot because of flashy investment trends that promise inflated returns.

Be careful with business expenses that don't pass muster. Consult with a CPA or tax attorney, and if it wasn't business related, skip the tax deduction. If you currently cannot afford a specialist to help you with your taxes, see above, and take advice from a trustworthy financial mentor.

Rushing into entrepreneurship with a sole proprietorship leaves you financially vulnerable if someone sues you. Form an LLC or other legal entity that provides personal financial protection and offers you the best tax structure for your business.

Keep accurate records and do not mix business money with personal money. Intermingling funds gets messy and muddies the waters for an accountant to help you with your taxes at the end of the year. If you cannot afford to hire a bookkeeper, there are plenty of effective bookkeeping software programs on the market.

File your taxes on time. It's the best way to avoid IRS late fees and penalties, and if you are entitled to a refund or tax credit, you can claim those funds that much sooner.

If possible, start long term financial planning early, in your twenties or early thirties. You do not want to depend solely on social security in your older years.

Being financially organized comes naturally for some people, and is more challenging for others. If you are not a person who is naturally organized, there are planners you can purchase to help you categorize and organize your financial records that you can then hand over to your accountant when it is time for taxes. It will make both of your lives a lot easier.

CHAPTER 6

—·—

WHY BLACK PEOPLE SHOULD BE INVESTORS AND NOT CONSUMERS

"Consumerism thrives on emotional voids." – Carolyn Knapp

I will never forget my very first business that I cleverly developed at the age of eight or nine years old. I was born in 1964, and eight years later technology wasn't exactly moving at lightning speed like it is now. I didn't have the ability to leverage a platform like Instagram, TikTok, or YouTube like some enterprising young people do today, but I was still quite ambitious and used what I had at my disposal. I started my own business selling slingshots, which I made from old wire coat hangers, blue jean material, and electrical tape. I began selling them to the neighborhood kids in my working-class neighborhood for a tidy profit of .60 cents per slingshot. At that young age I felt like I was in the money, and once I got the taste of how it felt to turn a profit, I was bitten by the entrepreneurial bug.

I have been building profitable businesses ever since, but what I learned as I transitioned from youth into maturity is that making money is not the whole picture when it comes to building wealth.

Earning money is only the first part of the equation, because without an income you cannot sustain yourself, let alone build wealth. However, you can earn all the money you want, and, mark my words, if you do not know how to manage that money you will not build long-term wealth. From Mike Tyson to MC Hammer to the late Marvin Gaye, there are countless examples of prominent figures, past and present, who made a lot of money and lost it all. These are talented, hardworking people with impeccable work ethics who simply failed to properly secure ownership of their own financial futures for myriad reasons.

From lack of financial education and lack of mentorship to poor career and financial management, you can be monetized to the hilt but lack ownership over your own intellectual property and/or lack the educational acumen to go the distance from becoming rich to building long-term generational wealth. Although these people got rich, they failed to take the proper steps toward building their wealth; whether it was poor tax planning, squandering assets, impulsive spending or lack of asset protection and lack of ownership over one's brand and intellectual property. These are the root causes of financial failure. Failure to build wealth and "going broke" doesn't just happen to people. The seeds of your future are sewn long before you reap your crops. The seeds you sow today will determine your future.

Conversely, people like Oprah Winfrey and Tyler Perry surrounded themselves with the right business and financial mentors and consultants, intellectual property and tax attorneys, and accountants. As a result, they grew their lofty incomes into the massive growth and astronomical wealth you see today. Did you know that although Oprah Winfrey has a team managing her money, she insists on looking at and personally signing every check before it goes to its recipient? You must value every dollar and you must be your own financial advocate. When you are able to build wealth, you don't just create security for yourself, you can also be a blessing to others. You can establish resources that can help to uplift entire family lines and entire communities.

If you want to know what some of today's billionaires think about money, debt, saving, and investing, take a look at these quotes:

"My father raised me to believe that debt was a terrible thing." **– Oprah Winfrey (estimated net worth $2.7 billion/Forbes)**

"Someone's sitting in the shade today because someone planted a tree a long time ago." **– Warren Buffett (estimated net worth $102 billion/Forbes)**

"Not everyone wants to make the sacrifice in the trade-off to become wealthier, and the first part of that trade-off is savings and investment and time." **- Robert F. Smith (estimated net worth $6 billion/Forbes)**

"I've never chased money. It's always been about what I can do to motivate and inspire people." **-Tyler Perry (estimated net worth $1 billion/Forbes)**

What can we learn from these people who have made their way into the billionaire club? Do not accumulate debt; if you want your family line to be able to sit in the shade tomorrow, it is up to you to plant the right seeds today and grow strong, solid trees for them. Building wealth takes discipline, delaying gratification, and focus. Informed investing is king. Make it your mission to chase what inspires and motivates you, contribute something positive to the world and the money will come.

You might be thinking that you have about as much in common with these people as a bullfrog does with a fruit fly, but let me tell you, not one of these people were born with a silver spoon in their mouth. Oprah Winfrey spent her childhood sleeping on makeshift beds and porches as she was shuffled from one distant family member to another. Her very first salary in television was $10,000 per year. Tyler Perry fought through homelessness and then financed his first stage plays using his modest $12,000 in life savings, before getting his creative works noticed by Hollywood. Robert F. Smith grew up the son of two school teachers in a middle class African American neighborhood. The point is, money is a byproduct of developing the right belief systems, a strong work ethic, a willingness to acquire financial literacy, and your behavior patterns with money.

For the average working American, learning the skills that can transform even the most modest income into long-term generational wealth is advantageous, and for Black Americans these wealth building skills are absolutely critical. Why? Because our very lives depend on it. Wealth equals the ability to protect oneself and one's family. It enables your family line to access better education, safer neighborhoods, quality medical care, and socio-political access to be able to affect change in the system.

Generational wealth helps you and your loved ones to be able to stand up and be counted by the people in power who have the ability to make decisions that impact your well-being in this country.

When it comes to Black America, money management skills go well beyond information and willpower. It boils down to transforming our cultural psychology, healing our emotional scars, and course-correcting our emotional cues that date back centuries. It's a tall order, so let's start by taking a look at some facts to gain a thorough understanding of how Black Americans earn and spend money, and the racial wealth gap.

According to research done by the Institute for Family Studies a few years back in 2018, "More than one-half of Black men have made it into the middle class or upper class as adults." The study goes on to explain that "millions of Black men are flourishing financially in America" to the tune of one-in-five *(or about 2.5 million)*. Black men who are in the upper-income bracket rose from 13% in 1960 to 23% in 2016, according to this IFS analysis.

Black families are now earning more than we ever have before in African American history. Where is all the money going if it is not building Black wealth? Why are Black families not building long-term generational wealth like their white counterparts?

The answer is generational social-emotional conditioning within the Black community. We have conditioned each other to associate our worth within this American societal construct with the things we own rather than our ability to positively impact our communities, our personal accomplishments, our integrity, our character, or even our experiences. We have been led to believe that owning expensive and flashy things is somehow our ticket to acceptance and a seat at the table. It is costing us, and it is costing our children, our grandchildren, and *their* children.

To unpack this issue further, when your lineage has been physically enslaved, mentally enslaved, and continuously sent overt as well as subliminal messages that you are somehow inferior, you have to find a way to survive. You are going to feel compelled to fill in those gaps and to find any way you can to cross that bridge toward the promise of higher self-esteem and validation, by any means necessary. If you look at how the late Steve Jobs dressed or how Mark Zuckerberg or Warren Buffet dress themselves each day, they are conservative and unassuming in their gate and manner of dress, because they are coming from an abundance mindset and feel they have little to prove. When you are showing up in the world with a lack mindset, you are going to try to overcompensate with your outward appearance.

As an African American man, I understand where you are coming from, and I know that pain. It is not your fault that, psychologically, you have absorbed by osmosis the ill effects of continued micro-aggressions and systemic racism. However, we must course correct. It is challenging when we are still dealing with systemic racism to this day, but I am telling you, this is the way out.

Yes, there are many African Americans managing their money well, owning their own intellectual property, saving and investing and building wealth, but we are in the minority, not the majority. We need to flip that statistic.

A widely read and shared August 2020 article published on the website BlackMenInAmerica.com, titled, *How Do Black Men Spend Their Money (The Racial Wealth Gap)*, paints an unattractive picture of African Americans as highly susceptible to advertising campaigns, financially self-centered (we don't consider our future generations), fiscally impulsive, and gaining a sense of self-worth through the purchase of material goods. The most disturbing passage in this article reads, "When shopping, African Americans are more influenced than the total population by store staff (34% more likely), in-store advertising (28% more likely) and merchandising (27% more likely)." Although I don't agree with this article in its entirety, the statistics are objective and non-emotional, and they speak to how much power the advertising industry has within our community to influence us by making us feel valued and validated if we possess certain material items.

If you are feeling angry while reading this chapter, you should be. According to the aforementioned statistics, if we as Black Americans stay this course, it is estimated that it will take us another 228 years to catch up to our white counterparts in terms of building generational wealth and closing the racial wealth gap.

To clarify the point, this alarming wealth gap is not solely due to the last 50 years or even the last 100 years. This racial wealth gap also cannot be completely pinned on you for that Louis Vuitton handbag you purchased, or the expensive car you leased. There is more to the picture that must be acknowledged. This racial wealth gap began and was put in play hundreds of years ago when generation after generation of African Americans invested their time, creativity, and labor for free; first as slaves, then as "free people" who were indebted to our former slave owners, and then to people who exploited our ideas and systematically stole our intellectual property and our ability to seek legal recourse as a remedy to these infringements.

Conversely, many white Americans have had a significant head start in building their wealth, which has been transferred from generation to generation in the form of money, real estate holdings, investments, business interests, inside information, networking, and educational opportunities for their children and grandchildren.

I would also be remiss if I did not mention the historical wage and salary disparities between African American families versus white families; another offshoot of the historical racial wealth gap. According to Statista.com's 2019 findings, the median household income for the African American family is $45,232 versus the median white household income of $76,000, the median Asian household income of $98,000, and the median Hispanic/Latinx household income of $56,000. Regardless of what your household earns, you still have to live and support yourself in this country which has the same fixed costs for everyone.

It is like someone who has already run several laps around a track asking someone who just got on the track to keep pace and log the same miles in the remaining allotted time. It would be impossible for the second person to catch up, because the first person already has X amount of miles on the second person.

If you are white and reading this book, I ask for your open mind and compassion as you read my words. Imagine for a moment that five generations of your family worked without getting paid, or having the right to vote or own property. And imagine that only two or three generations back in your family line, those ancestors were slaves and then trying to recover from the after effects of slavery as they negotiated the Jim Crow south during the 1960s. Now think about your actual family ancestry. Perhaps your great grandparents arrived on these American shores, and although they came here with little or no money, they were able to enjoy full equal rights, a certain level of education, and the ability to enjoy a profession and prosper so that all future generations could benefit from their sacrifice. There is a large chasm between the two scenarios.

And to my readers of color, we know that the racial wealth gap is bigger than you and bigger than me, but the future hedges on the decisions you make today and going forward, and that is most certainly on you and on me. My question to you is this: do you really need that expensive handbag or would investing that money into stocks serve to plant better long-term seeds? Do you really need to lease or buy that expensive luxury car to impress the neighbors, or would you be better served planting long-term seeds and investing that money into stocks? Or perhaps, toward building a business?

As a community, our historical desire for expensive impulse-driven consumer items that make us "look good" is not about a lack of intelligence. To the contrary, a 2016 *Psychology Today* article titled, *The Power of Emotions to Override Rationale Thought*, states that, as humans, our inability to switch gears or believe differently even when the evidence is right in front of us comes down to what the article labels "child logic" or "logic that is hijacked by emotion." As human beings, we all suffer from this affliction in one way or another. The article goes on to elaborate with an emphasis that "regardless of age or intelligence, we at times engage in magical thinking associated with earlier development" and that "it is as if the emotional brain and the rational brain are not effectively communicating with each other, whether emotions override logic or the rational brain is ill prepared to correct the surge of emotion. The result is impaired judgment."

Translation: Advertisers and the media are very effective at hijacking the emotional part of your brain and its reward centers, and convincing you that the emotionally-driven purchase you make right now is more important than your logical long-term financial goals. We need to re-write this programming so that the next time you are in a store, a car dealership, or maybe at a club that offers bottle service, you do not lose awareness of your long-term financial goals.

If I were to ask you if you would rather have a large sum of money in the bank but less flashy things, or *a lot* of expensive items but virtually no money in the bank and a pile of debt, your rational mind would take center stage and answer my question with something along the lines of, "Obviously, I'd rather have a lot of money in the bank."

So where is the disconnect? Why will so many of us spend money we don't have on cars, shoes, clothes, automotive accessories, beauty and grooming items, and jewelry that we cannot really afford, rather than looking after our financial future and the financial future of our children?

In my humble opinion the answer lies in our shared legacy living within a societal framework in America that has consistently told Black people that we are less than... less than human, less than acceptable, less than beautiful, less than capable, less than worthy of the right to receive justice when our life is senselessly taken out of racial prejudice.

Is it any wonder we have evolved into a group of people who feel the need to adorn our visage with status items that, in our minds, make us look more... *worthy*?

This is not to say that many Americans, in general, aren't swept up in the allure of status symbols. We see it all around us, from flashy cars to designer clothing, expensive fragrance, handbags that are the same price as an automobile, and shoes that cost a month's mortgage or rent payment. A lot of us want to believe we are living "the good life," because it is being sold to us on a regular basis, via Madison Avenue's slick advertising campaigns, since the day we were born. Now, add social media influencers and celebrities into the mix, and it makes for a seductive and intoxicating brew.

The difference is, we as Black Americans are behind, and as we know, it takes a lot more work to move the needle than it does to maintain what already exists. As I cited before, if as a community we continue going the way we are going, it will take Black Americans more than 200 years to close the racial wealth gap. That means we have work to do.

If you needed to lose 200 lbs., would you be able to eat the way someone eats who is simply maintaining their body weight? No. You would have to work a lot harder. That's the situation as it stands now.

One statistic that really weighs heavy on my heart is that many Black Americans are not just living paycheck to paycheck; they are actually borrowing against future paychecks. In essence, many of us are so broke, we are borrowing money from our future selves at punishing interest rates, and depriving that future version of ourselves with the ability to build financial freedom. When you borrow money against future earnings at a high interest rate or debtor's fee, you are actually stealing money from your future self.

Even when you borrow money at high interest rates for consumer electronics, furniture, flat screen TVs, expensive cars, or other "I want" items, you are stealing from your future self by taking money out of your paycheck and out of your pocket down the road that could be used to invest in your future.

When you wake up to the realization that it is of far more value to *be* wealthy than to *look* wealthy, your entire perspective shifts and your financial future begins to re-shape itself.

Did you know that Black Americans have the power to significantly impact some of the world's largest consumer brands' bottom lines?

According to the Selig Center for Economic Growth at the University of Georgia, "Black buying power will rise from $1.3 trillion in 2017 up to $1.54 trillion by 2022. This estimate for 2022 reflects a 5.4% increase over a five-year estimate and reaching $1.46 trillion by 2021. The 108% increase in black buying power between 2000 and 2017 outperformed the 87% rise in white buying power and the 97% increase in total buying power *(all races combined)* during the same time period."

The very fate of consumer-driven economics rests in our more melanin-effective hands. Yes, that is a lot of power, which is why so many brands, from fast food to fashion, specifically craft and design their advertising campaigns to speak directly to the Black community. They need our dollars, because our dollars make up the majority of their revenue.

But how has this helped our community? How has all of that money come back into our community to uplift us? How have all of those dollars we have spent helped our voices be heard or kept us safe? And how has it helped our people build generational wealth?

It hasn't. What it's done is make all of these companies and their executives and investors wealthy off our backs. To add insult to injury, some of the boards of these companies have publicly disparaged Black Americans, either overtly or covertly, as they continue to count our hard earned money.

Essentially, you have been investing in large consumer-driven companies for years, but at a 0% return rate. The trouble is, many of these companies, although they need your dollars, they do not respect your dollars, and instead, see them as a foregone conclusion. Your hard earned money is being taken for granted and not earned by these companies. If these companies respected your money, they would stand up for you, they would defend you, they would rally in support of your health, safety and well-being, and they would give back to Black and brown communities. It took the murder of George Floyd for many American corporations to start publicly expressing their support for Black and brown communities, and to declare that our lives do indeed matter. But it has been too little too late, and much of it was a PR move to appear lockstep with the current socio-political climate; born out of a PR and marketing board meeting. I, for one, would like to see non-Black owned businesses who profit off of the Black community taking action by giving back to our community with a percentage of the very money we put in their pockets.

Do not be passive. Research the companies and brands you frequently patronize and find out how they spend their money, who they support, and what their corporate culture is. If they are not for us, do not do business with them. Remember, THEY need YOU.

Please also understand that buying products based on what your favorite celebrities are flexing on Instagram is also a foolhardy venture.

An example that makes me "smdh" *(shake my damn head)* as they say is rappers who put expensive cars, clothes, private jets and jewelry in their music videos and on social media, leading their fans and would-be fans to believe they are living the multimillionaire's lifestyle, all in an effort to get people to buy in to what they are selling... literally. If you look behind the curtain, many of these new artists are receiving what is called an advance against royalties. This means that they receive a budget to produce and promote their album or their single. That money is an upfront advance against costs and what the record company anticipates that particular album will earn in projected sales. If the artist is a new artist, that advance will be much more modest than it would be for a more established artist.

Aside from fixed expenses including studio time, producers, songwriters, and a stipend for the artist to live on *(if they are lucky)*; there can be wardrobe stylists, photographers, music video directors, and a publicity and marketing machine to pay for. Then there is the cost of touring to support the album. And let's not forget music videos and everything that goes into their production. All of that needs to be paid back to the record company before that artist sees a dime of their royalties per unit sold *(or in this day and age, their streams/downloads)*. That is why it is widely known by insiders that an artist rarely earns a profit on their first album. Instead, they tend to get paid in the form of flashy perks like the ones you see in their lavish music videos, on magazine covers, and on social media.

Below, the popular website TheRoot *(via the "RIAA" Recording Industry Association of America's website)* breaks down the economics of being a first-time platinum-selling recording artist in great detail:

"Going back ten years ago, Courtney Love famously laid out the details of recording economics, where the label can make $11 million... and the actual artists make absolutely nothing. It starts off with a band getting a massive $1 million advance, and then you follow the money:

What happens to that million dollars?They spend half a million to record their album. That leaves the band with $500,000. They pay $100,000 to their manager for 20 percent commission. They pay $25,000 each to their lawyer and business manager.That leaves $350,000 for the four band members to split. After $170,000 in taxes, there's $180,000 left. That comes out to $45,000 per person.That's $45,000 to live on for a year until the record gets released.So, this band releases two singles and makes two videos. The two videos cost a million dollars to make and 50 percent of the video production costs are recouped out of the band's royalties.The band gets $200,000 in tour support, which is 100 percent recoupable.The record company spends $300,000 on independent radio promotion. You have to pay independent promotion to get your song on the radio; independent promotion is a system where the record companies use middlemen so they can pretend not to know that radio stations -- the unified broadcast system -- are getting paid to play their records.All of those independent promotion costs are charged to the band.Since the original million-dollar advance is also recoupable, the band owes $2 million to the record company.If all of the million records are sold at full price with no discounts or record clubs, the band earns $2 million in royalties, since their 20 percent royalty works out to $2 a record.Two million dollars in royalties minus $2 million in recoupable expenses equals ... zero!"I could go on, but you get the point.

Much of the luxury goods you see on or with these rap artists is either leased, borrowed, or gifted to them, and they are being used by corporate America to instill a feeling of envy or FOMO *(fear of missing out)* in the would-be consumer to stimulate sales. The artist or celebrity is being used as a human billboard or conduit to sell to you, their fans and followers, to get your money. Even if that artist crashes and burns in their career and personal finances, these corporations have already made millions and even billions off of their backs by selling to YOU.

Point being, please do not assume that what you are seeing is completely authentic. Please be inquisitive enough to look behind the curtain and think for yourself. And, most importantly, now that you know better, let's DO better.

We have exhaustively diagnosed the problem and how much it is costing us as a community. It is time to learn how to think differently about money, not as a tool for making expensive status-driven purchases and impressing others, but as a wealth building tool that will promote you and the generations that come after you.

What does it mean to build wealth? When the money that you have earned starts its journey toward making you *more* money, you are on the road toward building wealth. When your money is just being spent on non-income-producing products, leading to a deficit that requires you to go out and make more money to replace that deficit, you are not on the road toward building wealth. You are simply a consumer.

Yes, we all have monthly expenses that require us to spend money. The average American has a housing payment *(whether rent or a mortgage)*, a car payment, various insurance payments *(car, homeowners, renter's, life, health, etc.)*; and expenses for food, gas, children, pets, and other life-related incidentals. However, with a monthly written budget, those expenditures should not exceed your monthly income. In fact, each month at least 30% of your take home income should be paid to *you*, the person earning that money, in the form of long term savings, an emergency fund, and investments, in order to stay ahead of yearly inflation and to build your future security and legacy.

As your finances gain more and more health, this dynamic should actually flip to where seventy percent of your money should eventually come from passive and investment income, while only 30% of your income should come from your day-to-day work/labor/time.

If you are hearing all of this for the very first time, your mind is likely spinning, and all of this may seem foreign and overwhelming to you. Do not fear these thoughts. They are the first step toward waking up to a different way of viewing your money, and we are going to go through each of these points, step by step.

Let's Talk Income

The equation is quite simple, not easy, but simple. A good analogy would be weight loss. The equation for losing weight is to expend more energy than you consume. When it comes to building wealth, the equation is to save and invest more than you spend. Make sense? I promised to start with the basics, and I am a man of my word. For those of you who fancy yourselves financial sophisticates, I can tell you this, even for the most savvy among us, "repetition is the mother of skill," as Tony Robbins would say. It doesn't hurt to hear it again. We all need a swift kick in the rear from time to time.

If your income currently leaves you with a surplus at the end of each month, you have a considerable head start, because even without a monthly written budget and a specific formula, you are managing to save money each month. If your current income barely covers your monthly expenses or you are in the minus, there is more to unpack here.

Either way, let's start with a budget, and while we are at it, let's de-stigmatize that word. Budget? *Eeeyuck*! It is probably one of the least fun words in the English language. Afterall, so many of us associate that word with "poor," "cheap," or "unsuccessful." Ironically, it is just the opposite, my friend. Fortune 500 companies have budgets, movie productions have budgets, record companies have budgets, and yes, many wealthy people have and adhere to budgets. A budget holds you financially accountable and lets you see in black and white if, at the end of each month, each quarter, each year, you are profitable. This is business, people. You are running the business of your life. You are the CEO and CFO of your life, and, perhaps, your family's life. I would like to think that you would want to know if you are profitable. And if not, how to tip the scales in your favor to get into the black *(so to speak)*.

How many of you were taught about budgeting in public school? If I were in the room with all of you, I would probably be hearing crickets right about now. If you grew up in a family, as many of us did, where your parents were doing all they could to just get by from month to month, praying that the bills got paid, or borrowing from Peter to pay Paul, finances tend to get sloppy and the whole operation is being held together with prayer and some spit. I get it.

If we put the emotions aside and get out a piece of paper and a pen and write down what your monthly expenses are, what amount of money is coming in, and we dispassionately analyze the expenditures versus income, we can get a clear and objective picture of your current financial situation. Then and only then, can a plan of action be created to begin to close that gap, and eventually shift you into a surplus *(and yes, it can be done)*.

Let's take on a really tough scenario and say that you make $30,000 per year. That is a gross monthly income of $2,500 and $2,250 per month after federal income tax is taken out. Your rent, food, gas, insurance, utilities, and incidentals currently total $2,650. That's right, your newly written out budget outlines that you are in the red by $400 each month. Remember, energy in, energy out. Income in, income out. So how do you save and start investing? You will need to find a way to cut anywhere you can from your monthly expenses, while simultaneously expanding your income streams. Again, simple, though not easy.

Your first order of business is to see if there is anywhere you can cut. Your next order of business is to find another source of income to close that gap and make yourself profitable. Remember, you are in the business of YOU. Do not take your finances personally. This is business. You will have to lean on your pain points rather than avoiding them, and learn to defer gratification, temporarily. You will also need to work harder for the time being, but imagine living a life with money in the bank, not relying on debt, and the feeling of satisfaction you will have once you are able to start investing a little bit each month. In this particular scenario, ideally, you will want to shave your monthly expenses by $300, while upping your take home income by $700, giving you an extra $1,000 per month.

Start freelancing, wait tables, babysit, dog walk; do whatever it takes to raise that extra $700 per month.

Let's break this down:

Your original net *(after taxes)* take home income was $2,250.00 per month. You now found a way to bring your monthly income up to $2,950.00 per month. After expenses you now have $1,000 in surplus per month after eliminating $300 in monthly expenses. That $1,000 should be divvied up into emergency savings, long term liquid savings, and a long term retirement investment like a 401K, or a Roth IRA mutual fund if you are self-employed. A diversified fund is a great entryway into investing. It allows you to get your feet wet with minimal risk, because these funds are invested for you with a portfolio of diverse public companies with solid track records.

As things progress, you can consult with a broker or do some research and due diligence into different promising or established public companies that you might want to invest in each month. Typically, when we think of stocks, we think of famous companies like Facebook, Amazon, Coca-Cola, PayPal, and that ilk. However, there are many promising technology companies out there whose shares are more affordable and poised to go up. Within my own company, Solomon RC Ali Corporation, we work with some of the most promising and innovative companies within their respective spaces, helping these companies to raise capital, scale their operations, build out their infrastructure, and in some instances we help take them public. The point is, if you don't set aside a third of your money each month, it won't matter which stock is doing what, because you won't have the money to invest, and you won't have the opportunity to build any wealth.

Another thing you can do, if you are working with a shoestring budget, is to pool your monthly surplus with a small group of likeminded people who are also looking to invest and build long- term wealth. If you were to put $250 each month into your emergency fund, $250 per month into another long term savings account, and save $500 per month for one year toward an investment opportunity, that would give you a total of $6,000 to invest by year's end. If you pooled that money together with a group of ten other people who also each put in between $2,000 and $10,000, let's say, you could find yourselves with a pot of $50,000 or more which can be invested into the purchase of a business.

Each investor in your group is given an equity stake in the business, equitable to the size of their personal investment in this venture. You will need to hire an attorney and a CPA *(certified public accountant)* who can iron out the details and ensure that all parties are properly vested and protected in the investment. The great news is, as the business grows, so does your investment, and owning a percentage of something substantial is better than owning 100% of nothing.

If you are thinking, "Solomon, that all sounds great, but does that mean I can't get my hair and nails done? Or, I can't buy that pair of earrings I've had my eye on?" If you're a guy, you might be thinking, "Does that mean I can't take my girlfriend to that five star restaurant we've been wanting to try? Or I can't get that custom paint job for my car? What about bottle service at the club?" The answer is, if it takes away from that 30% you need to start building your personal wealth, I am afraid you are going to have to defer gratification for the time being.

The good news is, those luxuries will seem that much sweeter when you are not behind the eight ball. When you are able to make a splurge purchase that amounts to only a small percentage of your total net worth *(yes, you will eventually have a net worth)*, you can relax and truly enjoy, knowing there won't be a price to pay for your splurge later on.

Now, let's upgrade our scenario:

Suppose you are a single professional earning $100,000 per year and taking home $76,000 after taxes. This gives you a monthly take home income of roughly $6,300.00. Let's say your rent or mortgage payment is $2,200 and your other monthly essential expenses total another $2,500. You are looking at a monthly surplus of roughly $1,600. You are pretty well on track toward having 30% of your take home income available to pay yourself in the form of building your emergency fund, building your long term liquid savings. and investing some of your money for retirement. Your exact 30% would be $1,890, but I won't nitpick. Now, if you want to take the ball and run with it, I would encourage you to see how you can shave your monthly expenses by $290.00, which would give you exactly 30% to invest in your future. In your scenario, it all comes down to choices and shifting your thinking about money.

You might be thinking, "That's fine for a single person, but I have a spouse and kids, and the money goes out as fast as it comes in. I'm lucky to break even each month." For the average family of four, it's true that there are always unexpected surprise expenses. Children have continuous short-term needs, and they also require long-term financial planning for things like college, a car, and other milestone expenses. But guess what, that is all the more reason to have your financial ducks in a row. For short-term child-related expenses, the name of the game is a well-stocked emergency fund that you can pull cash from to pay these expenses as they come up and then replace that money the following month. You must always pay yourself back for any money you take out of your emergency fund. If you are scrambling, putting things on credit cards, getting expensive payday advances, or hitting up family members for a loan, it is because you haven't been allocating your 30% up until now. Now is the time to change that, so that six months or a year from now you are covered. If you have to start in baby steps by paying yourself 10% or 15% for a while until you get your sea legs, I am okay with that. Just be sure that within six to eight months' time, you are paying yourself 30% a month and allocating those funds toward building your emergency fund, your long term savings, and your investment portfolio.

While you are building your financial future, you may have to get used to uttering the following words to well-meaning friends and family who try to coax you into reverting back to your free-wheeling spending days, so repeat after me: "Sorry, I Can't Afford It Right Now."

Did you say it out loud? How does it feel? It takes some getting used to, especially when you feel like your pride is on the line. But here's the deal, as you become accustomed to having money in the bank to cover life's emergencies, as you grow to feel safe knowing you are saving for you and your family's future, your definition of what it means to be able to afford something will shift. You will begin to set the bar quite high as you come to respect every dollar that passes through your fingers. You will be aware that each of those dollars could be a building block toward financial security, or just another dollar earned and spent on the American merry-go-round of hyper-consumerism.

When we buy things, who are we paying?

Our dollars are not turning over within our own communities like they are with other races.

Inflation

According to Statista.com, prices increased by .62% across the board in 2020. And 2022? Well, don't get me started. Inflation is now the highest it has been since 1982! To be exact, "U.S. Inflation Hit Fresh Forty Year High of 7.9% Before Oil Spike," cries Bloomberg.com. It certainly stacks up over time, and before you know it, your money is not going nearly as far while your wages or salary stays stagnant. If you are living a life of work, spend, and work some more, you will find with each passing year that you would have to work a little more and a little harder just to continue the same rate of spending, and barely the same quality of living. That is why it is imperative that your money start to make money.

An interesting factoid: 85% of Black American spending power is in the personal beauty and grooming industries, specifically haircare. As a young boy, I remember watching television and casually observing just how many television commercials were geared toward a Black audience. To state the obvious, there were plenty of advertisements that depicted blonde, blue-eyed models with ultra-fair complexions as the 20th century beauty ideal, with little effort on the part of Madison Avenue toward inclusion. Even in my young mind, I felt the most egregiously offensive television commercials were the ones peddling beauty products to the Black community by using women of color, namely African American women, with lighter skin, more Caucasian-like features and long hair. They were presenting these commercials and print advertisements to a population of people who mostly had darker skin, larger and more Afro-centric features, and more natural tightly coiled hair. The message was clear, "Your natural skin tone and hair texture is not good enough, so buy our products." We've been plunking down billions of dollars in our quest to anglicize ourselves ever since.

In a June 2020 Newsweek article written by Seren Morris, titled, *From Shea Moisture to Carol's Daughter, This List of Non-Black Owned Hair Brands May Surprise You*, calls out thirty-one, yes thirty-one, Black haircare and beauty brands not owned by Black people. Two of the well-known companies name checked, included *Dark & Lovely* and *Carol's Daughter (as mentioned in the title)*. The point is not being made to disparage these companies, but to illustrate that many of the large companies dictating to us how we should look and how much we should spend to look that way are not Black-owned companies. Therefore, the money is not staying within our own community. Black Americans should be able to build equity in these companies with their dollars in the form of a portion of their monetary contribution helping to build infrastructure and resources within Black and brown communities.

Their bottom lines are going up because they are well versed in who they are advertising to and how they promote their products. These companies know, based on their marketing research, that you are going to keep buying from them because you want to be accepted and validated. They know how to make you feel like not enough, and how to present their product as the elixir to this self-esteem issue they have taken part in creating. Non-Black owned companies who manufacture and market products to the Black community should be donating a portion of that wealth back into the Black community. Do your part in holding them accountable to that standard by only supporting companies who do this.

For many people of color, the enormous sums we spend on beauty and grooming products, more specifically what we spend on haircare products, speaks to our desire to feel better about our appearance and our eagerness to facilitate a greater comfort level for white people who are around us in social/professional settings. I am sure, were it up to many white Americans, we would all have lighter skin and longer, smoother-textured hair. It is not their fault, per se. They are societally conditioned to find these aesthetics more palatable. Some food for thought: if we were all white and aesthetically homogenized, what a boring place this country would be. America is a melting pot, which includes people of color who have helped the United States of America build itself into the superpower it is today. We continue to do so through our collective buying power. Our diversity of skin color, culture, and spirit is what makes America.

In fact, corporations are now beginning to realize that to homogenize their companies by appearance is not only unethical and insensitive, but also unlawful. In 2020, The Crown Act was passed in Congress, and named for the CROWN *(Creating a Respectful and Open World for Natural Hair)* Coalition. The Crown Act makes it illegal to discriminate against someone at work or school over the way they wear their hair. I understand that long-held hair insecurities run deep and will not evaporate overnight, but you can rest easy knowing that you are now legally entitled to wear your hair any way that feels authentic for YOU, and there are legal repercussions if you are discriminated against for doing so.

I could get preachy and tell you that beauty is in the eye of the beholder and that Black is beautiful, but that digresses from the matter at hand, which is money. Every dollar we spend is a vote that tells the world how we wish to be treated.

I am about to knock you over, so here goes. An October 2019 *Essence* article titled, *The Industry That Black Women Built*, states, "African Americans spend $1.2 trillion each year, and that number is projected to rise to $1.5 trillion by 2021." Gulp! We are now in 2022 at the time of this writing, so you do the math. In 2018 the Black haircare industry raked in an estimated $2.51 billion, as Black consumers have progressively made the switch from general products to those that specifically cater to them.

The takeaway is that African Americans are likely now contributing close to $2 trillion dollars to the national gross domestic product (GDP). Our collective spending power is so humongous that we could make a dent in the American national debt, create our own country, send spaceships to Mars, re-train and re-organize police departments, house and feed every homeless Black American and Black underprivileged child, create and invest in more Black-owned publicly traded companies, put more Black Americans through college and graduate school, and put more Black Americans in key positions in congress... should I go on?

This is your wake-up call. No, you cannot reach every other Black American and attempt to pool your money with 40 million strangers. What you can do is vote strategically

with your dollars, support Black-owned companies when you do decide to make consumer purchases, insist that non-Black-owned companies contribute back into the Black community, research Black-owned publicly traded companies, pool your money together with people in your community or within your inner circle, and invest together. Begin to share this knowledge with your friends, family members, and colleagues that Black people are soon to be worth $1.5 Trillion to the national GDP. That means we wield some serious power. What has been sorely lacking in our community are the skills and focus to leverage this power.

We continue to give our power away. Why does each Black-earned dollar remain in Black hands for less than 6 hours before being turned over to other communities? TV One's Roland Martin shared, "The lifespan of a dollar in the Asian community is 28 days, in the Jewish community the lifespan of a dollar is 19 days, and the lifespan in the African American community is approximately 6 hours."

Aside from supporting businesses outside of the Black community and/or businesses that do not care about our community as is demonstrated overtly or covertly, this is partly because when people of color receive their paycheck, or any monies owned to them, there is always an outstanding obligation that needs to be fulfilled. Since many of us have gotten caught up in a cycle where we borrow against our future earnings, many of us have been unable to invest our own money, either in personal investments or within our local communities. If you owe rent, a car payment, credit card debt, payday advance debt, personal loan debt, or any other variety of multiple monthly debts, there is a good chance your money has already left the community.

While we are on these subjects, let's briefly cover how this country has separated people of color from white communities and how ghettos were created. According to Wikipedia, "The origins of these areas are specific to the United States and its laws, which created ghettos through both legislation and private efforts to segregate America for political, economic, social, and ideological reasons: de jure and de facto segregation." Therefore, if you are currently living in an underserved urban community, you need to be aware of the fact that your current *("current," meaning subject to change!)* circumstances were created, not by accident, but by design.

A 2017 NPR article titled, *A Forgotten History of How the U.S. Government Segregated America* states that "the U.S. government initiated a state-sponsored system of segregation" as part of Franklin Delano Roosevelt's New Deal after The Great

Depression. The article goes on to state that the United States government's post-depression efforts "were primarily designed to provide housing to white, middle-class [and] lower-middle-class families. African Americans and other people of color were left out of the new suburban communities and pushed instead into urban housing projects."

Welcome to redlined America, people. Author Richard Rothstein, in his book, *The Color of Law*, examines the local, state and federal housing policies that mandated segregation. He notes that the Federal Housing Administration (FHA), which was established in 1934, furthered the segregation efforts by refusing to insure mortgages in and near African American neighborhoods, a policy known as "redlining."

This is why many of our communities are financial deserts. We must go and purchase even the most basic necessities, like food, outside of our own community. The problem goes even further. Most shopping centers in Black communities are not owned by our people. Therefore, even if the shop owner is Black, only a small portion of the money you spend in that store stays within the Black community and a large percentage of it leaves in a matter of hours or even minutes. Those dollars then go to manufacturers, utilities, landlords and other parties that are likely not within the Black community. This is not to slam non-Black landlords, manufacturers, and utility companies. This is a call to action for communities of color to start saving, pooling our resources, and investing so that one day our shopping centers will be owned by us, the products we sell are made by us, and the utilities we use are owned by us.

Like anything else, the answers are often simple, but not easy. One might say, "Open more Black-owned businesses within Black communities and keep the money "in house," so to speak. Unfortunately, here is where we come full circle, which is what people of color have been talking about for years: lack of access to capital for African Americans and all the red tape that comes with it. Fortunately, all is not lost, and we are living through a dynamic point in history where our ship is poised to make an about-face. Throughout this chapter I have cited some pretty powerful statistics about the increase in Black income, as well as the astronomical amount of money African Americans pour into our American economy each year. The money is there people. Now we have to use it more wisely.

Within my company, Solomon RC Ali Corporation, I do not like it when someone on my team comes to me with a problem without offering a solution. Therefore, I will not spend this entire chapter, or this book for that matter, speaking ad nauseum about the problem without offering some real solutions. It is just important for all of you to see the problems we face in full living color, and from thirty thousand feet up, so that you can get the full scope of the challenge that lays ahead and why it is so critically important to meet this challenge. We have to turn Black American economics around in the 21st century.

My company's online presence, www.SolomonRCAli.com offers a vision and a goal of elevating our community and allowing financial access to those who may have bright ideas and want to contribute to our community, and to the world. My team and I share with you the basic requirements for acquiring capital, because knowledge is power. Rome wasn't built in a day, and you may encounter frustration when you add up what investors look for against where you are currently at, but you have to look at it like this; five years from now you can be five years older and in the same financial position you are in now, or you can be five years older and more profitable. It's time to learn the right steps and to *take* the right steps.

When one looks at the full picture it should be clear that borrowing money from your future self is no way to build a community, or to even sustain yourself. We must understand where we have been and where some of our self-destructive habits derived from and how it affects our lives today. Systemic racism, social and financial brainwashing, and self-hatred are poisonous seeds that were planted on this land hundreds of years ago. We are in the greatest information age in America's history. Books, podcasts like my *MBA: Minority Business Access* podcast, YouTube videos, documentaries... the information is there. We can no longer be kept in the dark, and that also means we no longer have an excuse to remain complacent.

How Celebrity Influence Has Changed the African American Community

I believe that celebrated public personalities from entertainers to athletes have indeed played a major role in how black people are seen and accepted within this American construct.

Although their role has largely been a positive one, there are some negatives. In more recent years we have seen Black actors win coveted awards for playing leading roles in films and on television shows that have portrayed our community in a positive and constructive light. I believe this has been extremely helpful to our younger generation. They have earned more money in recent years, helping young aspiring actors to see their dreams come true. Due to their social and financial status, they have also had a major impact by speaking up for the voiceless and in having a major influence in creating social movements that bring perpetrators to justice.

The flipside of that coin is that they often represent their own point of view, which is at times narrow and fails to represent the majority of Americans. On the other hand, when those celebrities speak up and stand in solidarity for and with their own people and it is not in sync with the system's agenda, powers that be will ensure the celerity is reprimanded and made an example of. Whether you support Colin Kaepernick or not, he was stripped of his promising and very lucrative football career when he chose to stand up and speak up against racial injustice. He has suffered financially and mentally, though his life will forever stand for necessary resistance and civil disobedience in the face of hypocrisy and injustice for Black Americans.

Now let's examine the other side of that situation. If Colin Kaepernick was a white man, would he have been treated the same way? How many white Americans have protested against authority to take a stand for something they believe in? Was the personal and professional cost nearly as great for them? I will let you be the judge. People of color typically do not possess the same entitlements as their white counterparts and are therefore punished for their points of view. The overriding message is, "Your constitutional rights are a privilege, not a right. You're an unwanted guest in this country so do not step out of line or else." How do we change that? Black wealth; institutional Black wealth. The more wealth a community has, the more insulated you are and the more your rights are protected.

Three Things African Americans Can Do Today to Change Our Destiny

1. Education. You must study money. In addition to this book, you can tune into our *MBA: Minority Business Access podcast*, visit us at <u>www.solomonrcali.com</u>, search YouTube, ask successful people, take a course, read more books. Learn how money works: how it is earned, saved, invested, insidious ways that money is divested *(stripped from you)*, and how money is used to influence everything from our local communities to our state and national politics.

2. Stop spending money you haven't yet earned! Stop stealing from your future self, from your children, and from *their* future children. Stop borrowing against money that you haven't yet made. Period.

3. Close your income to debt ratio and start saving at least 10% of your monthly income with the goal of saving

30% of your monthly income as: liquid savings, long-term invested savings, and retirement savings *(typically not usable until the age of at least 55, without a withdrawal penalty)*. Get your money earning money by investing in various stocks, and in an existing business or businesses.

Investing – Where to Start

In addition to listening to YouTube videos, podcasts, and reading books to begin to reshape your financial mind, it is also helpful to align yourself with other people who share your current and future money values and goals, and who will support your financial journey. You will also want to study and begin to understand the power of speaking things into existence and the power that each of us possesses to manifest things into the material world through the universal Law of Attraction.

One of the things that my team and I have done is to create a platform for potential investors to do their research and due diligence at an affordable price. We have found that typically people of color cannot afford to pay the hundreds of dollars per month that is necessary to do the research on a company they may wish to invest in, or to thoroughly vet an industry you wish to learn about with the intention of investing your money. Many people of color also do not have the luxury of time to spend jumping from website to website to investigate a company or its management team. By providing you with affordable resources like this book and my podcast, my personal goal and wish is to provide you with tools to save you a lot of time and money and maximize your seeds so they may grow into trees. I want to help you begin this journey toward becoming a successful financial strategist, a successful investor, and to put you on the path toward making a profit on your hard earned money. The goal is for you to find a sound place to put your money that is going to put it to work, where your risk will be minimal and calculated, and your potential gains will be maximized. I feel that if you are only working for your money aka trading your time and labor/energy output for money, you will always be just a board above broke. I do not want you to spend your life treading water, because you only have so much stamina. None of us can tread water forever. If your money is working *for* you, it should be like a river flowing with no end in sight.

You must understand that money is a tool. Imagine your money to be a seed that, if planted in the right soil, has the potential to grow into a strong tree with many branches and leaves, bearing fruit that you can continuously eat from. Now you have fruit in abundance and seeds in abundance that can bear more fruit. You should now begin to see the correlation between the money you earn and fruit bearing seeds. As you properly place money in the right investments *(fertile soil)*, the investment will start to yield you a generous and fruitful return.

Through your discipline, you will repeat the investment strategy starting with your due diligence, looking into companies that will yield a return because their management team will have shown through your investigation that they have a proven track record when they compare to other management teams who are in that same industry. Your investigation into a company should also reveal things about the industry, itself. Is it a growing industry with huge possibilities? Sometimes you could be excited about a company, but through your due diligence you will find that the company is actually in a shrinking industry that is primed for extinction in the coming years. If the company's industry is on the upswing, identify the things they do well and what they do not do so well. This will allow you to pick a company with a solid management team that not only operates as a finely tuned machine, but one that readily identifies solutions to existing problems within their industry. We call this "Meeting the Need."

Next, you want to identify this company's growth potential and how that growth potential stacks up against management's ability meet that growth through the ability to scale its operation. Management must be willing to reinvest the company's profits back into the business as they stay focused on growing that business, either organically or through making strategic acquisitions.

This last point is also critically important. Do Not, I Repeat, Do Not, transfer emotionally charged impulse purchasing from consumer items to investment products. When we purchase items like beauty-related products, clothing and accessory items with prestigious labels attached to them, flashy cars and car accessories, and the like; these are emotionally driven, ego-building purchases. That is fine within the right context and when you have the money. However, when you are making a decision to purchase a business, purchase a stock, or any other financial product, ego and emotion will not get you where you need to go.

Investing is a science and needs to be respected as such. The best and most profitable investors do their homework, ask questions, follow, and study industry trends, research companies, and don't invest what they cannot afford to lose.

<u>I will use one of my most successful investments as a case study</u>

I have invested in many companies throughout my career, including a significant investment in the intellectual property that is currently used by Amazon for its popular smart home "Ring" doorbell. If you don't have one on your front door, you probably know someone who does. When I initially invested in the company that invented this now patented two-way video technology, no one knew that the intellectual property we held in our hands would soon find its way onto millions of front doors and smart phones throughout the United States. No one had yet heard of the Ring doorbell or knew it was even possible to have a video doorbell that you could monitor from your smart phone.

As part of the due diligence process, I researched doorbell market trends and smart home industry capabilities, as well as the doorbell industry as a whole. That is how I ultimately made the bold decision to invest in this emerging technology that would eventually take over the world. I studied both industries to ascertain if there was even a need for this type of product. Discovering that there was nothing like it that existed at the time, I then looked into and studied the management team of the company that had developed this technology. Although management had not demonstrated a track record for scaling companies, nor introducing new products to market, I chose to take a calculated risk based on market potential and made my decision to invest.

I trusted the company's management, of which I became a part. My due diligence informed me that what they lacked, I was able to augment with my own capabilities, which would help us bridge the necessary gaps and bring our patented technology to market.

Next, I looked at the company's willingness to invest its own money back into the business, which is a big pre-qualifier for me, because it is a sign that management believes in the business and what that business is doing. As an investor, I have been lazar focused on observing if the company is willing to invest back into their business. After all, who would invest their own money into a business and not fight like hell to get that money back, in addition to a profit on that money? You want them to have skin in the game.

When you see this in relation to publicly traded companies and their stock, the investing public tends to have more confidence investing into a company that is investing back into its own growth and innovation. It seems like this would be common sense, but you would be surprised at the lack of attention to this detail. As I dove deeper, my further due diligence revealed two additional facts:

- The company had the ability to grow by triple digits. Although many investors are happy to see double digit growth, I have always prided myself in making sure that the companies I invest in have the potential to garner triple digit growth.

- I was further amazed that the doorbell industry had been stagnant for some time and was poised for a product like this to come in and be disruptive. In 2022, nearly everyone has a smart home doorbell outside their home or is in the market to get one.

Successful investing often means putting your emotional reactions on the back burner, focusing on fact-based data first, and doing the work. Believe me, it took more than thirty years of trials by fire to earn the right to impart that bit of wisdom. Research is key. There are no experts, college degrees, or even years of experience that can make the final call for you; at least not that I have seen in my thirty plus years of experience in this arena.

When you are ready to invest in a company, the best place to start is to check out what the top five industries in the world are doing. Next, you must give a company's management team a letter grade (A through F) and compare that assessment to the top five players in that industry in their performance.

Questions to ask yourself about a company's management team include: How has their operation run up through present day? Do they have the ability and the skillset to bring a product to market, scale their operation, and handle growth? Do they have access to capital? Do they have a history of investing their company's profits back into their company to grow their business? Does the company have the potential to grow, and even more importantly, is there potential for triple digit growth *(yes, this is an ambitious metric, but we are in it to win it)*? Is the industry a growth industry or a stagnant, or shrinking industry?

CHAPTER 7

EVOLUTION OF A SELF-MADE MAN

"Success is to be measured not so much by the position that one has reached in life as by the obstacles which he has overcome." –
Booker T. Washington

The title of this chapter might seem like it is filled with hubris, but if you think its contents will recount a flawless roadmap to riches without some significant bumps in the road and life shattering losses, you would be sorely mistaken. I have been an entrepreneur since the age of eight, and over the past forty-eight years it has been a challenge to "make it." I have earned a fortune, lost a fortune, and eventually through self-examination, re-organization, and a renewed mindset, and many hours of prayer and tithing; I've been fortunate to have made it back during some very trying and difficult times. My past missteps and landmines now serve as a golden roadmap that I can pass along to you so that you can enjoy a smoother ride than I did.

I spent the earlier part of my childhood in the eastern district of the city of Los Angeles, also known as South Central LA, up until the age of ten. I would imagine, similarly to my neighborhood, in many other neighborhoods across the United States, kids would play games of "Tag, you're it." I can remember running from house to house, recruiting kids to come outside to play. We would share stories about our day, what television shows we were excited about watching, or just simply shoot the breeze in the easy kind of way that kids do. There would always be one or two houses where someone's parent would provide fun snacks like ice cream or popcorn, as we entered their home. Not all days were breezy days, and I recall one occasion when I got into a fight. My grandmother was sitting on our porch chatting with a friend. I rushed to the porch where she was sitting, hoping for some consoling when she stopped chatting with her friend, picked up a broom that was next to her, and swatted me off with it, telling me, "You better fight back and don't come back until you win the fight." She didn't want to see a defeated grandchild lose a fight. If I'm being honest, I don't remember if I won the fight or not. It was a lesson to be learned; not about fighting, but about not running from a challenge. It wasn't about being violent or glorifying fighting. It was about never giving up or quitting on myself. This was one of many lessons I learned from my grandmother. Another lesson my grandmother shared with me was that someone is always watching.

With today's technology, everyone has a camera readily available. You are being watched even when you don't think you're being watched. This is the type of *watching* my grandmother was referring to. She reminded me that God was always watching even when *she* wasn't. To me, my childhood was relatively simple and carefree. Growing up, I had no idea if my family was poor or working class. What I do know is that I was surrounded by too much love to even know or be concerned with it.

My parents decided to move to the all-white neighborhood of West Covina during my early teenage years. It was a "step up" to move to the valley and an entrée into middle class white suburbia. I remember having to memorize our new home address and new phone number, but that was the least of it. The culture shock was the biggest change to acclimate to. My parents had worked hard to make this move and felt that it was a better environment for my brother and me. I was engulfed in the pain of leaving my friends behind. This new neighborhood might as well have been a different planet, because it did not offer me any friends that looked like me, nor were they warm or welcoming to my arrival. I could not share my dislike of our move with my mom, because I knew she was determined to do what she thought was best for our family.

My siblings and I played with the other kids on our street, mostly our next door neighbor's three kids: two girls and one boy. We swam in their pool and went to the movies together, and we even walked to the neighborhood gas station together to hang out. I recall one memory of my siblings and I swimming in their pool which had crystal blue water that enticed me to the point of getting in over my head, literally. The neighbor's eldest daughter had to jump in and save me, because although I was a pretty good swimmer, I had suddenly panicked when I could not tell where the bottom of the pool was with my feet.

I had not known that our neighbor was harboring some racism because in addition to swimming in their pool, from time to time we would eat at their table, go to the store with their kids, and generally hang out as a group of kids around our neighborhood. It was only after our neighbors had moved, six months after we moved in, that we heard chatter about their father despising black people. We would have never known the reason for their move had it not been for the loose tongue of another neighbor of ours sharing this information. Apparently, she had heard it from our neighbor's wife who did not have a problem with us living next door and was reluctant to uproot her family. But the father was insistent. He did not want to live next to us, have either of his daughters potentially date me or my brother, or have his son continue to play with black kids.

As kids, we did not understand what any of this meant, and I always wondered how those kids turned out. Are they harboring racial bias as adults just like their dad, or did they turn out like their mom who was accepting of other races? When I look back now, I cannot help but think that it was that image of his oldest daughter rescuing me in their pool and our close proximity in that moment that set him off and set the ball in motion for their move. I'll never know, but I do know that you can interact with someone on a daily basis and not know what they really think of you.

Looking back now as an adult, I do understand my mother's decision to move to West Covina. At the time, I was angry and confused to feel so racially displaced and I had to just deal with it. As I attended this new school and did not have a single friend besides my brother, some of the other kids decided to pick fights with me because I was the only black kid in my grade, and I looked different from them. Somehow, my different hue made me the enemy in their eyes.

During the 1960s and 1970s, Black culture had not gone mainstream in the way that it is today. In their eyes, I was simply a different kind of bird and didn't belong to their flock. I can recall one time when two guys at school took me into the bathroom, trapped me, and tried to stick my head in the toilet. As you can imagine, I had to defend myself, and subsequently *I* got into trouble with the school system for my "actions." I may have been disciplined by a shortsighted school faculty, but I adhered to the lesson my grandmother taught me about defending myself in the face of injustice. My grandmother passed away later that year when I was twelve. I am desperately still in need of her guidance; however, her lessons resonate with me to this day.

It's a challenging time, emotionally and spiritually, when one of your childhood heroes begins to deteriorate. I can remember my grandmother being bedridden and needing help to be transferred from her bed to her wheelchair. Although she was mostly homebound toward the end of her life, I remember her being in the nursing home, my mother by her side caring for her, making sure she was comfortable. My mother would change her bedding to make sure she had fresh sheets. It was the transfer of care and guidance from one generation to the next that has stayed with me to this day.

Challenges come in many different varieties throughout our formative years. As a young boy, I played little league baseball. My team was in the championship game for first place. We were down by one or two runs and I was up to bat with the bases loaded. I remember looking at all of the people in the stands, and thinking, "I am not going to disappoint everyone and cost us a championship game," so I slammed that ball as hard as I could. I didn't know you don't bunt with a four count. I didn't know the rules and that what I was doing was unorthodox, and maybe that was a good thing. In my mind I focused on not striking out, so I bunted the ball with two outs. If I would have struck out, we would have lost. I didn't want to be the one everyone was going to remember as that kid who struck out in the championship game and caused us to lose by one point. The move I made was totally unexpected. I didn't know exactly what I was doing, but two runs scored. The runner from third base went home, the runner from second base went to third and then home, as I slid into first base. You can imagine how shocked and excited everyone was with my unorthodox approach. The pitcher was baffled as to where to throw the ball. He threw it to home, but the guy on third already slid into home. The catcher then threw the ball to third where the guy coming from second was already safe on the third base – the third baseman threw the ball to first base where I was safe, and the third baseman made it home safely. The next batter up struck out. The game was over and we WON. I'll never forget my mom in the stands screaming to me after the game, "You gave everyone a heart attack in these stands!" But I won us the game. I realized then and there athletics would be my key to social acceptance in the white suburbs of West Covina.

This memory may seem relatively insignificant, but it is the small wins along the way that shape everything from our self-worth to our strategy to our life skills. It is those little wins that have shaped me to do what I do each and every day. I push through those challenges.

The turning point came for me in high school as an athlete. I finally began getting accepted into the social fold at school and getting invited to parties with schoolmates. One of the things that struck me was that all of the girls suddenly wanted me to attend parties with them. So much so, they would stop by my house on the way to the parties so we could walk into these parties in groups. As a shy and introverted kid, I was starting to feel accepted. I was finally being noticed as a person. One day, one of my friends who I played some of my favorite sports with, including baseball, pulled me to the side and said, "You need to stay with your own kind." He had a sister who came to all of our baseball games and she was a very cute girl. I always wondered if that was the motivation behind his warning to me. Looking back, I don't think it was malicious so much as a sad sign of the times and a kid regurgitating what he had probably heard at home. A bit naïve and just happy to finally seemingly be fitting in, I was not sure exactly what he meant, and so I asked him for clarification. Emboldened, he made himself crystal clear and flatly stated, "You need to date your own kind and leave white girls alone." Have you ever had a moment when a cold shiver runs up your spine and you are so shocked that you cannot even form words to respond? That was how I felt in that moment; gob-smacked. I was not actively dating anyone at school. Although, there were some very attractive girls at our school's social gatherings, I was certainly not pursuing them. Again, this was the era where racial fights in school were not an uncommon occurrence. It was very sad because this was happening almost every week. For those of us who played sports, we tried our best to steer clear of any fights, because it would affect our play time. But sometimes we had to defend ourselves, and at times we involuntarily defended our teammates.

The strangest part, and of course it is not so strange in retrospect, is that I was accepted as a guy who played sports, but excluded and picked on when I was just a regular student. As a result, I did not know where I belonged. As a high school freshman, I remember some of the students in my art class making fun of my nose and my lips. My art teacher, Mrs. Bacon, intervened and stated to those students how beautiful my features were. That bolstered me and made me feel special. I can remember when those kids were making fun of me, what it felt like, as if it was yesterday; the shame and embarrassment and pain. No one wants to feel unattractive, and when you don't look like everyone around you, you are already insecure about your appearance. Mrs. Bacon coming to my defense didn't just make me feel really good, it was a defining moment for me. It was the difference between damaged self-esteem and my ability to feel resilient. I wish there were more educators like her to help and protect students from being bullied and picked on because of their features, or other personal characteristics. These precious moments, when I beat the odds to achieve something great or when I was defended and complimented in an otherwise racially hostile environment, gave me a sense of calm and hope.

I remember feeling good about myself as I heard Mrs. Bacon say how beautiful my lips and nose were. Not only did it change my outlook of myself, but it also changed how I viewed white people as a whole. For her to be a white woman complimenting my appearance and my physical characteristics in the face of racism, she gave me an appreciation for human beings. In that very moment, I concluded that not everyone is the same and sweeping generalizations don't always apply.

Recently, an old friend was visiting my parents and they were going through pictures and saw all of the trophies, plaques, and ribbons I had won for playing various middle school and high school sports including track, varsity football, baseball, and basketball. I can also remember teaching myself gymnastic by watching the 1972 Olympics on television, as I practiced my tumbling on an old mattress. Mind you, I was only 10 or 11 years old at this time. Six years later, during my freshman year in high school, I tried out for the gymnastic team and I made junior varsity. This was a huge deal because I did not get any formal training like other kids who attended camps and other specialized training facilities. I learned by watching. Exceling at sports and athletic activities played a pivotal role in shaping me and making me the man I am today.

There are some memorable moments that become life lessons that make you rethink your decisions. My freshman year in high school, I attended a party after one of our Friday night football games. I was excited because, once again, I had that feeling of fitting in. My friends were drinking alcohol as this was something they were accustomed to doing at their Friday night gatherings. I was offered a drink. I'd never consumed alcohol in my life. I was feeling the social peer pressure of fitting in with everyone else in high school. I can remember I had on my letterman jacket, and I wanted to fit in and be social, and "act the part." I can't remember how many drinks I consumed that night. The concoction I was offered tasted sweet like Kool-Aid, but no sooner did I drink it all down, I started to feel funny. The room was spinning, I staggered as I walked. My friends knew I was drunk and made sure I got home safely. The next morning, I had football practice, which on that particular morning only consisted of watching film from the previous game and reviewing our plays. Since we were only going to be watching film and reviewing plays, it didn't seem like a big deal, and I thought, "I'll be fine and power though." That wasn't the case at all. The effects of the alcohol had my stomach hurting and my head pounding.

Every sound was magnified times ten. All I wanted to do was get out of practice so I could go home and go to bed. Practice was finally over and I was on my way home to sleep this awful feeling away. But as soon as I got home, my parents had other plans for me.

When I came in that previous night, they didn't come out of their room. I found out later that my mother was about to come check on me and my dad said to her, "He's drunk. Don't worry about it. We'll handle him tomorrow." And boy did they! As soon as I got home from practice, I was given a list of chores to do. This list consisted of chores I typically wasn't asked to do and I knew something was up. My parents knew I wanted to sleep the hangover away but they wanted me to regret the decision I made the night before. They needed to make me suffer and learn from my behavior so that I would never do it again. Those chores were excruciating, because I could barely stand up, not to mention how many times I threw up as everything around me continued to spin. But it worked, and I never drank alcohol again until I was in the military. Looking back, it's cool how they handled it, but going through it, I was mad. They didn't whoop me or say, "You're grounded." But they got their point across and I didn't drink anymore for the rest of my high school career.

I joined the military my sophomore year of high school and three days after my high school graduation, I was at Fort Jackson base in South Carolina reporting for basic training. When I got off that plane and stepped out of the airport, the southeast humidity hit me like a ton of bricks. My first assignment was with the 51st signal battalion in Fort Gordon in Augusta, Georgia, and then I was shipped over to a place they called K-Town, over in Germany, which was my next duty base.

I was stationed overseas in Germany at the age of 19, and it was during this time that I got drunk for the second time in my life. I was out drinking with my brothers in arms and having a great time, so much so that I began mixing different alcoholic drinks. I got drunk and became sick, once again. It was like déjà vu, but much worse this time around, because I consumed so much more alcohol. That was the last time in my life that I ever got drunk. I learned an important lesson once again. The universe sends you a sign that something is not for you and does not serve your life's path. If you don't listen, it will show up again, more dramatically, until you take notice and cease that behavior. Another lesson for the books I do enjoy the occasional fine drink, but I know my limit and strictly adhere to it.

As my high school years progressed, the drama continued. During my sophomore year I was enrolled in a class that offered electronics, primarily because my uncle was an electrical engineer and a certified pilot, and that intrigued me. He also regaled us with tales of the history of professional baseball, and specifically of black baseball players entering the sport and breaking records for the MLB. Black pilots were also not the norm back in those days. He would tell us about the few Black pilots at that time. I did not quite grasp the passion of his stories, but my brother and I enjoyed listening to him. He had just gotten back from Vietnam and he would buy us baseball gloves and baseball bats. He would also take us flying with him, which was unheard of back in those days.

I can't stress enough that my brother and I did not grasp the full effect of how truly gifted our uncle was. He was so passionate and dedicated in his time spent with us. All in all, my uncle spending time with us, mentoring us, investing in our spirits and our minds, and exposing us to the gift of possibility, brought me so much joy and still does.

Sometimes we don't realize the value of the precious time our family and friends spend with us, the healing words they speak into us, and something they show us that awakens something within us which ultimately leads to our life's path. But it is these moments that can change your life if you allow them to. Whether as an entrepreneur, a friend, a mentor, or a parent; please expose yourself to history and culture, and pass along your knowledge to the next generation. Teach your kids as early as possible as those things can shape their life. It is no less important than the nourishment food provides to their bodies.

Learning about all that life has to offer whether through education, family, or mentorship is imperative. A good friend of mine who was exposed to the wonders of chemistry as a girl, grew up to become a chemical engineer; a testament to the importance of being exposed to possibility, combined with an instilled belief system of what you can achieve can lead to greatness.

Oddly enough, as the semesters and years rolled along, I never became part of a particular social group. Rather, I saw value in spending time with many different groups comprised of people with different ideas and interests; different demographics if you will. As my adolescence progressed, I enjoyed the chess club, the radio club, and electronics classes. Although I did not dabble in illegal recreational drugs, I must admit that I did spend some time with that crowd as well. I eventually even ran for class president one year, but sadly, lost by a landslide because when it came time to give my speech to the class the words would simply not come out. I froze like a deer in the headlights. Today, my staff likes to joke about how they cannot get me to stop talking. I guess I am making up for lost time.

Academically, I struggled, as I was a poor speller. In fact, I don't think my grades alone would have afforded me more than a C in my classes, so I found alternate ways to improve my grades and my standing in my teachers' eyes. I had to do extra credit work. I completed extra assignments going to school early, before football practice, or during lunch. I knew I needed to complete additional projects so I could increase my GPA. I built a strobe light, built a radio, and did several other projects for various classes in order to get by. Though the other kids did not have to do all of that because they just seemed to "get it," I knew I had to find another path toward graduation. It was an incredible lesson in thinking outside the box and a definite foreshadowing in the storyline that would become my adult life. I have always had to find my own path to success.

I soon learned another lesson in emotional intelligence and the destruction and self-sabotage that can come from fear and prejudice. One of my teachers, my electronics teacher, Mr. Weaver, was probably the best teacher I had during my high school years. I have a painful memory of feeling that I had disappointed him when I earned a C one particular quarter. The other Black kids in my class had been gossiping about Mr. Weaver, branding him a racist. Ashamed of my less than acceptable grade point average, I decided to follow suit and call Mr. Weaver a racist as well. I figured, why not go along with the popular narrative and dodge all personal accountability for my poor grade in his class.

I eventually apologized to him, but to this day, I can viscerally remember the pain I caused him because of my inaccurate statement. Looking back, I knew better, and when the other Black kids spoke negatively about Mr. Weaver, I should have chimed in and said that he was not racist and that they were, in fact, just being prejudice toward *him*.

Mr. Weaver was a stern teacher with a strict set of classroom values and rules, and he took pride in upholding these rules with every student that entered his class. I knew better, but I chose not to do better until my conscience got the best of me, and I corrected course. In that moment, I learned the value of self-accountability and the importance of apologizing when you know you have been wrong.

In reality, Mr. Weaver had gone out of his way to help me, and in fact, that C would likely have been a D or worse, without his dedication and help. Eventually, I ended up with an A- in his class because I put in the work.

Today I believe that falsely judging or accusing someone based on ego, pride, and idle gossip is wrong, and when an injustice is taking place I feel compelled to speak up. I also learned the power of words to heal or injure. Do not say anything that you cannot take back. Mr. Weaver went out of his way for me because he believed in me, just as my uncle believed in me and my brother, just as my grandmother believed in my ability to stand my ground and stick up for myself. One person believing in you can make all the difference in your life, and in your ability to create a better internal dialogue to begin to believe in yourself. I would experience this lesson later on, in the military, and once again with my (now ex) wife in young adulthood.

My father was a hard-working 9 to 5 guy, but my parents were always enterprising. From the time I was very young, they had begun investing their hard-earned money wisely. They eventually owned investment rental properties, and they had my brother and me help them to maintain these properties. My brother and I would spend our weekends and some of our after school hours helping my parents to clean the units to get them ready for the next tenant to come in. If they had any issues with a tenant, they would take us along with them so we could hear the conversation and learn by osmosis. I remember there were times when a tenant would have an issue with their apartment or a problem paying the rent, and my dad would have to respond to the situation. Sometimes my mom would need to step in and try to mediate things, and I would witness the different conversations taking place. As I matured, I was able to handle some of the tenant issues, myself, using the tactics I watched growing up.

I remember my dad would be very strict with tenants who were not paying their rent on time, as my mom would try to extend them the courtesy to see if they could catch up on their rent. I would sometimes be called upon to fix various bathroom and kitchen issues, along with my mom, if my dad couldn't accompany her on a particular day. Later, they would have me go and pick up rent for them, which is when I began to model a combination of my mother's and my father's best communication skills. I took what I felt was the best of each of them. I can remember certain instances where a tenant did not have a phone and I would have to sit and wait outside their apartment for them to come home, which could sometimes take hours.

Tagging along with my parents to clean and prep rental units, helping to fix broken kitchen and bathroom appliances, and bearing witness to conversations about rent payments were tedious at times, and at times I even resented it when I just wanted to hang out with friends like any other normal kid. Many of the most valuable experiences in our lives cannot be truly appreciated until we see them from thirty thousand feet, and many times, years later.

I didn't just learn how to fix a toilet, put in a new window, and replace electrical outlets. I learned how to plan ahead, make decisions, and think on my feet. I learned how to run life like a chess game; always thinking multiple steps ahead. I learned how to address issues before issues became problems. My parents were trying to teach me something and they did. I learned everything from communication to problem solving to some of the basic building blocks of business. So yes, I was a junior landlord in training.

When I was in 7th grade, my mother began teaching me how to pay household bills and how to manage money. When financial or bill-related issues arose, she would allow me to listen to those conversations and then have me make the call to a utility company to get the situation resolved *(with her coaching, of course)*. She taught us to make sure an issue was resolved on that phone call, whether that meant asking for a supervisor or hashing it out with the original party on the other end of the phone. Her motto was, "You don't get off the phone until the issue is resolved."

With all those executive and managerial skills; surely everyone could see I was poised to take on the world, right? Wrong. My high school guidance counselor did not offer me much in the way of guidance, or a vote of confidence for that matter. I walked into her office one day and was told that instead of colleges or universities, I should perhaps consider going to a trade school. I think she sized up some of my earlier academic struggles and the fact that I was a person of color, and wrote me off as not college material. She should have taken the time to get to know me, evaluated the improvement of my GPA and recent test scores, and taken the care to see where I fit in best. She did none of that. As a seventeen year old young man, I did not have the benefit of wisdom or foresight, and that fateful meeting with my high school guidance counselor resulted in me turning my back on any hopes of getting into college. I internalized her critical voice and sentiments, and took her opinion as fact

I felt my parents could not afford to send me to college even if I had felt the inner pull to apply. I was not aware of the existence of HBCUs *(Historically Black Colleges and Universities)*, financial assistance, or many of my own abilities. Without even broaching the subject with my family, I announced to them that I had decided to join the military. I was very fortunate to have parents who advocated for me and uplifted me. Later in life, I was also fortunate to witness another guidance counselor do her job well and evaluate a child to see where they fit best. I can truly say that I witnessed a good guidance counselor in action and I know what one looks like. She was passionate about her job, passionate about her students, and deeply invested in their futures. This is just one example to illustrate that every profession requires you to do your job to the best of your ability, and to do right by the person you are serving.

In recent years, I have been involved with many young students and I always ask them to get all of their options on the table before making a pivotal life decision. What I realize now is that my parents didn't get involved in my high school and potential college career decisions, but it was not because they didn't want to or because they didn't care. They didn't know they needed to get involved. In their naivete, they trusted my high school's guidance counselor as a professional to help their son navigate through the process.

To anyone who has chosen to make the United States military their career, I salute your service, and please understand, this is not directed toward you. My decision to join the military wasn't because I felt moved to enlist and passionate about taking my life in that direction. I made the choice by default; a combination of misguidance, not communicating with my support system, and not having all of the facts at my disposal. One of the good things that I remember about my military experience is that it helped me with problem solving. The military afforded me an opportunity to course correct, and to learn who I was and what I had to offer the world. For someone passionate about the military, this could be a way of achieving their dreams faster. Being in the military taught me discipline and gave me the tools needed to get things done efficiently. The military teaches you that you may not be passionate about certain things, but you get things done and completed because you have been trained to do so. It trains you to complete what you've started with, you guessed it, military-like precision.

Unfortunately, still to this day, there are many opportunity gaps in communities of color and no one steps in to close those gaps. From parents lacking the funds to support their children's extra-curricular activities or personal one-on-one tutoring where academic challenges exist, to distracted parents who are working multiple jobs to make ends meet. These obstacles can be challenging when wanting to be present throughout their children's educational experience. I, myself, have been working hard to correct this broken dynamic through helping entrepreneurs obtain funding, through my podcast, *MBA: Minority Business Access*, and hopefully through this book.

You may be asking yourself how this is all related to business. Imagine that you are a business owner with little to no understanding of what guidance you need to scale your business.

You hire a professional to assist and guide you in this endeavor, but because you don't know to ask the right questions or to look for the right milestones to be completed successfully, the "professional" you have hired may not be giving you their best work. You are purely operating on a trust level. My team and I have experienced this at times when witnessing the operations of companies we have elected to invest in. We are able to see where our client may not know what to ask their team of advisors. Fortunately, we are able to provide direction to our clients on the best course of action with regard to scaling their businesses.

Identifying the people who have your best interests at heart is a skill that you should learn and develop as early on as possible. When people are mediocre at their job, or they don't take the time to research or develop their skillset to do anything other than just get by, that was my high school guidance counselor. That mediocrity is dangerous, because it can negatively impact you or the people around you, so be careful.

Here is the thing: I do not believe that we can miss our destiny. Have you ever been driving somewhere using your smartphone's navigation system, you get distracted for a moment and pass your signal to your turn, or you may even turn down a completely wrong road? What happens? Your navigational system immediately re-routes you and suggests an alternate route to get you to your ultimate desired destination. But here is the caveat: if you continue to disregard your navigational system's attempts to re-route you, and you consistently make wrong turn after wrong turn, or you refuse to pick up the cues to make a turn when prompted, you will not arrive. We are all allowed one or two wrong or missed turns, and the universe will happily re-route us.

CHAPTER 8

TAKING ON THE SEC

"The battle of life is, in most cases, fought uphill; and to win it without a struggle were perhaps to win it without honor..." –
Samuel Smiles

As far back as I can remember I'd wanted to play a pivotal role within a big company that would impact society and change the way we do things. That was my dream, much the way others grew up dreaming about becoming a famous entertainer, professional athlete, doctor, or attorney. I had visions of being a business owner and running a large publicly traded company coursing through my veins as a kid, even before I really knew what that was or what it entailed. I knew it was a steep mountain to climb and the only way to get there was to do the work. Throughout my younger years I devoured every book and article I could find on business and financial strategy and searched tirelessly for information to help point me in the direction of exactly what type of business I wanted to use as my vehicle to achieve my dreams.

Growing up in South Central Los Angeles with hardworking parents who had to hustle every day to eventually lift us into the middle class, my mother, who held multiple degrees from the University of Southern California (USC), endlessly preached that having a college degree was non-negotiable. Her voice echoed in my head as I opted for military service in lieu of college and then went straight into the business world. I know her goal was not to instill insecurity in me, but to impress upon me the value of higher education. Unfortunately, her voice in my head became a point of insecurity throughout my twenties and thirties, as I constantly assumed that if the person next to me held a college degree, they were better than me and would perform their job better than I could.

With entrepreneurship (and a lack of patience) in my blood, I knew heading straight for the real world was my path. This burning in my soul to get right down to business could not be ignored. I knew I didn't have it in me to delay my desire by four or more years, and so all I could do was outwork the next guy to close what I saw as the "college gap," and quiet my mother's voice in my head. "You may have your degree, or several degrees, but you're not going to outwork me," was my constant mantra. It meant late nights, eighteen hour days and precious few weekends. I knew where I belonged, but I needed my mother to validate my choices, and I needed her to believe in me.

When I found myself, at a relatively young age, becoming an officer and director of three of the sixteen Black-owned publicly traded companies on the stock exchange, it gave me the opportunity to be part of a very elite group. You can imagine how elated and honored I felt, and I wanted my mother's stamp of approval that I'd made it.

Sadly for me, and for all African Americans, this distinguished accomplishment and the accolades that came with it couldn't shield me from racism or grant me complete acceptance in the eyes of white America. Instead, I ran squarely into people's cultural and racial biases. I never believed or understood the power of people throwing a rock while hiding their hand, or failing to stand up for what was right. Similar to an NBA player or famous entertainer from decades past, he was good enough to play ball or sing a song for cheering crowds, but after the game or the show had ended, he would be ushered through the back door and told he could not use any of the venue's facilities or even walk through the lobby.

No matter how hard you work to achieve your goals, and no matter how much you have earned your place at the table, as a Black person in America, you will butt up against a certain ilk who want to see you fail and will work toward that end because they do not think you belong in their circle. They see you as a person of color or a "negro," though they are too skillful and politically correct to ever use those words or allow their true colors to be seen. They look like nice people and blend right into the politically correct fold as they attain positions of power in the business and financial sectors. Therefore, some of these people hold yours and my destiny in their hands.

Knowing these facts, I had a decision to make. I will admit that I was, and still am, scared about what the future holds for me. But as someone who has played sports throughout my life, I am wired to get out there and attack my opponent; to put my fear aside and to carry the ball to a resolution. With all of that being said, I am aware that the title of this chapter is an ambitious one. Why would anyone in their right mind undertake such a battle? If your sole interest is protecting your own hide, taking on the SEC is a horrendous idea. Afterall, what started out as a routine witch hunt in which the Securities and Exchange Commission wanted to fine me a relatively modest sum of $50,000 and have me sign a document stating I admitted to no wrongdoing, while also barring me from earning a living in my chosen profession for five years.

I turned down their "offer" and continue to endure in my chosen profession while I play the part of David fighting Goliath. What has this fight cost me? It's incalculable, but monetarily speaking, I have spent seven figures, to date, fighting to be acknowledged as innocent of any wrongdoing.

I feel a responsibility to a cause much bigger than myself. I want to be part of the solution in setting a new precedent regarding the validity of Black wealth in the United States of America. As foolish as it may seem from where you are sitting as you read this book, my integrity and dignity are not for sale. Moreover, why would the SEC allow, and even encourage, me to sign an official notarized document stating that I admit to no wrongdoing if they truly believe I did something wrong? And why would I go along with such a staged farce? The answer is, I wouldn't and I didn't. Instead, I choose to keep fighting.

Google my full name "Solomon RC Ali" and somewhere in the mix, you might see a listing about ongoing litigation between me and the Securities and Exchange Commission, also known as the SEC. For the uninitiated, the SEC's official website states the following:

"We work together to make a positive impact on America's economy, our capital markets, and people's lives. For more than 85 years since our founding at the height of the Great Depression, we have stayed true to our mission of protecting investors, maintaining fair, orderly, and efficient markets, and facilitating capital formation."

In summation, the SEC is the government regulatory body that ensures all investments remain above board for the protection of the public.

According to their official information statement, I am supportive of the Securities and Exchange Commission's mission to protect investors from fraud and harmful market irregularities. I do not blame an entire governance body for what I have gone through over these last five years. I believe any organization is made up of people, and people are imperfect with cultural and emotional biases that are next to impossible to quantify. Additionally, institutionalism sets in, and while individuals may not have racist inclinations, certain principles and practices instituted by a few racist individuals become part of the bureaucratic ecosystem. They take root within an organization or government body and dictate procedure henceforth.

Countless people have asked me what happened between me and the SEC, and why it happened. Truthfully, no one ever knows what brings on an investigation, but here is what I do know; selective justice is practiced on many levels and I am living proof of this unfortunate dereliction within our legal system.

In late 2010 and into early 2011, the Board of Directors of a then little-known technology company called Revolutionary Concepts (ticker symbol: REVO), through an introduction at the Charlotte, North Carolina Black Chamber of Commerce *(as we discussed earlier)* elected me to be a board member and an officer of their company. They were familiar with my reputation for helping companies raise growth capital. By that point in my career, I had raising capital down to a science. I knew how to identify the potential for profitability and how to package a business to be attractive to investors.

Last I checked, there are roughly 13,900 publicly traded companies, and you have 16 publicly traded companies that are Black-owned or controlled; yes, 16 out of nearly 14,000 publicly traded companies are Black-owned. With this appointment, I was now the only African American to sit on the board of three of those sixteen companies, that we know of, while simultaneously holding officer positions in each of these companies. Out of the three, two of them became profitable industry leaders. The facts speak for themselves. Why would the SEC want to sabotage that kind of success and track record? It is the same thing institutionalized racism has done for hundreds of years. People in power feel threatened and they like to disenfranchise.

In my position as a board member and newly appointed vice president of Revolutionary Concepts, I was put in charge of raising capital and investor relations. I arranged growth capital for the company and helped them to strategically build out their business infrastructure, develop and secure their technology patents, and put a strategy in place toward monetization for these technology patents. Plainly put, my job was to help a financially sputtering company raise a lot of money so they could protect, market, and ultimately license their technology to larger companies to make a profit for their shareholders.

Because of our combined efforts, you can thank Revolutionary Concepts every time you push or look at your Amazon Ring or Sky Bell smart home video doorbell or receive a text message from your local bank branch. Those are just two of the technologies REVO developed and licensed out for the benefit of the public. I wonder if any of the guys or gals at the SEC have a Ring doorbell on their front door to protect their home and family, but I digress.

When I entered the picture, Revolutionary Concepts had no funding or revenue to speak of, but just an idea and some technology they had created *(Sound familiar? How many of you out there are currently nursing underfunded dreams?)*. They also had a pile of debt; not uncommon for a mostly bootstrapped tech startup with a CEO who was not sure how to properly manage what little funds they did have.

Through the acquisition of capital, the company was able to pay their bills, meet all their obligations, and eventually grow. Additionally, I oversaw investor relations to keep shareholders informed about what the company was doing. SEC regulations state that whatever management believes is factual and accurate, you are required to disclose to the public and to investors. So, we put out press releases with what we believed were factual, material events that the public and our shareholders needed to know about.

Sometime in late 2015 and into the beginning of 2016 the SEC decided that they were going to investigate Revolutionary Concepts' financial activities as a public company; perhaps as the result of a complaint made by a single shareholder or some other party. Nevertheless, do we feel, or do *I* feel, anything wrong or improper occurred? No. Under SEC rules it states, and I am paraphrasing, "If you believe when you are putting out a press release that it is going to be material that investors and shareholders needed to know or should know, then management should put out that press release." A public company can be exposed to liability under the securities laws if a press release contains any material misstatement or creates a misleading impression when viewed in the context of other publicly available information.

When we first received the official complaint from the Securities and Exchange Commission (SEC), I felt resolute that they would do their due diligence, and in my naivete I knew it would all be okay because we had the facts on our side. As the process rolled along, and began to steamroll right over me, it dawned on me that they did not care whether I did something right or wrong. Just the fact that I was now on their radar, they were going to come after me by any means necessary to collect what I began to understand in my opinion to be government sanctioned extortion.

If you ask any high-profile CEO, they will tell you that one of the ways these government backed regulatory agencies make money is through frivolous fines they are able to enforce through intimidation and the threat of litigation. Many people pay it and keep it moving. "The cost of doing business," they rationalize. Call me stubborn, but I have taken a different route.

It was devasting to realize that a respected regulatory body such as the SEC, which was put in place to enforce securities laws and to protect the rights of investors, would have that kind of animosity against any one individual. After all, this is the same regulatory body that investigated and ultimately brought the case against the biggest and most profitable Ponzi scheme fraudster in United States history, Bernie Madoff. A fun fact about Bernard "Bernie" Madoff's Ponzi scheme: he cheated and defrauded his clients out of a total of $65 Billion according to CNN Money. The reason I bring up Madoff's case is because during his decades-long tenure as a multi-billion-dollar Ponzi scheme mastermind, the SEC continuously received tips that something was not quite right about Wall Street's golden boy.

They turned a blind eye for more than three decades as Madoff enjoyed praise as a financial genius, and even held a position as Chairman of the Board of the National Association of Securities Dealers (NASD), a self-regulatory securities-industry organization. I believe it was not until the economy crashed during the Great Recession of 2008 and 2009 when a lot of nervous investors requested to cash out of Madoff's fund and he could not produce all the money, that the SEC knew they had to act and act quickly before they were exposed as complicit. Prior to that, he was largely protected due to what I believe was willful ignorance on the part of the SEC. That is my opinion and I am not alone.

Speculatively speaking, it bears pointing out that the late Bernie Madoff, of course, was not black. If you know your black history, you are aware of our historical exclusion from Wall Street, securities, and the world of venture capital and private equity investing dating back to the Tulsa, Oklahoma massacre of the early 1900s. Black people created their own self-contained "Wall Street" in the Greenwood District of Tulsa, Oklahoma, only to have it burned to the ground in 1921 by an angry white mob. As a black man involved in this world, I am still seen as a fluke and an outlier by much of the financial establishment.

It is the same racially and culturally biased dynamic that effects police behavior when they are attempting to detain or arrest a white person verses a Black person. As we have witnessed many times, there is a wide behavioral and procedural gap in how police departments handle these situations. Their defense is always, "We were doing our job," or "I was in fear for my life." I am not trying to compare money to human life, but this draws an important parallel in how systemic racism can play out.

With me, all it took was one or two complaints by a couple of shareholders who did not understand the law and that Revolutionary Concepts was actually making them money, and what I believe to be a healthy dose of racism. "This Black man couldn't possibly be operating above board," was the sentiment. That was all the SEC needed in my case to bring down the hammer. At the risk of being accused of having a flare for the dramatic, what happened to me, and is still happening to me, is a modern-day lynching. The powers that be have grown more sophisticated in their pursuit of people of color. Rather than kill us, and they do that as well, cutting off our ability to create and establish generational wealth is the more effective modus operandi of modern-day. Black people can get rich in this country, but getting rich and building generational wealth are vastly different.

So there I was, five years ago, sitting in my office when I got the news that the United States Securities and Exchange Commission was investigating me for failure to disclose information to shareholders. I, and several close colleagues of mine, were being investigated, collectively. At the time, I was resolute in my assumption that the situation would be rectified and taken care of, and that the truth would prevail. One by one, I watched as the rest of my colleagues settled with the SEC, paid their fines and took their lumps, all in the name of not making waves. I understood and respected their decisions. Afterall, what I have been through financially, professionally, and emotionally, has been more weight to carry than the average person could probably handle.

The SEC, in their pursuit of me, called twenty-six different witnesses to testify, one being my ex-wife. What they did not count on were all twenty-six witnesses attesting to my solid character and insisting that I had followed the letter of the law in terms of my business practices and what I had and had not disclosed to investors. I have a saying I am known for, both, in my personal and professional circles: "You don't have to lie, cheat, or steal. You just have to do the work." I live by that motto. For the government to accuse me of the opposite cut me to my core.

Yes, we had a creative and different way of doing things, but all of our activities adhered to legal parameters. If anything, perhaps the SEC feels I am guilty of having a thorough understanding of the law and having the intelligence and the advisors in place to assist me in using the law to my advantage.

To be embarrassed and have my name dragged through the mud as though I had to cut corners because I was incapable of doing my job properly was devastating. My mental health suffered greatly as I began to question myself every day. Then to have a handful of shareholders make all kinds of negative comments out of ignorance, threw me deeper into emotional turmoil. The most perplexing aspect of the complaints is that if I did not do what I did to arrange the necessary capital for our company, they never would have had the opportunities they have had, nor would they have made a return on their investment. That is when I learned another valuable lesson. Some people operate on herd mentality. If one person complains or spews negativity, it becomes a contagion, and others fall in line with that narrative *(just look at Twitter for proof of concept)*. When you are investing money into a company, you fully understand the risk involved with your investment. Those who have spoken badly about me are those who were very well aware of this risk.

Please allow me to share with you the policy and rules that were created to be followed by all people. This policy states, "In the U.S., an Accredited Investor is anyone who meets one of the below criteria: Individuals who have an income greater than $200,000 in each of the past two years or whose joint income with a spouse is greater than $300,000 for those two years, and a reasonable expectation of the same income level in the current year." Of course, anyone can invest in a company, but an Accredited Investor must show proof of a certain level of income as stated above.

Some of the shareholders actually, explicitly, complained that I was a man of color doing the things I was doing. One shareholder actually said to me, "What are you going to do? Go buy some fancy clothes and a pink Cadillac?" I thought, "Wow! At least they're being honest about the root of their hostility." This small group of people were then able to go onto various online message boards and say whatever they wanted to say, perpetuating incorrect, libelous information that others would then co-sign and spread. It really knocked the wind out of me.

What exactly happened and why? Let's get into it so you can form your own fact-based, opinion.

The short story is that I was previously a principal in a private equity firm called Rainco Industries. During that time, I accepted a position as Vice President of a struggling publicly traded technology company called Revolutionary Concepts (ticker symbol: REVO) as we have discussed. In my position I was tasked with investor relations and raising capital. Consequently, I resigned from my position at Rainco Industries, turning it over to my colleague Nicole, and signing ownership of all of Rainco's assets over to an irrevocable trust. Once financial assets are signed over to an irrevocable trust, that irrevocable trust operates independently in the best interests of the trust and is overseen by a designated trustee. According to law, a beneficiary of an irrevocable trust (in this case, myself) cannot have ownership, either directly or indirectly, of the assets of the irrevocable trust. Therefore, I no longer had any direct or indirect decision-making power, ownership, or governance over any of these financial assets or financial decisions. I was now simply a beneficiary of these funds, as the trustee sees fit to disperse said funds. That would make Rainco Industries an independently acting, third party investor in Revolutionary Concepts. That is not according to me, this is according to the law, both state and federal. In the interest of transparency, I put out a press release stating all of the above.

The newly appointed trustee of Rainco Industries felt it advantageous to invest $3.5 million into Revolutionary Concepts over a period of time. Revolutionary Concepts' then-CEO negotiated the details surrounding Rainco's investment in

Revolutionary Concepts. Revolutionary Concepts' board of directors which included myself, accepted the investment. To reiterate, as per United States and Georgia state trust law (the state in which Revolutionary Concepts operated) I did not have a legal say in this decision. The decision to invest in Revolutionary Concepts was the decision of the trustee in charge of the irrevocable trust.

Was this my money? Yes, because it was given by me to the trustee in the form of cash and assets that may have been liquidated over time at the trustee's sole discretion. This is all in keeping with trust law that was created hundreds of years ago. According to trust law, these assets are no longer settlor's (my) assets. This information can be found in publicly accessible Trust Law, and one only needs to Google what an irrevocable trust is to access this information. Did I have legal decision-making power over how Rainco invested these funds, or direct ownership over said funds? No. Therefore, there was no conflict of interest, whatsoever, according to the law. Could you make the argument that I leveraged Trust Law to my advantage? Yes. However, last I checked, this was the United States of America and leveraging laws to one's advantage is how business has been conducted on this soil since this country's inception.

With all of that being said, the SEC's assertion that I owned or controlled Rainco Industries, thereby creating a conflict of interest with my positions as both a board member and officer of Revolutionary Concepts, was not factual under state or federal law. As Rainco Industries was turned over to an irrevocable trust,

I could not own any assets of that irrevocable trust, either directly or indirectly. Even if the SEC's main argument was that I had an obligation to disclose activities associated with Rainco Industry's investment into Revolutionary Concepts, the irrevocable trust clearly states that according to the law of the land, I had no ownership, directly or indirectly, in Rainco Industries. Therefore, there was nothing to disclose. One can only assume that the Securities and Exchange Commission chose to single me out as a man of color for using my knowledge and wisdom gathered over the years, and what many white capitalists have used since the beginning of trust law.

How can you say these things, Solomon? You are accusing the Securities and Exchange Commission of being racists and conspiring against you.

I am not accusing the SEC of being racist and consciously conspiring against me. What I am stating is that any official regulatory or government body is made up of people. People come into their jobs with myriad cultural and emotional biases, not to mention trunk loads of personal life experiences that might serve to confirm those biases. Just as we all do, people entrusted to serve the public good in positions of authority can carry racial and cultural biases with them into their respective positions. These biases, whether conscious or unconscious, inform decisions and behaviors. Unfortunately for African Americans and other peoples of color in this country, these biases bleed over into the decisions made by people who make up large governing bodies. It is not the governing body that is racist, per se, but many of the people who make up that governing body. And very often it is the everyday decisions made by these people in power that effect the fate of other human beings in immeasurable ways. Men of color are shot because of these preconceived notions and biases.

The SEC's second erroneous assertion against me is that Revolutionary Concepts was solely funded by Rainco Industries. This is also false. Like many technology startups, REVO was funded through several private equity firms, including Rainco Industries, Magna Capital Group, Asher, and Fair Hills Group, rounding out REVO's total initial funding.

This is where the confusion begins, when a government agency such as the SEC is granted the power and authority to violate other laws, especially when they have the authority to oversee and interpret the constitution. How could one agency, the SEC, come back and say that I had this arbitrary obligation to do something when it has already been made clear that there was no obligation to do so under irrevocable trust law?

This is the ongoing dispute and battle I have been fighting for more than five years and which has cost me a considerable amount of time and money, not to mention many sleepless nights and a great deal of stress. I am actively defending, not just mine, but all of our ability to defend our God given right under the United States constitution as law abiding American citizens.

Lastly, I was accused of exaggerating successes in various press releases that Revolutionary Concepts distributed. Not one press release was exaggerated. We composed and distributed what we believed to be factual. We expressed how we saw the facts and how we believed certain material events should be disclosed to our shareholders and investors. It was always up to the shareholders and investors to do their due diligence to determine whether or not our company and its technology would be a good and sound investment for them. This much was also disclosed in what is called The Safe Harbor Act, within all of our press releases. The Safe Harbor Act states that you cannot depend solely on the information in a press release for the decision of whether or not to buy into a particular stock. We were simply relaying information to the public.

I do not believe that we were accused of inflating, deflating or in any way altering how much money we reported that we raised. We were never accused of pumping and dumping any stock.

Additionally, the irrevocable trust invested exponentially more money into REVO than all other shareholders put together, while not knowing if the investment would pay off or fall flat on its face. It was a calculated risk that Rainco made based upon some of REVO's promising technology. Regardless of who invested, I believed that REVO's technology could be patented, licensed, monetized and really disrupt certain key markets. But, like any investment, there is risk involved. I have many talents in business and finance, but fortune telling is not one of them.

Ultimately, I was accused of not being transparent about Rainco's irrevocable trust and its overseeing trustee investing $3.4 million into REVO over a period of time, because the SEC felt it was my money, not the trusts, and I had an obligation to disclose that to shareholders.

Let's think about this together for a moment. Let's say I start a business and later sell it to you, or simply gift all rights to you. Then I decide to publicly disclose the things you are doing with said business, and how you were doing them, in the present. Remember, I have not been part of the business for some time, and therefore, I am not aware of your day-to-day activities. I then find out that I must publicly disclose information about your business as if it were my own. As you can see, this would be a problem. You as the owner would have the right to sue me for interference in your business. When you leave a company and are no longer a part of the company, it would be improper to disclose information about that company.

From a different point of view as an officer and director of a public company where I am an employee of that company, to go out and make such statements about a legal entity that no longer belongs to me would be wrong and misleading. To state that there is a current relationship with my previous employer, of which there is none, would be at best, an untruth. The only role I had was to introduce the CEO of Revolutionary Concepts to potential investors, whether they be private equity, bank or a venture capital firm, and to prepare the CEO for said meetings.

When I came into Revolutionary Concepts, the company was only worth about $150,000.00. They had patent pending technology, though they did not yet hold any actual patents. It was not until I helped package that technology and its potential, and helped arrange financing through introductions to CEOs of various companies that Revolutionary Concepts was able to borrow money to pay patent attorneys for the purpose of protecting their technology so that it could be licensed and monetized as it is today.

On more than one occasion my legal team and I have questioned what this case is really all about. Perhaps it comes down to a few ignorant shareholders who did not understand the concept of personal enrichment. I am a simple man, and I had a simple and straight forward goal. I brought in investors who invested quite a bit of money into a company that I believed in and wanted to see succeed. I could not tell the future and had no idea we were going to get lucrative licensing agreements with major companies. I put what I felt was Revolutionary Concepts' airtight strategy together, but nobody could predict what the outcome would be. I wanted to succeed, and I wanted the shareholders to win. My job was to create the value to get everyone to win. I was tasked with raising capital, building out infrastructure, developing proprietary technology, monetizing the company's technology, and making shareholders money. I did my job.

Some parties may have had a problem with my color and the diverse parties I brought to the table, and they may have believed that it would all benefit me, personally. Again, I cannot speak to people's biases or ignorance. However, I can say that it is a well-known fact that when officers and directors invest in their own company it shows a great deal of confidence that management believes in their strategy and they plan to move the company forward. They are placing their own money at risk in an effort to grow the company. In fact, historically, stock prices do tend to rise when shareholders see that vote of confidence by a company's management team.

Throughout this horrific journey of continued legal proceedings that I have been embroiled in since 2015, for as long as I can recall, people have, without reservation, taken it upon themselves to share their biases toward me and other people of color whom I consider close colleagues. Although many of these were ignored, some of them still hurt. Some of my white colleagues would dispassionately say that it comes with the territory, or remark that they were impressed with my thick skin. They cannot, nor do I expect them, to understand or relate to the pain that I have suffered because of racial bias.

I am sure some of you can relate to doing a job and doing it well, only to be criticized and picked apart by bullies, whether it be at your office, on social media, or perhaps, within your professional/social circle. On one occasion I heard through team members who regularly communicate with my attorney that one of Revolutionary Concepts' shareholders traveled from California to Texas to go sit in our attorney's office and throw around accusations about me. He demanded information based on hearsay and gossip, while yelling threats pointed toward me. I cannot completely blame any of these people, as the SEC was egging them on. I have also had to withstand many random indignities, whereby I have had to stand before some of these people to answer questions where I was accused of having two different names, as though I was attempting to perpetrate a criminally motivated, illegitimate alias.

I have heard my name change thrown around quite a bit, in a derogatory manner as if to say, "And on top of everything else, he went and changed his name." In fact, I had legally changed my birthname prior to being professionally involved with REVO, or with my other public company affiliations with UniversalBio Energy and JMI. I elected to legally change my name from my birthname of Richard Carter to my adopted name, Solomon RC Ali, for personal and symbolic reasons that are important to me.

In the SEC's mind, my name change, which took place before I became involved with any public companies, was a nefarious attempt to create an alias with which to commit white collar criminal activity. They tried to paint this illegitimate picture, and even attempted to prove that my chosen name of Solomon RC Ali was not legally changed. When they were proven wrong and presented with evidence that my name change was legal and predated my involvement with REVO, they never apologized or admitted to any wrongdoing. It was another arbitrary, racially motivated attempt to poke holes in my character and credibility.

It takes a lot of time, work, and care to build a house, but you can tear a house down in a day. That is kind of what they did to me, and my fight with the SEC continues.

It did not matter that I did not take any money from Revolutionary Concepts, nor did I receive a salary. And it did not matter that my work was benefiting the shareholders. It did not matter what state or federal law dictates about irrevocable trusts. The law did not matter; only what the SEC wanted mattered, and that was to get me and destroy my character and my legacy by rewriting a false narrative and claiming that they are doing their job. When officers of the court can manipulate the system to verify false and untrue narratives otherwise known as lies, and the judge accepts these lies as true and factual, is this not systemic racism at work?

Allow me to share with you just one small example of the false narrative that has been constructed and weaponized against me. The SEC presented false information regarding the day and time of when a particular press release had been issued by Revolutionary Concepts. When the press release in question was pulled by me and my legal team to show the judge that the SEC's assertions regarding the particulars of this one press release were false, the judge stated that I was being argumentative. Another clear example was an assertion made by the SEC stating that I failed to disclose that I had a relationship with Rainco Industries. However, a press release had been issued to the public, investors, and shareholders aka all relevant parties, stating that I had resigned from Rainco in 2011. The disclosure of my involvement with Rainco Industries and my resignation from Rainco Industries and the transfer of all of Rainco's assets over to an irrevocable trust could not have been clearer.

I still struggle with a lot of emotion, hurt, and disbelief that, in this day and age, people would still have those kinds of biases and are allowed to hold a position of power which enables them to push their personal agendas to these extremes. I am in a unique club, being an officer and a director and in charge of raising capital for three publicly traded companies. The SEC has never seen a person of color who looks like me moving in this way. We did break the mold, or perhaps we shattered the mold, but we never broke the law or the rules, only the glass ceiling. That should be a good thing, not a punishable offense.

My ongoing battle with the SEC has caused me countless personal and professional problems and interruptions, some of which I will discuss, and some that are too painful or private to address publicly. I am currently forbidden from becoming an officer or director of a publicly traded company. This has caused me to lose possible future employment and was intentionally done to prevent me from helping myself, my family, and other companies who could have greatly benefitted from my experience and expertise. You see, beyond the SEC's ability to harm my own professional prospects and earning capacity, by harming me in this way, they are preventing me from either directly or indirectly helping other entrepreneurs and business owners within minority communities who suffer from a lack of working capital. You've taken the first Black man who has ever held simultaneous director and officer positions at three publicly traded Black-owned companies and severely handicapped his ability to continue helping other Black business achieve this kind of success.

The SEC's actions also caused me to develop physical illness that I hadn't experienced before, due to the enormous stress and countless sleepless nights I have endured since 2015. A while after the SEC's aggressive legal investigation began, my stress shot through the roof, my health suffered greatly, and I was diagnosed with Type 2 Diabetes. My doctor was shocked at the diagnosis, because I was a fairly healthy and active person who worked out consistently.

I continue to be resolute in my passion for helping minority-owned and operated companies. The SEC's attempt to sabotage and sink us, I would like to say has not prevailed, but it has caused me a great deal of time and resources, not to mention lost opportunities. This, in turn, has potentially affected many entrepreneurs and business owners whose companies could have been helped by me. This help could have resulted in hundreds, and possibly thousands of jobs within minority communities. What is the SEC's goal here? I have always believed that if it walks like a duck and it quacks like a duck, it's a duck.

Reflecting back on the monumental progress that REVO made, both, financially and technologically, at times I grow weary in this fight against a giant (the SEC). They cut off our heads by placing our stock on freeze, which was counter-productive to all involved who were harmed by their actions. Our shareholders need to hold the SEC accountable for destroying the company and its future potential. We have had many instances where companies did not want to do business with us because during the process in negotiations known as "due diligence," they would see the SEC filing on REVO. We have had companies pushing to settle with us for lower amounts of money to continue to license our hard earned patented technology because they knew we were being attacked, and they leveraged this fact to push us to settle for pennies on the dollar while they were clearly using and profiting from our technology. In case you are wondering, there is no empathy in big business. When they smelled blood in the water, they circled the carcass looking for their own pound of flesh to feast on at our expense.

The SEC put out a summary judgment, presenting their five best complaints they think will allow them to win this case against me. As for my side, under the rule of law I only needed one complaint to stick for this case to go to trial and be heard by a judge. They said I had control or influence over the irrevocable trust. The law states I cannot have any influence over it, directly or indirectly. That is the law in the state of Georgia from which this case originates. Do you think the truth is going to come out and it is all going to be alright? Well, for a Black man in America, more times than not, it is not alright. You never get the benefit of the doubt. It is always suspected that you are doing something wrong. When it comes to us there is no truth. It is only what they want it to be.

What many of these government regulatory bodies are missing is that in addition to enforcing industry regulations, they are responsible to put in place regulations stipulating that all Americans are to be treated with equal measure, irrespective of race, color, creed, religion, sexual orientation or gender; and that they should have a system in place to police themselves and be held legally and constitutionally accountable for any actions that go against this constitutional policy. Because at the end of the day, who is holding *them* accountable?

For the extra inquisitive, here is another kernel of information that might surprise you. A few shareholders' perspectives is that I was trying to steal Revolutionary Concepts by way of the irrevocable trust. Their lack of understanding of the irrevocable trust is at the root of this assertion. I could not have taken Revolutionary Concepts, directly or indirectly, due to the laws that govern irrevocable trusts. I would encourage anyone reading this book to educate themselves further on revocable and irrevocable trusts as they pertain to all financial matters, both in business and in personal finances.

It stands to reason that many shareholders would have appreciated an officer of Revolutionary Concepts helping save the company and their investment from losses. However, only people without prejudice and bias could be thankful and appreciate someone doing good for them.

My attorneys and I presented unequivocal evidence to prove that an irrevocable trust owns and decides all matters pertaining to Rainco Industries and their investment in Revolutionary Concepts. We also proved that assertions made by the SEC that I made untruthful claims in certain press releases were, in fact, not made in any press releases. We presented ample proof to substantiate that I did not have to disclose my previous ownership or previous legal involvement with Rainco Industries since an irrevocable trust owns and operates the trust, not me. And we proved that when I gave up ownership and decision-making power at Rainco Industries, I announced it through a press release issued to the public and to shareholders and other investors.

Let's take the SEC out of the equation for a moment and shift to something much more universal. If you are a man of color, I am sure you can recall being pulled over by a police officer as your thoughts start racing, your heart starts pounding, and you scramble to try and figure out why you were pulled over. You experience anger at knowing you did nothing to justify being pulled over or being unnecessarily detained as you observe the aggression in the police officer's voice and in their body language, and you feel primal fear as America's history flashes before your eyes. You are aware that this can go wrong at any moment, and this police officer has the authority to take your life and find legal precedence to justify his or her actions.

Or how about a situation when you were in school, and despite having done your work to completion and having put forth your best efforts, your teacher may have been dismissive of your work because he/she did not like you, but there was no way for you to pinpoint or verify your experience?

Perhaps you were bullied at school for no apparent reason, but you found yourself being attacked by an adolescent mob; an early, pre-social media version of cancel culture. While others are watching you being attacked and mocked, they can't help you because of their own fear of being attacked or targeted in some way. They know what they are witnessing is wrong, but it is safer to not speak up.

Maybe in your adult life, you have witnessed a co-worker being mistreated, but you were afraid to speak up because that may cause you to be looked at unfavorably, or you feared losing your job.

If any of this resonates with you, you can relate to how I have felt throughout this entire ordeal with the SEC. I have had plenty of people around me who offered private support and who believe in me and see that the SEC's treatment of me is unfair, but are afraid to speak up.

As my attorneys and I continued to present proof of my innocence, the allegations against me continued to be a moving target, with the SEC continuously shape shifting their charges against me, determined to make something stick by any means necessary. I began to realize that this was not about the truth. This case was more about their reputations having been threatened. I have witnessed the SEC lying to the judge in an attempt to do what many members of law enforcement have been accused of over the years. The rationalization is that they are bent on a particular outcome even if it means framing an innocent man.

It is not my belief that all members of government agencies, law enforcement, or the court system are bad people, but we all know the bad apple theory. It only takes one to tank the reputation of a good and decent organization. If you are a person of color in this country, then you know that it is not enough for someone to "not be racist." We need to go a step further and foster an atmosphere of anti-racism, whereby people who witness racially biased views and actions within an organization stand up and say, "no more," and educate their partner, colleague or associate.

The conclusion to this unfortunate saga, is that after spending $1.3 Million on my legal defense, engaging the best legal minds in securities law, we sadly lost this case. The courts sided with the SEC on all counts, but like one of my attorneys stated to me that in all his years of practice, he had never seen such a strong bias against any one individual. He concurred that the facts were on our side and that this case should have been dismissed.

The judge did not dispute any of the facts we presented, but argued that I was being argumentative, a standard response to many people of color.

The judge said I had a living trust. I did not, I have an irrevocable trust. The judge said I failed to disclose certain facts when in fact I issued a press release making these facts common knowledge. While I was not shot dead in the street, my character was indeed assassinated, but in the face of systemic racism, I go on.

I cannot be an officer or a director or promoter on any penny stocks, meaning a stock under $5.00. If it's $5.00 or above I can be an officer and director. If you can't do one, you should be able to do the other. They have also not prevented me from loaning companies money as long as all the rules of proper disclosure have been followed. Can you make sense of this ruling? You didn't see the late Bernie Madoff being told he could oversee some investments and not others after he was charged with running the world's largest Ponzi scheme.

Chapter 9

An Ownership Stake in America

"40 Acres and a mule would be at least $6.4 trillion today." –
George Newman

The website Inequality.org did some digging on the numbers back in 2016 and found that "the five largest landowners in America, all white, own more rural land than all of Black America, combined." If this fact were based on a historical meritocracy, you would get no complaints from me. Unfortunately, this discrepancy has roots in slavery and systemic racism that date back hundreds of years. We all know this, so why do I state the obvious? Because as much as African Americans are aware of the broad strokes of racism and how it has trickled down through our lineage to affect everything from our families to our finances, most people are not aware of the detailed and staggering statistics that serve as an ice-cold shower and hopefully a wakeup call.

Do you remember the 2014 Ice Bucket Challenge to raise awareness for ALS research? Let the pages of this book and the information it contains serve as your metaphorical ice bucket over the head, waking you up. Let the inside information I share with you about building generational wealth serve as your marching orders forward.

A recent report put out by the United States Department of Agriculture (USDA) states, "[The tiny group of white landowners], a band that would fit comfortably in any mid-size sedan, owns more than nine million acres, while all of the African American population combined, over 40 million people, own just eight million acres."

At first blush you might think, "Well Solomon, you are splitting hairs here. White Americans may own nine million acres of land across the United States of America, but black people own eight million acres of land. That's not too bad."

Let's crunch the numbers by individual person. What this information is outlining is that just five White Americans have accumulated nine million acres of owned land. Theoretically, the five biggest rural white landowners across the U.S have a share of 1.8 million acres each between them. Our entire Black American population, 40 million people to be exact, owns eight million acres in total. If you divvy it up, that means theoretically our community owns just 0.2 acres of land per Black American. So much for 40 Acres and a Mule.

We do have the ability to catch up, we can, and we will. Here is my theory on how we can expedite this pursuit.

What exactly is ownership, and what does it mean to have an ownership stake in America? The American narrative would have you believe that it starts and ends with home ownership, when that is only part of a much bigger equation. Homeownership has its place in the fabric of the American dream but owning a piece of America goes far beyond a white picket fence, especially if you are Black.

When it comes to securing ownership of the ideal family home on the ideal American street, historically, millions of Black Americans have been left behind. Redlining, an unscrupulous real estate industry that is invested in perpetuating the continuation of racial segregation, and wage disparities have created much of the problem. Now, we need to focus on real solutions that empower and enrich our people.

Follow me for a moment as I attempt to explain my viewpoint on real estate as a personal investment. When you put down 10% of your own money to purchase a piece of residential property to live in, that down payment is no longer working for you. Instead, it is providing you with the leverage needed to borrow the other 90% to buy that home. The home you purchase becomes collateral security for the lender. That is okay if this step is taken at the right time and for the right reasons. The right time would be when your credit score, proof of income and liquid *(easily accessible money with no early withdrawal penalty)* emergency fund are in order. The right reason is when you are able to hold on to the home for a considerable amount of time, preferably a decade or longer, and if you have devised a plan for leveraging your mortgage debt to either earn money on your debt or subsidize yourself to offset some or all of the interest on your mortgage debt.

Before accepting an offer through a bank or mortgage broker, you should do your homework on the going interest rates and what your credit score and debt-to-income ratio qualifies you for. For starters, you will want to get a fixed rate mortgage and not an adjustable-rate mortgage *(ARM)*. You want to know what your monthly obligation is and what it will be for the next decade so that you can plan and budget accordingly. You should <u>not</u> pay points, and you should consult with a real estate attorney to find out what you should be paying for your closing costs on your home. A good rule of thumb is that your closing costs should not be more than 3% of the cost of your home. If you are a first-time home buyer, research first time home buyer assistance programs and down payment assistance programs in your state.

This equation does also vary if you are attempting to purchase property in a redlining district, *yes, they still exist*. In fact, Long Island, New York's top circulated newspaper, Newsday, recently conducted a three-year investigation of ninety-three local real estate agents over 240 hours of secretly recorded meetings, whereby 5,763 residential real estate listings were analyzed. The newspaper uncovered widespread evidence of unequal treatment by real estate agents toward potential home buyers based on race and ethnicity.

The biased behavior and manipulative maneuvering were found to be perpetrated against Asians 19% of the time, against Hispanics 39% of the time, and against African Americans 49% of the time. Homebuyers were guided away from specific communities, and toward other communities based on race. The Newsday exposé states, "The investigation reveals that Long Island's dominant residential brokering firms help solidify racial separations. They frequently directed white customers toward areas with the highest white representations and minority buyers to more integrated neighborhoods."

Whether you live in a predominantly white neighborhood, or a neighborhood with a large minority population, should be your choice to make and not a realtor or a lender's choice. Anything else is unconscionable.

Additionally, when people of color are guided toward minority neighborhoods by a professional, they put their trust in, that neighborhood is not necessarily thriving in terms of the public education system, the crime rates, or the property values. This is why it is so important to be your own advocate, do your own research and make the best decision for you, your family, and your financial future. Do not blindly put yourself in the hands of a realtor, no matter how warm and fuzzy or helpful they appear to be. If you do, you might find yourself in a less desirable neighborhood with lower or decreasing property values if you cross paths with an unscrupulous realtor who deliberately pushes you into less valuable neighborhoods in an effort to keep white neighborhoods and neighborhoods of color segregated from one another.

When shopping for a mortgage to purchase a home, you may also find that lenders may loan you far less money, if they decide to loan you money at all. You will need to circumvent their unconscious racial bias sand tactics with a solid credit score, a healthy bank account, a favorable debt-to-income ratio, and a reliable income that is documented via your annual income tax returns and/or W2 documents. Don't have some of these things yet? We'll address this in a bit.

Many decades back, post-slavery, it would take years and years for black people to pay off a property and many folks could lose their property due to an act of God or other events destroying their crops, therefore losing their property as well as their original down payment. Racial discrimination also played a role. Many who were able to take their crops to market would notice that their crops were valued at far less than those of whites, thereby creating more financial hardship. These circumstances would often lead to seizure of the crops and the property.

Because the narrative has historically been so focused on owning residential property, the average American, no matter their color or creed, has failed to see a few important points.

One point to consider is how business ownership translates to an ownership stake in the American Dream, and if approached properly, can lead to successful home ownership and/or the successful acquisition of farmland, commercial property, or residential investment property.

If one purchased a business using the same 10% down payment that we cited earlier when speaking of a down payment on a house, that business could be an invaluable tool toward providing steady cash flow for you and your family at a much faster rate than a home can. The business can provide you with income and equity and provide financial longevity. Remember, money is a marathon, not a sprint. The business would allow you the ability to purchase land or an investment property, and to service the mortgage debt on said property while your other tangible asset, your business, increased in value as you simultaneously draw an income from it.

And here is an important caveat to homeownership that no one tells you. Once you own a home and have placed it up to the bank as collateral, you must begin to make additional investments into that property so that you can use your residential property as a wealth building tool from which to make additional income, <u>as you are living in the property</u>. Your "investment" in real estate, if it is your primary place of residence, is the slow boat to China, so to speak. The home may provide considerable returns for you after a decade, or two, or three *(though there are no guarantees)*. In most cases, with the exception of extreme market volatility, you will not see a return on this investment any time soon. An example of real estate market volatility that could work in the homeowner's favor is when the real estate market crashed in 2008 and 2009. If you purchased a home in 2010, 2011, or 2012, at the bottom of the market, and then sold that same home seven or eight years later once another real estate bubble had begun to develop, you would walk away with a considerable profit in less than a decade. If that is you, congratulations, but that is the exception to the rule.

If you already own a home, a financially sophisticated move would be to create an income stream from your residential property. Reason being, you never want to be the one servicing your whole debt, and a mortgage *is* still debt. You want to create an additional income stream that services that debt, and possibly even makes you a profit beyond servicing the debt.

The type of land that has the most potential for earning you money is rural land. With rural land, you can raise cattle, grow crops, rent out space, and the like. Urban and suburban settings are a bit more challenging, though not impossible.

Just some of the ways to turn your primary residential property into income that services all or part of your mortgage debt:

Rent a small portion of your property to a tiny house or mobile homeowner

Cultivate and sell crops locally

Offer outdoor classes on your property

Rent additional parking

Take in a thoroughly vetted roommate or tenant

Purchase a mother/daughter style home and rent out one floor to a family member, friend or vetted *(after a complete background, employment, criminal, financial investigation)* tenant

Take advantage of agricultural tax exceptions by inquiring if your land can be classified as farmland

According to SmartAsset.com, "You don't have to be a full-time farmer to take advantage of agricultural tax breaks that will help you with your property taxes. In some cases, all you need is a piece of land that's not currently being used. You can say that the land is preserved wilderness or put it to some kind of agricultural use to save on property taxes."

If you are not a full-time farmer, you will need to consult your local laws, speak with a tax accountant, and possibly a homeowner's association *(HOA)*, to make sure the moves you intend to make are all above board. It is always important to dot your i's and cross your t's before making any significant financial or tax-related moves.

The point is, wherever possible, try to avoid using a significant portion of your paycheck to pay your own mortgage and create extra income streams with your property to service or offset at least a portion of your mortgage debt. Now you are living in and enjoying your long-term investment, while simultaneously creating an extra income stream with that property.

If you choose to first build credit, equity, and income through the acquisition of a business, there are some important things to be aware of, and pitfalls to avoid. The acronym "CEO" is a coveted one within the African American community. The thought of being the boss, writing the checks, and calling the shots is alluring. The privilege of holding the position of Chief Executive Officer or President of your own company comes with significant responsibility. If not handled properly, it can enslave you with mounting personal debt from borrowing money with personal guarantees attached to collateral. If you attempt to self-fund a startup, you will find yourself pursuing personal debt in the form of credit card purchases and business loans with personal guarantees attached to collateral, such as an existing home or other important personal assets.

I know many of you are thinking, "What is the difference between getting a loan to purchase a business versus getting a loan to purchase a home? First, many of you are not using, or did not plan to use, your land as a business, but as solely as your primary residence, thereby eliminating the opportunity to create any enterprise value or tax savings. We must keep in mind that most real estate is used for single family residential purposes and not business purposes. Therefore, a much slower return on your investment will exist.

I, for one, chose not to borrow, but to become an investor in businesses. Although this path is initially more difficult, it is far more rewarding. Investing in an existing business, either by yourself or by pooling your money with a group of co-investors, can provide ongoing short- and long-term returns on your money.

One of the greatest strengths we have is our ability to commune and pool resources. There is strength in numbers because where I am weak you may be strong, and where you are weak, I may be strong. Combining resources such as income verification, credit scores, skills, networks, and savings expedites our cause in every capacity.

Community Building as a Means of Creating Ownership

Pooling economic resources has long been a tactic of innovative African Americans who seek economic freedom, and a sense of safety and community. It is also a way of circumventing a lot of the bias, marginalization, and institutional racism that has resulted in many of us having limited personal resources to begin with. Just imagine what could be accomplished if you pooled two incomes, three incomes, four incomes, or more.

That is exactly what nineteen African American families recently did when they collectively purchased land just north of Atlanta and dubbed their newly minted community, "Freedom, Georgia." As ABC News reported about the pioneering community back in September of 2020, Freedom, Georgia is currently just a "campground on red clay under the hot sun. But for the Black Americans who are moving here, it's a dream," and one with the immense potential for establishing a thriving Black community that puts the dignity, civil rights and personal safety of its citizens first. The ABC News piece goes on to state, "So far, about 19 families, most of whom are from Georgia, have pooled their money to buy the nearly 97 acres of land in Wilkinson County, which is located about two hours south of Atlanta. It's their escape, they said, from the everyday racism that feels like a part of life in the United States."

Speaking to ABC News, one of the founding investors in Freedom, Georgia, expressed, "We came together, and we said, 'You know what, we don't like being slaughtered in the streets. We don't like our children being there, being at the mercy of some psychopath that wants to tackle us and arrest us and bang our heads. We don't want that. So how about we just come together and build our own,'" said Dr. Tabitha Ball, a licensed clinical psychologist from the Atlanta suburbs.

Coming from all walks of life with one common goal, "the people in Freedom include a range of professionals from doctors to real estate agents. Still, the group needs to build roads and establish running water and electricity before it can start building homes."

This may sound like a daunting and overwhelming venture to the average American of any color who is content to avail themselves of readily established infrastructure and luxuries that we have all grown comfortable with, but are you comfortable with the idea that you or a loved one could be shot in the street like a dog because of the color of your skin? Are you comfortable with continually trying to climb up a ladder that is spiked with racially bias booby traps, without the support of a village of likeminded people and pooled resources?

Life is about choices, and from my perspective, the people of Freedom, Georgia have made an empowered one.

Think Like a Bank

I challenge you to look at a bank and how they continue to prosper from all of the loans they make, receiving far more money than what the collateral was worth. Banks prosper, period. Ask yourself why. A recent article on the website MoneyUnder30.com explains the business model of a bank very well:

"Banks use depositors' money to make loans. The amount of interest the banks collect on the loans is greater than the amount of interest they pay to customers with savings accounts—and the difference is the banks' profit.

For example: You currently have an emergency fund of $10,000 in a high yield savings account that may pay 1.50% APY. The bank uses that money to fund someone's:

- *Mortgage at 5.50% APR*

- *Student loan at 6.65% APR*

- *Credit card at 16.99% APR*

Now, think about this process repeated with millions of banking customers and billions of dollars."

The way you beat the bank at their own game is by following their business model, which has proven to be one of the most profitable business models on the planet. It is time to think like a bank. In a nutshell, that is how you stake your claim to the American dream, no matter the vehicle you choose to invest in.

Banks make money by accumulating money from various sources and loaning that money out at moderate to high interest rates. For example, you place your money in a basic savings account at your local bank branch and earn a paltry yearly return of 1% while the bank is leveraging your money by lending it out to other people, or to businesses, and charging them anywhere from 3.5% to 16.99%. They may be paying you $150 per year on your savings account but they are servicing that miniscule debt owed to you, plus making a considerable income on your money, by leveraging your money to loan out at much higher interest rates than they are paying you.

Whether you are borrowing money to purchase a business, a home, a car, or a piece of land, you must re-train your brain to think like a bank would think. Who will service that debt and how will it be serviced? How much interest are you paying out per day, per month, per year? How can you re-compensate yourself for that interest you are paying out, or even make money on that debt? Here are a couple of possible scenarios to consider:

Many urban areas throughout the United States have developed what are dubbed "Mother/Daughter homes" or "Two-family homes." Some other homes in certain parts of the U.S. feature generously sized walk out basements. Purchasing this style of home can enable you to either purchase the property in partnership with another party or create an apartment for a tenant. The separated space can also allow for office space that can be written off as a business expense or partial commercial space. It can also serve as space for some other business-related venture. This way, you are offsetting the mortgage interest and other expenses that comes along with this type of long-term investment.

If you choose to pool your money with other parties to purchase a business, you are sharing in the service of the debt and other related expenses, as well as mitigating your risks associated with the business.

If you have the means, you can simply offset any debt interest through placing the sum of money you owe on that debt into a relatively safe investment that won't go gangbusters, but that will earn you a decent return on your money, equal to or surpassing the interest you are paying on the debt. When wealthy people are deciding whether to pay for a significant purchase in cash or to finance the purchase, they always ask themselves if they can take that same amount of money and earn greater interest than the interest they are paying on that debt should they choose to finance. They do this by investing the money elsewhere. That is thinking like a banker and thinking like a wealthy person.

Example: you are in the market to purchase a used vehicle that has between 10,000 and 40,000 miles, and your budget is $15,000.

You can either A. purchase the car outright for cash or B. finance the car with interest. The only time it is more advantageous to finance the car is if you can take that same money you would have used to purchase the car outright and invest that money to not only cover the cost of the interest, <u>but to earn a profit on top of that interest</u>.

Let's now delve a bit deeper into Black homeownership in America. A 2019 Urban.org article paints a grim picture in the racial homeownership gap, which gained unfortunate traction after the Great Recession of 2008, from which African Americans have been the slowest to recover.

According to that same article, here is how it breaks down:

The current 30% black and white homeownership gap as of 2019 was larger than it was just prior to the passing of the 1968 Fair Housing Act.

If Black homeownership was the same today as it was back in the year 2000, America would currently have 770,000 additional Black homeowners.

Homeownership is currently lower for Black college graduates than it is for white high school dropouts *(Did you just hear the record skip? Me too!)*.

Here is the biggie!

"Black borrowers are less likely to meet the traditional credit standards necessary to qualify for a mortgage." The article then goes on to say, "These differences in credit scores by race can be at least partially explained by the forces of structural racism within the financial system. Research has shown that the legacy of redlining and community segregation has limited black borrowers' access to traditional credit and exposed them disproportionately to predatory lending sources."

Not to mention exposure to more crime and inferior public education.

Additionally, according to HudUser.gov:

"Minorities who do save enough for a down payment are often assessed higher lending fees that make the mortgages unaffordable."

A 2019 CBS News article delves into this racial bias mortgage rate disparity, proclaiming that technology is now allowing minorities to get more comparable mortgage rates when applying online rather than in person. The article states,

"A recent analysis of nearly 7 million 30-year mortgages by University of California at Berkeley researchers found that Black and Latino applicants were charged higher interest — an average of nearly 0.08% — and heavier refinance fees when compared with white borrowers. That was in face-to-face transactions. When applying online or through an app, minorities still ended up paying more, though terms were slightly better than when borrowing in person."

Slightly better when lenders cannot see our faces and the hue of our skin, but still not the same rates as white borrowers. So how do Black and brown borrowers even the playing field when shopping for a home loan?

The CBS News piece goes on to say, "Latinos and African Americans paid almost one tenth of a percentage point more for mortgages between 2008 and 2015, the study found — a disparity that sucked hundreds of millions of dollars from minority homeowners every year. For example, a black homeowner with a $429,000 mortgage would pay an average of $640 more over the life of the loan, said Nancy Wallace, one of the Berkeley researchers.

An amount that equates to an extra $20 a year may seem small for one household, but "it's still outrageous to pay more because you're a different race," Wallace said. And it adds up: the higher mortgage costs amount to an additional $765 million a year for Black and Latino borrowers."

We also get rejected at higher rates. "The Berkeley study found that both face-to-face and online lenders rejected a total of 1.3 million creditworthy Black and Latino applicants between 2008 and 2015. Researchers said they believe the applicants "would have been accepted had the applicant not been in these minority groups." That's because when they used the income and credit scores of the rejected applications, but deleted the race identifiers, the mortgage application was accepted."

The UC Berkley study on fairness in lending concluded that one fact working against Black and Latino borrowers is that, unlike white borrowers, minorities tend to stick with one lender as opposed to shopping around for the best rates. The article concludes, "The biggest takeaway for both the Latino and Black communities is you should shop around for your mortgage. You should not accept the first option."

As stated above, making your first investment into a business and building credit, equity, and income through that business will allow you the financial leverage and necessary credentials to then purchase a home or investment property as a stronger candidate. Pooling financial resources with another party can also place you in a stronger position, because combined and augmented credentials can also place you in a stronger position to access quality lenders.

I said this chapter was going to feel like a cold ice bucket poured over your head. I know it's a lot to take in, and if you are anything like me, your mind is likely spinning right now as you think of all of the things you feel you have done 'wrong" up until this very moment. You might even be looking for someone or something to blame for not knowing certain things, or you might just feel angry at some of the statistics shared with you in this first chapter.

That is okay, because I now have your attention and you are ready to keep learning and make the necessary changes in your life to meet your financial goals. If you need to re-read this chapter, please do. In fact, I would suggest treating this book as a workbook. Highlight, re-read, make notes.

Your life is about to change.

CHAPTER 10

MANAGING YOUR MONEY LIKE THE ONE PERCENT

"When money realizes that it is in good hands, it wants to stay and multiply in those hands."- *Idowu Koyenikan*

My professional and financial journey of the last thirty-four years has taught me several things about money. How to see and define it, what to look for when investing in other people, and how to avoid those people and situations where money is being mismanaged.

Let me start off by saying this. If you are like me, and there is a good chance you are, at one point in time you had very little to no money. Maybe you were born into this world without so much as the clothes on your back. Even if you were born into a large inheritance, we all start in the same place in that we are born with no money. We may be born *into* money or into families that have accumulated money and elect to give us an allowance and a head start. We may take jobs and work to receive a paycheck once we are able to get a student work permit at the age of sixteen. But that is not what I am talking about. I am talking about money that lasts and goes out and works for you. No, I am not talking about your 401K or another retirement plan that you contribute toward monthly, nor am I talking about the business you are trying to build as an entrepreneur where you anticipate generating a certain amount of money in exchange for your sweat equity.

My point, and I cannot stress this enough, is that <u>money must go to work for you</u>. This is a fundamental principle that I have learned along the way. Being that money has always been a passion of mine, I have read many books on the subject and I can tell you that the best book that describes and outlines the concept I speak of is none other than The Holy Bible. Yes, you read that correctly. I would urge every one of my readers to read the Bible and its principles pertaining to money, for the Bible gives you many principles about money that, brilliantly, are as relevant today as they were thousands of years ago. "Solomon, biblical principles may have worked for you, but I am not a Christian."

Understood, and you need not be. You can read biblical messaging and principles about money with purely academic intentions if that is your wish. Do not throw out the baby with the bath water. This book is training you to think and behave the way wealthy people do, and with that being said, I am going to ask you to set aside your dogmatic principles and focus on the prize; the prize being the roadmap to building generational wealth.

I would then add *The Richest Man in Babylon* to your shortlist of reading materials. The principles presented in *The Richest Man in Babylon* were made simply and clearly, as most powerful messages typically are. Please understand that my aim is not to preach, but to give you the information that can help you to advance and promote yourself.

Through these reading materials, including what you hold in your hands right now, you will first find yourself in a state of seeking and trying to better understand money. You may feel overwhelmed and that is okay. Give yourself a great deal of credit for shifting your perspective from earning, borrowing, spending, and accumulating debt, to your awakening to the idea that there is more to learn. Congratulate yourself on this newfound desire to move toward building wealth.

In an initial effort to try to understand money and become better acquainted with it, you will find yourself searching. Some of you may even look up the definition of the word "money," as I did once upon a time. Let me make it simple for you. Money is a tool. That is it. It is a tool that, when placed in the right hands, can do great and wonderful things for you, for the people you love, and for humanity. One must utilize it as a tool that is no more important than a carpenter using a hammer, drill, or saw. It is to be applied at the right time and with the right principles behind it. Being an entrepreneur is not enough.

Being an entrepreneur can sometimes even cost you more than you wish to spend. Although being a reasonably successful entrepreneur can potentially take you far, it will also keep you longer than you want to stay. It will wear out its welcome in your life if you do not then pivot toward making your *money* your employee.

What I have come to realize after many years is that it is not enough to earn money, even if you are earning a nice sum of money. Money must go to work for you, because as the months, years, and decades roll along, you won't always be able to go to work. Money must become your servant and faithful employee, meaning, it exists to serve you. This is the beginning. Some of you may be thinking that what you have just read sounds far out or weird, and some may even say it is arrogant. It is not. This is part of Capitalism. Capitalism holds the objective of obtaining the least expensive labor possible with the highest possible returns of profit on investment, in the safest manner possible, and with the best possible returns. My job is to be a good steward over this entire process. What does a good steward do? A good steward of Capitalism and of their own money should find a home for that which he is responsible for. I am responsible for a great deal of money, and I am the steward of that money. You are responsible for being a good steward of your own money. It is a seed to be planted. When planted, it must be watered, it must be nurtured, and it must be placed in a safe environment. It must be handled and given to others to handle in such a manner that it should return back to you, multiplied.

There is a story in the Bible that I am paraphrasing *(The Parable of the Talents; Matthew 25:14-30; Luke 19:12-28)* where a farmer was leaving on a journey. He entrusted his money ("talents") to three of his servants, which he divvied up to each of them according to each of their known abilities. Upon the farmer's return, he asked each of his three servants how they handled the money they had been tasked with managing. The first two servants immediately set about multiplying the farmer's money. Upon his return the first two servants each proudly presented the fruits of their good stewardship over the farmer's money, while the third servant confessed to not multiplying his master's entrusted money at all, but simply burying it in the ground.

The first servant explained that he took the five "talents" he was entrusted stewardship over and multiplied it into five more talents for a total sum of ten. The second servant also proudly explained that he took the more modest two talents he had been given stewardship over and gained two more, making for a total sum of four talents. The third servant who was entrusted with one talent was fearful, resentful, and angry with the farmer for expecting to multiply his fortune sans any time spent or manual labor on the farmer's part. The third servant explained that he simply buried the one talent that he had been given stewardship over and did not multiply it at all. In fact, it lost value in its inability to multiply *(a reference to our modern-day inflation)*.

While the first two servants were now granted even more talents to be stewards of, meaning the wealth they would now be entrusted to oversee on behalf of their master, the third servant was stripped of the one talent that had originally been given to him, and he was banished for his shortsightedness and the "evil and lazy" manner in which he presided over what was entrusted to him.

Let's break this down.

This parable is symbolic of God or the universe *(whichever you prefer)* entrusting us with stewardship over resources. As temporary human beings of this earth, nothing is permanent and nothing truly belongs to us. We are merely humble stewards over that which we are given.

He who is able to multiply what is given to him is considered a good steward, and more will then be given to him.

Honoring and respecting money, saving money, and ultimately, taking some calculated risk with the higher purpose of multiplying that which is given to you is blessed and multiplied even more. Your money deserves to be multiplied and grow as if it were seeds placed into your faithful hands. Now what does it mean to make a calculated risk to invest your money in order to gain fruitful returns and multiply what is given to you? Education and due diligence are necessary in order for you to be a good and faithful steward of your money in this life.

Are impulse purchases that garner no returns and subtract money from your account a good way to multiply what you have been given? No. Are impulsive and emotional investments a good way to multiple what you have been given? No. Is spending money to impress other people or garner their social acceptance a good way to multiply what you have been given? No. Spending money on enjoyable things and meaningful experiences is fine within its proper context, for the right reasons, and when that "spend" is a small percentage of your total net worth. We cover that throughout this book.

Now that we have established that your money should be invested and multiplied, we need to do a deep dive into how, why, and when to invest your money.

There are many people out there who will want you to invest your hard earned money into various ventures for one reason or another. Their ideas may sound attractive and enticing, and they might be tricksters, meaning they have tricked themselves into believing that their idea is a money maker without any real knowledge or consideration of a tried and true formula. There is a formula to determining the quality of an investment and its ability to provide you with a return on your money. Beware. Beware of any investment opportunity that is run solely on emotion and hype. That is not where you want your money to be. Do not follow the crowd, do not follow the hype, and do not follow emotion.

If you understand what it is you are investing in and why, you will understand the risk versus reward equation more thoroughly and clearly, and you will be a better steward over your existing money. Stewardship over money is earned and flourishes over time. It is a rite of passage, and it is how the universe entrusts you with more and more money. Wealthy people, for the most part, understand this concept. When you understand the sacrifices that come with making money and the sacrifices that others have made to accumulate their money, you will have a healthy respect for it, and that is what you need on your path toward building wealth.

How do the one percent choose their investment opportunities?

First you need a story; a story that makes sense and a story that you understand. I don't spend my money foolishly because I have had more ups, downs, and ups, and more downs than many of you. I look at things and I invest in them for one reason and one reason, only; because I can see certain possibilities that are backed by an equation that has been cultivated over a period of years. These possibilities are shaped or look as follows:

Probability of Safe Returns - even in the case of failure

Good Collateral

Books and Records

MDNA - management discussions

A Well Thought Out Plan

Probability of My Money Returning with Friends

Let's Break This Down.

Probability of Safe Returns

If a company has $1 million in assets and/or a $1 million valuation, the most I would invest in that company would be $250,000. This investment equivalent to 25% of the company's valuation provides me with assurance that in the event of a company's failure to thrive and my need to sell off my investment in a fire sale *(pennies on the dollar)*, I can sell off these assets at $500,000. The $500,000 is 50% less than the company's total valuation of $1,000,000, but twice as much as my financial investment in said company. With this time-tested mathematical equation, I am able to recover my initial investment of $250,000 plus a significant return on that investment *(I have still doubled my money)* by selling it off as a distressed asset to a separate party. And this is in the event of a "failure." The acquiring party is getting a deal because they are buying a distressed asset at 50% of its original valuation, and I am doubling my money and walking away from the table. This is how experienced investors view investments. If a company wanted me to invest $1 million into their venture, they had better be able to show me a valuation of $4 million in order to meet this same mathematical equation of risk versus reward.

Good Collateral

Good collateral varies from company to company. Historically, solid collateral was just that, meaning that it was of the brick-and-mortar variety. Real estate holdings/property values and inventory would be good examples of brick and mortar or physically tangible collateral. In the age we are currently in, that can still be the case, as can collateral in the form of a company's member database, proprietary information, patents, or trademarks, which would fall under the umbrella of intellectual property (IP) collateral. This is up to the discretion of the investor.

A Well Thought Out Plan

A business plan, that is. I have to be able to see what I am investing in, and how I am getting my financial returns. I also need to see that if everything goes to pot, there is a clear path forward for the company and for me as an investor in that company. Business is more than a notion, more than an inspired idea. It takes preparation. Part of that preparation begins with fleshing out all of the things you can possibly think of that can potentially go wrong. Most people, whether they are seeking an investment or seeking to invest their money, think only of what will go right. I look for every single thing that can go wrong, how it can go wrong, and why it can go wrong. Then I look for potential solutions to hedge against those things. It puts you in a better position to predict and course correct with minor adjustments along the way. Chances are your business or idea is not new, it is just new to *you*. There is nothing new under the sun, but you very well might be introducing, or are introduced to, a new approach to doing something that can indeed bring value to a market. Most businesses fail because of a lack of capital. The question is: What are you going to do in launching, running, and growing your business that is going to keep you from running out of capital? The answer: You need O.P.M. - Other People's Money. You get that in one of two ways. You can get access to other people's money in the form of debt financing or in the form of equity financing.

Debt Financing is exactly what it sounds like. You are receiving capital as a loan, which can be structured a multitude of ways. But the bottom line is what you must repay with interest the monies that have been loaned to you.

Equity Financing means that you are given capital in exchange for equity in your company. The more capital you receive, the more watered down your own stake in the company becomes. This is not a bad thing, because, as I have said and will reiterate throughout this book, a smart business owner knows that, for example, owning 30% of $30 million is far better than owning 100% of nothing. That is simple math.

Hybrid Financing is when you do a combination of the two. Although many companies tend to opt for one form of financing over the other.

The Probability of My Money Returning with Friends

When money is employed into a good business, it could go from one unit of operation, or one location, to several locations. When money is properly used to move a business enterprise forward, that is how it is achieved. Invested capital, whether you are the investor or the person receiving an investment, should not be used to pay back previous mistakes, debts, and obligations. On the contrary, the money should be used to build out management, scale operations and grow revenue. Owners must be willing to listen to their investors and advisors. They may know how to run their business but running a business and growing and scaling a business are totally different animals. How do we put systems into place so that it feels seamless? Although a business has scaled from one location to fifty different locations, it still feels like one location.

The average business owner is not equipped for this undertaking. When my team and I come in and evaluate a business for potential investment, this is what we look for. How are things currently being run? And is the current team coachable to be able to listen to consultants to move the ball forward? Some businesses want to keep doing things the way they always have, simply because it is comfortable, even if it inhibits growth. This is a non-starter. There needs to be a shift in the company's culture and in its structures and systems, to allow them to ease into growth and scalability.

MDNA

The next thing is called the MDNA or Management Discussions. If a company has no management discussions, then I will read their business summary several times before taking a look at their competition. Who is in the industry? What are they doing in the industry that is different? Take the top five companies within any industry. As you identify the top five companies in the industry, you are looking to see exactly what can be done better and/or differently than what is currently being done within that industry. These are the steps that are necessary.

Books and Records Tell the Story

I look at the company's bookkeeping and records. I try to ascertain what the company's records look like. Why has the company made certain decisions, and what did they base these decisions on?

The interesting thing about financial statements and records is that it is like reading a book. It tells a story. It is always a very interesting and unique story that is being told to me, the investor. This is why I am diligent in my pursuit of reading the financial statements and looking for the story in it. You are looking for things that can be easily adjusted and corrected in the future. You are looking for new opportunities that management might be too close to the project to see clearly. You are also looking for growth opportunities within the company's respective market that management may not know exists.

If you are looking to start investing your money, this is valuable intel to incorporate into how you think about investments and why you would or would not choose to move forward with a particular investment. If you are seeking capital in the form of an investment, please heed this advice in preparing your credentials completely before pursuing investment capital.

This is how the one percent invest their money into a company, and this is how future one percenters will get their ducks in a row to raise capital. Whether you are investing in the stock of a public company or a private startup, emotion takes a back seat to this tried and true formula. When I think of a plan, my approach is very simple. I look at the investment opportunity that others wish for me to take on and I ask myself, "What is the possibility that this management team can actually pull off what they say they can do?"

"How does this management team compare to others within their industry who are considered industry leaders?"

I will grade the company's management team and see if they have the ability to continue to run their business successfully? And, as mentioned above, if they have the ability to grow and scale their business. What are their shortcomings? I will note their strengths, but their strengths are not where my risk lies. My risk lies with their shortcomings, and by the way, this is exactly how banks think. This is not about negativity versus positivity. Investing is not a glass is half full/glass is half empty game of perception. When it comes to money, and when you are playing in a large pond with big players, it is all about assessing risk.

Financially sophisticated people understand this, and do not take it personally one way or another. I want you to understand this and apply it in your own financial life.

Another important thing I look for, and some might say this is a bit far reaching or controversial, but I look for triple digit growth. It sounds like a lot and it is, but I want to know that this company, even if it fails to hit the mark, still has the ability to achieve a return on my investment. An example is the ability to take a company from three locations to nine locations within a reasonable amount of time. This is important to me, because I want to be a part of something that will be in a continuous state of growth. I am a good steward, like we spoke about earlier, and all good stewards should want to be a part of something that will be larger than themselves, both in mission and in multiplying.

Lastly, and this is critically important: is management willing to invest its monies back into the company to insure growth and the success of the company? If management is looking to pay off previous bills and debts from the monies they are given, that makes no sense to me. If they are looking to instantly fatten their own pockets rather than investing money back into the company, that, in my opinion, is also crazy. That is bad stewardship. I can't pay for someone else's bad decisions nor can I pay for their greed and lack of ability to delay gratification.

Never take your seeds *(your hard earned dollars)* and place them in bad soil. You will not reap a healthy harvest that way. Bad soil is where seeds go to die. I place my seeds in good, fertile ground. Management must be willing to use all of its resources to move the company forward and to develop the company's products and services, not to pay for its previous mistakes or play a game of catch up. Whether that means creating new locations, a new product, developing out technology, monetizing, creating competitive strategies, and ultimately selling or bringing a company public; these things should be the focus.

Consistency is key. Management must be consistent. Also note that although management has an obligation to you as an investor, you as the investor have an obligation to the management team of that company. An investor's obligation is to meet the responsibility of good stewardship. There is only one way to meet that responsibility. Good stewardship starts with educating yourself. And now we come full circle. As you educate yourself and understand what it is that you are looking to do and why you are looking to do it, then and only then, will you understand what it is you are trying to achieve with money.

As you move along through these chapters, I will continue to share information about my relationship to money and how it has prospered me. Please never mistake simple financial principles as being simplistic, too easy, or too elementary. Some of the best and most time tested principles are simple in nature, but difficult in practice, because they require thought, education, discipline, and consistency of behavior. None of those things are easy in practice, but they are necessary if you are going to win with money. The one percent know this.

To drive my point home, let's work with an analogy. If I know a guy who can do 100 push-ups and I can only do 50, I will not challenge him while I can only do 50 push-ups. I may have to continue to work up to doing 130 push-ups before I am willing to challenge him. What does that mean? That means I have to do the work. That means I have to continue to exercise and workout until I build myself up and can compete in that arena. If I can work my way up to 130 push-ups, that means that even if all of my push-ups aren't accounted for, I know that I can do 130 and I will still exceed his number, because he probably got complacent at 100. I need to know who my competition is. Due diligence is extremely important.

Another important book, titled, *Millionaire Mind* by T. Harv Eker, illustrates a few differences between how the poor think and how the wealthy think, *and all wealth begins with how we think*. Now, before you read these bullet points, bear in mind that you might just feel like you've gotten stung by a wasp after reading them. That is okay. Remember that you are learning, growing, and shifting your mindset:

"Rich people get paid by results. Poor people get paid by their time."

"Rich people focus on net worth. Poor people focus on working income."

"Rich people learn and improve themselves constantly. Poor people stop learning when they graduate from college/high school."

Yes, these are very black and white statements and, perhaps, you have dipped your toe into the waters of how the top one percent think from time to time, but now it is time to dive in. For example, have you ever considered your net worth, and do you know how to calculate net worth?

Your net worth is the total dollar amount of your assets, minus your liabilities *(like your debt)*. It is a fairly simple equation. I do not care if your total net worth is currently in the negative. Remember, we are shifting how we think about money, so whether your current net worth is high, average, low, or abysmal, it is time to stop equating worth solely with your paycheck, and time to start considering how to increase your total net worth.

Right now, as you read this, let's examine how you get paid. If you are like the majority of Americans, you currently get paid for your time and your energy output, as we discussed earlier. The majority of the one percent get paid by the results they produce, along with the results that their investments produce *(passive income)*. In other words, many of us get paid a great deal of money as a direct result of our ability to make other people a lot of money, or as a direct result of our ability to help a large number of people solve a problem in their lives. But the majority of the one percent do not earn the bulk of their money by exchanging their time and labor. And, again, we are shifting our mindset.

With that being said, I would like you to start to think about ways in which you can start earning some money based on results, based on the result of an investment and/or by helping a group of people solve a particular problem, or increase their quality of life. Do not feel discouraged if lightening doesn't strike right away. Remember, we are building the muscle of a changed mindset, and wealth begins with how we think and view money.

Let's talk about education. The ability to pursue higher education is a phenomenal opportunity, and if you are fortunate to have a college degree, or a graduate or doctoral degree, my hat is off to you and I congratulate you on your hard work and accomplishment. But here is the thing. Even if you hold a high school diploma, we are living in the greatest information age in human history and you owe it to yourself to take advantage of that fact to propel yourself forward every which way you can. Between endless shelves of books like this one, podcasts, documentary films, online courses, lectures, YouTube series and more; your ability to self-educate, or to continue your education, is boundless. It is stymied only by your reluctance to seek more knowledge. Wealthy people across many different disciplines never stop learning, never stop practicing, never stop creating, and never stop sharing the knowledge they have accrued with others. They also never stop taking calculated risks.

When you set aside time each day, each week, each month, each year to expand your mind and continue learning new things, both within your profession and for personal enrichment, you are telling the universe that you are ready, willing, and able to handle more wealth and prosperity. When you share that knowledge with others, you are sending a message to the universe that your "cup runneth over *(Psalms:23:5),*" you are divinely blessed, and you have an overabundance of wealth to share with others.

I am going to supplement author T. Harv Eker's three bullet points, above, with three of my own additional bullet points about how the rich think, versus the poor:

Rich people focus on abundance and making more money. Poor people focus on bills and more debt.

Rich people focus on gratitude. Poor people focus on lack and complaining.

Rich people think they deserve to be rich. Poor people think they deserve to be poor.

"Ouch! Another wasp sting Solomon." At first blush, you may deny the above bullet points, but if you are currently experiencing lack and debt, feeling poor, or wondering why you are not getting ahead with money, let's break the above three bullet points down and see if some of it applies to you.

When you think about money, what is the first thought that comes to mind? If your first reaction is to think about financial stress, debt, bills, the fact that your kids need braces and college tuition, or that you can't stand your job *(or all of the above)*, then you are not thinking about making more money. You are thinking about all of the money you do *not* have, all the money you owe, and, perhaps, how annoying it is to continue to earn the money you do make. You feel put upon by money.

It is not that you lack intelligence, willpower, or positivity. It is that the day-to-day stress can take over even the brightest mind and hijack what you are projecting out into the universe. A little known fact about the human mind that escapes most people is that the mind is not designed to make you happy. The human mind is an instrument that has evolved over millennia to help you survive. The mind is a survival tool. According to a 2019 *Psychology Today* article, "The human mind has a negativity bias."

Why? Because it has evolved itself to recognize and avert threats in order to keep you alive so that you can reproduce. We are working with a machine that was designed to find and try to thwart and stave off threats to our survival, not to make us happy. This is where our work comes in. On an energetic level, we are bound by the laws of the universe, and what we tell the universe is what will be mirrored back in our life experience. Many rich people know this. Through all of the interviews I have conducted with people in the top one percent across many walks of life, one thing these people have in common is their ability to visualize what they want to accomplish so completely and so convincingly, that their subconscious mind figures out a way to make it happen. I, myself, practice the discipline of visualization on a daily basis. Whether I am preparing for a meeting, a presentation, or I am looking for a particular answer to a question; I will close my eyes and visualize things playing out, detail by detail, exactly as I want them to go. Nine out of ten times, it goes that way.

Whether you are a religious person, a spiritual person, or even an avowed atheist; no matter. The fact is, we all pray. We all try to impose our will on the universe and try to plead our case to get what we want in one way or another. Whether you are praying to a tree, a statue, to science, or to God; the question is, how do you pray and what do you pray for? Rich people tend to pray in gratitude, giving thanks, and declaring their abundance. Poor people tend to beg for things, wish for things, complain about things, and treat prayer the way children communicate with Santa Claus before Christmas. You have probably heard the saying that it is important to "be in an attitude of gratitude." The fact is, gratitude attracts love, support, prosperity and opportunity; and the wealthy know this.

If you listen to most rich people speak, they will let you know in one way or another that they feel they deserve to be rich. They think they deserve to make money, to have money, to grow their money. Rich people feel entitled to wealth and prosperity. Poor people, and many middle class and working class people, believe at their core that wealth is out of their reach and something that other people get to experience. It is obviously an erroneous belief, because if that were true, the Forbes list wouldn't be made up of so many self-made multimillionaires and billionaires. Only a small percentage of Americans inherited their wealth. Regarding millionaires, according to RamseySolutions.com, "Only 21% of millionaires received any inheritance at all. Just 16% inherited more than $100,000. Most wealthy people were born into poor, working class, and middle class families.

Poor People Can Chase Money Away by Viewing the Rich as Crooked, Bad, or Greedy

Do you hold the belief system that rich people must have somehow taken advantage of people, stolen from people, or are greedy and amoral? If you do, you are not alone, and you are also not moving toward a path of wealth. A 2019 Yahoo! Article titled, *We Asked Americans What They Think About the Rich – And Their Answers Surprised Us*, proclaimed that most Americans have a "love/hate" relationship with the rich. GoBankingRates.com also surveyed more than 500 adults to gauge how they view the wealthy. This survey found that ¼ of Americans have negative or very negative feelings toward the rich. The same survey found that one in three Americans think the rich are greedy, and the majority of Americans are for higher taxes for the rich. That same sampled population believe that the government favors the rich.

The problem is, how do the above sentiments and belief systems help you get and stay rich? The answer is, they don't. If you spend any amount of time complaining about the rich, resenting the rich, and vilifying the rich, you are sending a clear signal to yourself, everyone around you, and to the universe that you believe that wealth is a bad thing. This will be reflected back to you in your life experience.

The website Harveker.com sums things up perfectly with their article titled *13 Differences Between a Rich and Poor Mindset* (please note the operative word "Mindset." Why? Because wealth starts with the right mindset, which you are gaining through reading this book):

"Rich people are <u>committed </u>to being rich. Poor people <u>want</u> to be rich.

Most people don't get what they want because they don't know what they want. People with a rich mindset are clear that they want wealth. They are unwavering in their desire. They are fully committed to creating wealth. As long as it's legal, moral, and ethical, they will do whatever it takes to have wealth. People with a wealth mindset do not send mixed messages to the universe.

It means being willing to do whatever it takes for as long as it takes. This is the warrior's way. No excuses, no ifs, ands, buts, or maybes. Failure is not an option. The warrior's way is simple: "I will be rich, or I will die trying."

In my experience, getting rich takes focus, courage, knowledge, expertise, 100 percent of your effort, a never-give-up attitude and, of course, a rich mindset.

Are you willing to work 16 hours a day? Rich people are. Are you willing to work seven days a week, giving up many of your weekends? Rich people are. Are you willing to sacrifice *(at least for a period of time)* seeing your family, your friends, and giving up your recreations and hobbies? Rich people are. Are you willing to risk all your time, energy, and start-up capital with no guarantee of returns? Rich people are.

It's simple — you will be paid in direct proportion to the value you create in the marketplace.

If you have a wealth mindset, you know your life is not just about you. It's also about contributing to others. It's about living true to your mission and reason for being here on this earth at this time. It's about adding your piece of the puzzle to the world.

Most people are so stuck in their egos and think everything revolves around them. But if you want to be rich in the truest sense of the word, it can't only be about you. It has to include adding value to other people's lives.

Part of your mission in life then must be to share your gifts with as many people as possible. That means being willing to play big.

Wealth is more than financial wealth. As you share your gifts and help others, the "richer" you become — mentally, emotionally, spiritually, and definitely financially.

Rich people see opportunities and focus on rewards. Poor people see obstacles and focus on the risks. Rich people see potential growth, take responsibility for the results in their lives, and act upon the mindset that 'it will work because I'll make it work.' Rich people are committed enough to do whatever it takes. Period.

Rich people focus on what they want, while poor people focus on what they don't want.

Did you know that there are no straight lines in the universe? Life doesn't travel in perfectly straight lines. It moves more like a winding river. More often than not, you can only see to the next bend, and only when you reach that next turn can you see more.

Bless that which you want. If you see a person with a beautiful home, bless that person and bless that home. If you see a person with a beautiful car, bless that person and bless that car. If you see a person with a loving family, bless that person and bless that family. If you see a person with a beautiful body, bless that person and bless their body."

The One Percent See Every Dollar as a "Worker"

I look at every dollar as a "worker" or a "seed." You can assign whatever visual works best for you. Whatever word you choose, you should begin to look at every dollar in your possession as a tool that serves you and that goes out and multiplies itself, bringing back friends. This is the only way to look at money if you are to build wealth. If I plant a seed, I believe it will grow into a tree and I believe that tree will blossom and bear fruit. It will in turn, give me more seeds to work with. This is how money grows. Just as you work at a job, a worker provides energy output in the form of productivity. Energy should produce something. You don't go to work to *spend* money. You go to work to *make* money. My money should provide energy that produces something. Yes, my money is also the fuel for someone else's energy to go out and produce more fuel. The money has no energy in and of itself, but when you give it to the right person, that person adds energy to the money and goes to work to produce something.

Every wealthy person is aware that as life progresses, our energy output becomes more limited, but if we are good stewards of our money, we now have money to invest in other people's energy output. Their energy output can, in the right hands, multiply our money and bear more fruit. This is what it means to be a good steward over money. Your job is to ensure that your money has a good and solid job to go to, to earn more money which will return to you at the appropriate time. One percenters understand this concept and employ it consistently. Our money should have reliable, growth-filled employment, when it returns it should not return alone, and we should not have to go out hunting for our money. We should be aware and accountable for our money at all times, even when it is in the possession of others who have borrowed it. We also understand deferred gratification, which is putting off the things that we may want for a later date, and utilizing all of our time and our resources to maximize our effort for greater returns in the future.

Additionally, we understand that time is our greatest commodity and we do not allow people to monopolize our time. We understand that everything that is glitter and sparkling is not solid gold. So therefore, we are very cautious when looking at things and careful not to take them at face value. Wealthy people look under the hood, so to speak. Shine is great, but shine does not equal a solid investment. We listen carefully to the words and the things that are *not* being said as much as we listen to what is being said.

We listen intently and understand other people's projects, perhaps, better than they do because we are willing to do the research and look into all of the blind spots that they do not. I have also heard some very similar pitches over and over again. Along the way, I have picked up many more things and logged many more data points than the person who is pitching me.

To this point, we have talked about many things and I have shared my journey. It is my hope for each of you to have a better understanding of money and the use of it. Money has no more power than a hammer or a saw. In fact, it takes human thought and energy to put it to work to generate returns. No, money is not evil nor is it good. If you choose to spend your money and complain that you do not have enough to invest, you are as the wicked servant that God took the talent away from, and gave it to the blessed servant to multiply it.

Being a good steward is putting your money to work and being grateful for all that you have. Take this as a wake-up call, a harsh but necessary one, to begin to change how you perceive money. It truly does not matter when you start. As I have mentioned, and will continue to re-iterate as a guidepost for you throughout these pages, I lost everything and had to start all over again with $250. I know you can do it to.

CHAPTER 11

— ꞏ —

TIME STEALERS AND OTHER DISTRACTIONS

"Time is more value than money. You can get more money, but you cannot get more time." – Jim Rohn

Time stealers come in all forms. They can be your family members, co-workers, business colleagues, or your friends. If you are a business owner, these people can even be your employees or vendors. They are people who take your time away and distract you from the things you are doing. Up until now, you may not have viewed time as that precious of an asset. A friend talks your ear off about the same old problem but doesn't take your advice on how to fix it. A chatty co-worker stops by your desk to gossip when you are trying to complete a project.

A family member continuously sucks you into the latest family drama. An employee steals a bit of time here or there from your wallet and your company's productivity output with extra-long lunches and too many coffee breaks. And lest we not forget a significant other who is in need of quality time and another vacation. As much as we love them, it can be a struggle giving your family the time they need and still meeting those ever-important deadlines. Yes, I said it.

Family is first in our hearts, after God, but sometimes work does come first. It's not popular to say, but our livelihoods provide the grease that keeps the machine going, and it can be a challenge to express that to our loved ones.It all adds up to one thing: an asset that you lost and cannot get back. Yes, time is our greatest asset next to our health. You can make more money, but you cannot make more time. That five minutes here, twenty minutes there, an hour or two here and there, or even a day. You will never get that time back. I cannot stress this enough: you can make more money, but you cannot make more time. This is not to say that there aren't worthy things to spend your time on, and worthy people, but stay aware of who and what you are giving your time to.

I will share a story of a time when my mother came to visit me for a week but ended up staying for more than ninety days. While she was visiting me over an extended period of three plus months, I still had to work, but I made a good amount of time for her while she was in town visiting. After a few of months of my mother staying with me, I politely asked her when she was leaving. It was not a comfortable conversation to initiate, but I knew that my mother's extended stay was inching toward four months at that point, and the push and pull of accommodating her visit and my business responsibilities was creating an imbalance that was detrimental to my overall productivity.

As I'm sure you can imagine, my mother told me I was being rude and selfish. What I feel she missed in our conversation was that because of my love for her and loyalty toward her, I was bending over backwards to accommodate her in every way I could, while hurting my business and livelihood. It wasn't that I didn't care about my mother or that I didn't want to see her. It was just the opposite. That is why we have to set healthy boundaries, so that our emotional wants do not outpace our long term needs. Same goes for the challenging time difference with me living on the east coast and my parents living on the west coast. My parents live in a different time zone, and they often ask when I will be coming home to visit them. This process takes some thinking on my part, because in order to give them a clear and accurate response, my undivided attention is needed.

Often times, this would require my attention to be focused on responding to them. If I am in the middle of solving a problem with my partner or negotiating a deal, pertinent information can be lost or not captured. I have to make sure I carve out time for my parents, and as you can imagine this takes time to plan a visit with them. When you have given someone else your time right smack in the middle of a thought process, and you have been interrupted, it takes more time to get back to that same thought process or to get back into the "zone."

Going back to my mother's extended visit, months later after she had left and returned back home, I realized how much it had impacted, both, my personal life and my business life. I found little errors here and there in my business that were made during my mother's three and a half month stay of which I had to fix. Some of these errors did cost me money. Time is valued differently for everyone. My mother spending hours at a time with me was no issue for her because she had an abundance of time. For me, even blocks of thirty minutes or an hour of time is quite valuable because of the scarcity of my time.

The moral of this story is never let someone impose their perspective of time onto you. Whereas two hours of time might be in great abundance for them, for you it could mean the difference between major progress or a costly step backwards from your most important goals. Respect other people's time and ask that they respect yours.

Anything that is not helping you make money is hurting you. Of course, we have to nurture our health and our personal relationships. Sometimes things get draining and unproductive when we find ourselves giving time to those we love and care about. It may seem like they don't appreciate the time we give them. This is because they don't understand the sacrifice we have made to carve out that time. You will find some people in your life don't understand what it takes to make a business function. Often times, this may become visible in new relationships or even during a marriage if you have just become an entrepreneur. One feels they are being cheated out of time with you because they are not getting to see or spend as much time with you as they would like to.

As humans, we have a finite amount of energy that is granted to us by our Creator. If you are to achieve your goals, be it personal or professional, you cannot allow time and energy thieves to steal away that energetic output which you have been granted as a gift and a limited, nonrenewable asset. When you are trying to achieve something, you must stay focused.

Spending your time becomes counterproductive when the time you are spending is not yielding valuable returns in your life and in the lives of the people you love. Yes, I am drawing an analogy between your time and your money. Just like money, your time should yield returns in the form of revenue growth, good health, enhanced personal relationships, happy and healthy children, and enjoyable life experiences. That is how you will know your time is being well spent.

Being generous with your time doesn't have to be a bad thing. In fact, you can donate your time to a worthwhile cause that you believe in while using the opportunity to network. Spending time with your children, is an investment in who they will become. In fact, your children will often appreciate your time and attention more than any material things you can provide to them. Using your time to volunteer for causes that you are passionate about can be beneficial. You can spend your time, much like you spend your money, on worthwhile pursuits.

As an entrepreneur, you should always be looking for ways to maximize 24 hours. The name of the 24 hour game is productivity. Productivity makes you money, and money is your wealth building tool. Wealth allows you to establish security and to be there for those you care about.

My team and I have done some research with regard to time management. You may feel differently, but I believe this research will be an eye opener for most of you, and will help you establish more clear boundaries surrounding time, as you gain more time and more money without feeling guilty.

A 2018 Inc. Magazine article, titled, *New Study Shows You're Wasting 21.9 Hours a Week*, breaks down where people are stealing time away from their work week and their productivity. First, to be fair, the article points out that more than 400 executives, business owners, and entrepreneurs were interviewed about how many hours they put into their business per week, and the result was an average of 72 hour work week – definitely not your father's or your grandfather's "40 hour work week." In a joint poll conducted by Gallup and Wells Fargo Bank, it was found that 57% of small business owners work 6 days a week and over 20% work 7 days a week. With that being said, we are not a society of lazy people. The issue is not our lack of hard work or our willingness to work hard, it is in our inability to quantify, with a specific metric, how productive each of those hours really is. Here's why:

According to the aforementioned Inc. Magazine article, these studies found the following time wasters among these same "hard workers":

The business leaders we polled spent 6.8 hours per week on low value business activities that they could easily have paid somebody else $50/hour or less to handle for them. That means that they were wasting almost a full workday each week.

They wasted 3.9 hours each week indulging in what we might call escapist "mental health breaks" --streaming YouTube videos and checking social media.

They wasted 3.4 hours a week handling low-value emails and 3.2 hours a week dealing with low-value interruptions that easily could have been handled by somebody else on staff.

They spent 1.8 hours a week handling low-value requests from co-workers and another 1.8 hours a week putting out preventable fires.

Finally, they spent an average of 1 hour each week sitting in completely non-productive or wasteful meetings.

Total that up and we are looking at more than 21 wasted hours each week -- hours that are going up in smoke while you are doing things that contribute little to no value to your company, and/or career goals, and finances. Depending on the length of your work week, those wasted hours could account for as much as one third of your time."

Let's break down the above information by category.

Low Value Business Activities

These activities can range from opening mail, intercepting inter-office squabbles, organizing computer files, paying company bills, calling or emailing vendors, dealing with a repairperson, tinkering with a printer that's jammed up...you get the idea. These seemingly innocent time stealers are sapping 6.8 hours of productivity away each week from well-meaning, hardworking entrepreneurs and business owners. To figure out what that is costing in dollars and cents so you can apply it to your own life, figure out how those 6.8 hours can be spent to make you money, or simply take what you earn per hour and multiply it by 6.8. Subtract the time wasted and dollars associated with that wasted time and see where you are. Perhaps, an hourly wage worker who is put in place to take care of these ancillary tasks cannot only save you some of the money you already earn but will enable you to make more money in the long run.

Mental Health Breaks

This is a tricky one, because we all do need and deserve mental health breaks. In fact, it has been proven that, especially in creative and knowledge-based jobs, we tend to get our best ideas when our minds are at rest and feeling inspired, as opposed to when we are staring at our computer screen and "working." However, there is a caveat. Be honest with yourself. Are you in need of a mental health break or are you simply looking forward to watching that viral TikTok video everyone in the office is laughing about? If you legitimately do need a break, are you going to spend that break doing something productive like walking in nature, hitting the exercise bike, getting a massage for ergonomic purposes *(especially for all of you who work at a computer)*, or perhaps listening to a YouTube video or lecture that can help you improve an area of your life that needs attending to? How can you spend your mental health mini-breaks in service of your future self?

Low Value Emails (and Texts)

Whether it is your 20th solicitation email of the day or a back-and-forth email exchange with a loved one or persistent colleague, you need to know when to hit the delete button, when to ignore, or when to politely tell someone that you are swamped and will pick up the conversation at a later time. It is easy to get sucked into an enticing email or text exchange during the workday, or to take that five or ten minutes to craft a clever comeback to a rude or inappropriate email, but the fact is, you are wasting your time and your money. Don't do it.

Low Value Requests from Co-Workers

"Hey, can you come here and help me unjam this printer?" or "You have to come over here and take a look at this great Facebook post..." Whether you are an employee, an entrepreneur, or a larger business owner with your own employees, depending on your productivity and profitability, we have all gotten these low value requests from co-workers. Teamwork is important for company cohesiveness and social interaction can be good for business, but not at the expense of your future. Don't be afraid to delegate these tasks to someone else or to tell a co-worker that you will stop by their desk to look at that funny or interesting post once you come up for air. Set clear boundaries for yourself. Setting daily goals will help you create and stick to boundaries with potential time stealers *(more about this later)*.

Non-Productive or Wasteful Meetings

Don't sit in on meetings that don't concern you, and don't make other people sit in on meetings that don't concern them. If you are an employee, you may want to softly ask your employer if they feel you will benefit from sitting in on a particular meeting, or if they would prefer you complete an important piece of work instead. Ultimately, it is their call. Before getting on a call or into a Zoom, Skype, or Microsoft Teams meeting, have a clear agenda for the meeting. Most meetings should not take more than 30-60 minutes to complete. If a question can be answered by a quick text or email, do that instead. If a quick phone call would suffice, do that. Meetings are for instances when an issue or project requires either creative input and/or accountability from several different team members. Be personable and social, but concise and to the point. "Get in and get out" should be the mantra here. Don't drag employee morale down with endless meetings that go nowhere. Always have a clear and organized agenda for your meetings and have one team member run the meeting to stay on track.

Both long and even short term goals require four things: planning + preparation + time + energy. Just like Albert Einstein's famous formula e = mc2 *(energy equals mass times the speed of light squared)*, goals are no different. The planning + preparation + time + energy formula is non-negotiable in the science of time management.

Goal Setting Helps You Respect Your Own Time

Setting goals and writing them down is one of the most important ways you can safeguard your time and your money. Why? Because it helps you create a roadmap for yourself, outlining where you are and where you want to be. Once you put down on paper where you want to be professionally and financially in a year, two years, five years and so on, you will be more inclined to adhere to behaviors that fall in line with that path. According to a famous Harvard Business Study *(aptly titled "The Harvard MBA Business School Study on Goal Setting")* conducted over a ten year period by following 1979 Harvard MBA graduates from their date of graduation to their lives ten years later in 1989, "Setting goals and writing down objectives enhances your motivation and increases your likelihood of success." The study goes on to point out that companies with a written set of goals experienced a seven hundred percent increase in growth compared to companies that did not write down their goals. Breaking this study down to an individual level, "three percent of graduates from their MBA program who had their goals written down ended up earning ten times as much as the other ninety-seven percent put together, just ten years after graduation."

A 2018 Forbes article corroborates this study, stating, "Encoding is the biological process by which the things we perceive travel to our brain's hippocampus where they are analyzed. From there, decisions are made about what gets stored in our long-term memory and, in turn, what gets discarded. Writing improves that encoding process. In other words, when you write it down, it has a much greater chance of being remembered."

Let your written goals be your North Star when deciding where, when, and how to spend your time, and with whom.

Recognize Disguised Time Stealers

Time stealers can also come in various disguises. It can look as innocuous as a friend wanting to hang out. Maybe you were asked to play hooky from work, school, or your studies, and catch a movie or grab an extra-long lunch in the middle of a weekday. You think, "I could use a break." You are quick to agree, and they are quick to remind you that "all you do is work." This is not to say that we all don't need a break sometimes to recharge our batteries, but you know in your gut when you are squandering your time.

In situations like this, we can all fall prey to something called Confirmation Bias. According to *Psychology Today*, confirmation bias "occurs from the direct influence of desire on beliefs. When people would like a certain idea or concept to be true, they end up believing it to be true. They are motivated by wishful thinking. This error leads the individual to stop gathering information when the evidence gathered so far confirms the views or prejudices that one would like to be true." A good example of this would be purposefully looking for medical studies in support of consuming dairy products if you happen to love milk and do not wish to give it up. According to psychology, you will cease any further research on this matter once you have information in support of drinking milk.

It is easy for a distracting friend to "twist your arm" to ditch something important that is in service of your long term goals when you are already on the fence. You've been staying on track with budgeting and saving your money, and sometimes it gets hard to say no to what you feel is a well-deserved shopping spree. Then your friend who is frivolous with her own money convinces you that you do, in fact, deserve that shopping spree. You see her persuasive argument as a sign that you should loosen up and live a little, so you buy that $500 pair of shoes. Later that evening you have buyer's remorse as the reality sets in that you needed that $500 to reach your goal of going back to school or buying your dream home.

You really need to prepare for an important meeting that could help you land a big client for your firm, but a friend who always seems to be in crisis begs you to come over and be his/her shoulder to cry on. It makes you feel good to always feel needed, and you go running over there to be the hero. Later that night you toss and turn as you realize you could have used that extra hour of preparation for the next day's presentation.

You're sticking to your diet and you've got five pounds to go to reach your goal weight. You break your rule of preparing your own meals and agree to go out with some friends for dinner. They egg you on to splurge and you order that big plate of pasta and also scarf down some bread. Next the dessert menu comes and one of the other people at the table says, "You look great. A bite of cake won't hurt you," so you fold and eat the cake. The next morning you awaken to get on the scale and see that you have gained a pound. You realize you should have stood your ground and ordered the salad.

Why do we do this? Confirmation bias. The way we get around this psychological phenomenon is to write down clear and concise goals and to remind ourselves that what is true and what we wish to be true may be in direct conflict.

What I know to be true is this, what you apply your time and energy to blossoms and grows and what you do not put your time and energy into wilts – good or bad. There is an old saying about Two Wolves. You've got the Good Wolf who represents joy, love, generosity, prosperity, and light. You also have the Bad Wolf who represents fear, greed, envy, lack, and sadness. Which wolf will grow and prosper? The one you feed.

As the late philosopher, author, and motivational speaker, Earl Nightingale, famously said in his award-winning and critically acclaimed recording, titled, *The Strangest Secret*:

"Let's say that the farmer has two seeds in his hand - one is a seed of corn, the other is nightshade, a deadly poison. He digs two little holes in the earth and he plants both seeds - one corn, the other nightshade. He covers up the holes, waters and takes care of the land... and what will happen? Invariably, the land will return what was planted."

Allow me to interject here, and share a phrase that you may be familiar with from the Bible. "As ye sow, so shall ye reap."

Getting back to *The Strangest Secret*:

"Remember, the land doesn't care. It will return poison in just as wonderful abundance as it will corn. So up come the two plants - one corn, one poison. The human mind is far more fertile, far more incredible and mysterious than the land, but it works the same way. It doesn't care what we plant... success... or failure. A concrete, worthwhile goal... or confusion, misunderstanding, fear, anxiety and so on. But what we plant must return to us. You see, the human mind is the last great unexplored continent on earth. It contains riches beyond our wildest dreams. It will return anything we want to plant."

To interpret the above passage originally recorded and published by Earl Nightingale back in 1956, which sold more than 1 million copies at the time of its original release, you are an incredibly powerful creator. If you are fortunate, you have been granted a healthy working body, a healthy working mind, a finite amount of time *(your human energy and lifespan)*, and a fertile imagination. How you choose to use those precious gifts will make the difference between success or failure. If you choose to squander a healthy body, you will become ill. If you choose to squander your mind, filling it with negative and self-defeating thoughts or keeping it closed to new and valuable ideas, you will be limited in what you can create and achieve.

And if you choose to squander your time, you will find that the years and decades roll past you, and you will awaken one day to the realization that much of your health, creativity, and your life's purpose have been squandered because you failed to see each 24 hours you were blessed with as the priceless gift it is.

As you can see, I didn't make these rules. They are universal and well documented. If you water something and you continue to water it and nurture it and care for it, it will grow. It will bear fruit. Wasted time begets wasted time, and it will not yield fruit. If you neglect something valuable for even one day, you run the risk of it wilting, while that energy you put into something else will prosper.

You must be goal oriented and strategic with your time, and spend it only when appropriate on the things, people, ideas, and places you wish to see grow and prosper. If you do this, the rewards will be revealed to you as an inevitable byproduct of time and energy well spent.

Let's take an all too common example. If you place a great deal of your time and energy into purchasing items you cannot afford, while simultaneously putting time and energy into a job you dread going to every day, you are in quicksand and sinking fast. You will turn around and find that you are a slave to both your creditors and your employer. You are reaping the unfortunate harvest you have sewn for yourself from how and where you chose to focus your time and energy.

Money is the result of spending time wisely. Let's repeat that: <u>money is the result of spending time wisely</u>. If you spend your time wisely and strategically, people around you who continue to squander their time will begin to try and figure out how it is that you are able to eventually travel and enjoy your life, with so much "free time." When you are frugal with your time and dedicated to fulfilling your highest purpose with the time you have been granted by our Creator, you will enjoy more time and abundance in your later years.

"But Solomon, what's a day here, a week there, or two or three hours here or there? And exactly how disciplined do I have to be with my time, and for how long?" Well, just like money, $10 here, $50 there, $100 here or there can and does add up to a lot. If you squander $50 per week on nonsense, at the end of a year, that is $2,600 down the drain that could have been saved or invested and, therefore, multiplied. For many people, that could be half a month or even a full month's pay that you worked hard for. If you are fortunate enough to earn $2,600 per week, then that is a week of hard work, time, and energy down the drain. That money never got the opportunity to go to work for you. The magazines, the Starbucks, the wasted food, the extra pair of shoes you didn't need, the 20th lip gloss or keychain that will sit at the bottom of a drawer... the thoughtless small purchases that go unnoticed until you say, "Why am I always broke? Where does my money go?"

Time is the same. It will get away from you if you do not take control of it. If you waste 5 hours per week, for example, at the end of a calendar year, that is 260 hours that you could have spent furthering your relationships, your business, your career track, your health and fitness, and your finances. That is 260 hours you could have spent working on that long term goal or dream you have been nursing for years.

From my personal experience, it takes roughly 7-10 years of strategic time management to reap large rewards. Though you will, of course, enjoy small rewards along the way. I have been on my financial journey for 34 years and it has been a journey of ups and downs. Many people may have to work at a job for a total of thirty to forty years, or perhaps even longer, to continue to pay their bills and sustain their lifestyle. But who wants that? None of us do. I know I did not, but many of us don't know any other way of life. By controlling our thoughts, controlling our desires, controlling our time, and controlling our dollars, we empower ourselves to work toward and achieve our goals and dreams. We empower ourselves to save and invest our money in our future, and we empower ourselves to design and live our life, instead of merely existing in it.

Where our energy and time is spent is where we will manifest our results and achieve a particular outcome. If you wish to work diligently for seven to ten years, you can then be ready to retire, while your friends, family members, and colleagues are still working.

It may feel lonely at times when everyone is going to a party and you are at home studying or hard at work burning the midnight oil in service of your dreams, but later on when you are free to enjoy your family and your personal interests, or perhaps even venturing into a second career that is more in line with your personal passion, they will all still be busy working. They will still be enslaved by their circumstances. There is no getting around sacrifice. You can sacrifice now or you can sacrifice later. I learned this lesson twice in my life. When I was a younger man, I spent a lot of my time hanging out with my friends and sacrificing my business. I did not know I was sacrificing my business, and one day I recall reflecting on my earlier days as a much younger man in the military. During my military years, I recalled how disciplined I was with saving my money and my time, and not going out or doing things that were frivolous time wasters. I pondered, "how could I have been so mature beyond my years at the ages of nineteen and twenty, and become so immature and undisciplined in my thirties and forties?"

It was not until my fifties that I realized the error of my ways. Have you ever caught yourself regressing in an area of life that you thought you had mastered years earlier? It is a humbling event to be sure. How could I have been smarter in my youth than I was in my thirties and forties, in the area of respecting my own time?

I immediately made changes and I no longer spent my time with people or on things that did not yield positive returns. I do not spend my time on too many lunches, dinners or frivolous moments. I spend my time building my reserves of resources that I know will work for me and enhance my future. Some of my friends get it, some of them don't, and that's okay. I will often hear comments like, "C'mon, you can take a break for an hour or two." Let me remind you when you take a break for an hour *(or two)* you still have to come back, and it may take some time to come back to what it was you were doing. Additionally, if you have ever experienced what it feels like to be *in the zone*, creatively speaking, you know that this lightening in a bottle effect that I speak of cannot be replicated an hour or two later. The moment has passed and is gone. You are the same person and you have the same work in front of you when you return, but you are no longer in that exact space, mentally or creatively. Why? Because that exact emotional state you had achieved waned once your energy shifted away from it and toward something else. We are energetic beings. If we pull our energy abruptly away from that moment, the moment is lost.

Add up all of those breaks and distractions and you will find that many hours are being taken. You may find that if you did this consistently, out of every month, you would be losing a full week each month, or at least a few full days each month. Who among us has a full week to lose in a month when you could have applied it to your life's work? Most people don't look at it that way, and that is why they are not in that elusive group of people that are now referred to as the one percent.

One percenters think the way I have outlined throughout this chapter. We understand the value of time.

You might be reading this chapter and seeing my words as a revelation, or you might be thinking, "These are obvious points, Solomon. I don't like to waste my time either." But knowing and doing are two different things. Knowing and actually tracking each hour of your day, week, and month to gain control over your time and energetic output so that you can correct course if need be, are two different things. One is an objective and dispassionate acknowledgment of a fact, and the other involves making that emotion-driven connection.

If you told me you were struggling to lose ten pounds and during that same conversation you also mentioned that you know to stay away from junk foods and processed foods, and to eat healthy whole foods, I would suggest that you keep a food diary for a week and record every morsel that passes your lips. You might be surprised at the end of the week to discover how much of the foods *you knew not to eat* you had actually consumed, unconsciously, out of pure habit.

The Productivity Game

No, productivity is *not* a game, because you cannot make up for lost productivity. Large public companies must report their 1st, 2nd, 3rd and 4th quarter earnings to their stockholders, the public, and to the SEC *(Securities and Exchange Commission)* each quarter of a given fiscal year, in the form of four quarterly distributed press releases. If Q1 productivity and revenue was down, you can absolutely kill it during Q2, but you can never get Q1's potential back. It is gone for good. Should you move forward? Of course. But actions, or the lack thereof, have consequences. Do not move ahead without looking back to see where you fell short. Then correct it for the future.

Yes, you can try to work harder and harder to make up for it later, but you are now working at a deficit, trying to make up for something that you have done incorrectly. You are placing more stress on your body and on your mind. What works better? Studying for a test an hour each night for a week, or cramming seven hours of studying into one night? Eating well and getting moderate exercise on a regular basis to maintain one's weight and heart health, or going on a crash diet and trying to hit it hard in the gym once the doctor tells you that you are in danger of having a heart attack or becoming diabetic?

Since health is also wealth, we want to avoid unnecessary stress on the body and mind. Consistently good habits prevent extreme stress on the body and mind, because you don't have to scramble to correct what you have done wrong.

Perhaps you can relate to the fact that my weight has been a struggle throughout my adult life. Managing my weight with good eating habits and daily exercise has definitely required discipline, delayed gratification, and a lot of time management. I love all the sweet stuff, and it is not always easy to turn it down. As for my regular workouts, they can be tedious and exhausting at times, but it helps with relieving the stress that we all go through in addition to weight management and heart health. Let me tell you, there are days where I just don't even workout because I don't feel like it, but I do get back at it the next day and I don't allow one day to turn into two or three days. It is my goal to be as consistent as possible and hit the mark a minimum of 80% of the time. We age over time. Each year we get older and there's no way of stopping this. Our energy levels are not the same as they were in our twenties. Think about it, your smile may have been brighter, your eyes wider, your hair more flowing, you ran faster and jumped higher. Over time with age, we look at the gray hair we've sprouted and we feel the drop in our energy reserves. At some point, we may find ourselves thankful and happy just to get up and go for a walk. I speak to many young people and I tell them, "Do not take your youth and time for granted. Use it wisely. For it is a finite resource." Use that energy and direct it, like a ship, to achieve that which you want to achieve for your family, your children, your loved ones, and yes, even for your friends. They may not understand the time management skills you are developing, and the sacrifices you are making, but in the end it will all make sense. Sooner or later they will see your vision. At that point, what it was that you were doing may suddenly make sense to them.

What makes this time management journey challenging is that it does not end. It is ongoing. But what isn't? Each and every day we get up and we have to work. We have to work toward something. We have to work *at* something. We have to work on doing that which needs to be done to pay our bills, meet our obligations, and ultimately create and live fulfilled lives.

We are exchanging our time for money, resources, growth, and valuable experiences. I have always said, "Let your money work *for* you. Let your money be your employee. Let it go out and produce more money and bring it back to you." You, the human, cannot be solely in charge of making you money in the long run, because A. you deserve to live your life as a free person, and not as a slave; and B. you only have so much time and so much energy.

You, the human being, can only produce so much. On the other hand, your money's potential to produce is infinite. If, after twenty or thirty years of time and energetic output spent on "earning a living" you are having to get up every day and go to work, and still having to figure out how to pay your car note, your mortgage *(or rent)*, credit card bills, or your kids' education, your time has not been spent wisely. If you are currently having to work every day to try to figure out how to pay for smaller purchases like clothes, meals, and basic forms of entertainment, you are not spending your time wisely. You are living life as a slave, and you must look in the mirror and do an honest assessment, based on what we have spoken about thus far. You have likely, up until this point, deceived yourself into thinking you are spending your time well, when in fact much of your time, your most precious asset, is being squandered.

If you are still healthy and still breathing, you can change how you spend your time, but first you must identify where you are losing time. Time can be your trusted ally or your worst enemy and a terrible thief. We want to make time your ally and a valuable tool toward achieving success in all areas of your life.

What you do today affects tomorrow. The sacrifices that you make today will afford you more time tomorrow.

A January 26, 2021 article published by *UC Berkley* titled, *How to Structure Your Day to Feel Less Stressed: if you don't control your schedule, your schedule will control you*, touts the structure of a daily schedule as a way of reducing stress, telling readers to "let your priorities lead, create structure for yourself, use time blocking and task batching," and even encourages you to carve out time to "relax." Yes, schedule your well-earned relaxation at the end of a productive day. Highly effective people schedule time to relax and engage in something enjoyable, and they actually enjoy their relaxation *more* because of all they have accomplished during their day.

A September 5, 2017 CNBC article titled, *How to Schedule Your Day For Maximum Success, According to Science* attributes the success of highly effective people to their willingness to schedule their days rather than winging it. The article states, "Ultra-successful people realize the sheer importance that every minute plays in their day. They're able to schedule their days strategically, maximize their productivity, and enhance their well-being outside of work."

How I Manage My Own Time

I am going to share with you how I manage my time on a typical weekday, and how I keep myself honest with how I spend my time.

Most days it starts around 4:30 am. I take the time to pray by reading a chapter from the Bible or I listen to one of my favorite ministers on TV, and I meditate to get a clear head and visualize in great detail everything that has to be done. Afterward, I will grab a cup of coffee and eat a bowl of oatmeal before I head out to the gym. Around 7:30 am I will make sure I get my time in the gym for about an hour with my friend and personal trainer who is very passionate about health and wellness. He believes, as I do, that your heath is your greatest wealth. I ride my bike as much as 20 miles every other day.

Around 8am I have showered and I begin to touch base with each member of my team to get my itinerary for the day, and what needs to be accomplished based on priority. The most challenging thing as an entrepreneur is that the priorities change from day to day, or even hour by hour. It can be taxing for a leader and for team members, but the change-up can also be rewarding. I cover this in an earlier chapter, where I discuss hiring team members for your company and the importance of them believing in your vision as well as their ability to adopt a flexible state of mind. As a CEO, I am only speaking to my top leadership or those who are critical to the task. These conversations may take up to an hour.

By 11 am I may have calls with other CEOs or attorneys that have been put on my schedule. I will grab lunch from 12 -1 pm.

After lunch and by mid-day, I am taking inventory of what must be done today that cannot wait until tomorrow. I am always geared toward making things happen as soon as possible without procrastination. I have a "now" O'clock mindset, as in, "What better time than now?" unless, of course, something else takes priority in that moment. As a general rule, I do not like to put things off. Around 2 pm in the afternoon I am normally reading contracts and proposals as well as strategizing both short and long term business goals over the next 4-5 hours. One thing that I have adopted and try my best to make sure to do is to eat my dinner prior to 6:30 pm. This is not always the case if I have to meet people at a restaurant or when I am traveling. Around 7pm or so I try to take a walk or smoke a cigar to reflect on the day and what we have accomplished or what we could have improved upon, which can be implemented the next day.

By 10pm I am either in bed or preparing for bed, although there are times when I am still up until 1am due to unexpected conversations or commitments. Regardless, I still try to rise at 4:30 am, as my routine is set. Often, people ask me what I do for fun. If I have my cigar and if I can fit in time to go to the shooting range, I am pretty happy.

To some of you, my daily schedule may seem rigid or even punishing, but I assure you it is not. Budgeting and planning out how you spend your time can actually assure that all aspects of your wellness are attended to. At the end of the day, that leaves me feeling pretty good. I know that I have taken care of my nutrition, fitness, my business dealings, my finances, and I have fed my soul with something restorative that I enjoy at the day's close. So many people who insist on getting that extra hour or two of sleep, or who bristle at the idea of adherence to a schedule often find themselves feeling depleted at the end of their day. They may also feel discouraged or frustrated about the things that didn't get done. I'll take Plan A every time.

This is my schedule that I adhere to on most days. Of course, life happens and there are some days when my schedule is altered due to unexpected business dealings, last minute business travel, or other personal matters that need attending to, which brings us back to the number one rule of entrepreneurship: Be flexible when necessary.

Many years ago when I was a young man right out of the military and I had just started one of my first businesses, a maintenance company, I was a strict taskmaster when it came to managing my employees as well as my time. However, I didn't always have my priorities in order. I was ever so thankful to my parents, and to my time spent in the military, for instilling in me strict organizational and time management skills, so structure was never my problem. Structure is not a bad thing, as it keeps you at your most productive. But I can recall a time when my maintenance company staff and I had to go clean several apartments in one day. Well, on that very same day, as Murphy's Law would have it, I had a sudden family emergency. We all know how that goes, when two critical things collide at once and you are forced to make a split-second decision. As I am sure you have also experienced, sometimes you can go into an anxiety-fueled tailspin not knowing which way to go.

I had gotten a last minute phone call from my daughter's school that no one had shown up to pick my daughter up. I am not sure where the breakdown in communication was on that afternoon, and when I feverishly tried to get ahold of various family members, no one was answering their phone. In my twenty-something year old brain, this was maddening. Here I was trying to get all of these apartments cleaned so that my maintenance company could get paid on time, and I was in charge of overseeing everything. Now I was in a panic because I couldn't get in touch with anyone who could help me out. I was going to have to drop everything at work and drive forty minutes to my daughter's school and back again.

What did I do? I am not proud of this, but I wasted twenty minutes ranting and raving about the fact that I had to leave work to go pick up my daughter. In doing this, I wasted more time than I needed to, and I unloaded my stress and frustration onto my hardworking staff for no good reason. I had mastered structure and keeping a schedule, but I had not yet mastered flexibility.

Of course, my daughter was, and is, extremely important to me. That goes without saying. But in my mind, at that time, I felt that dropping the ball with my business on a crucial day could delay payment, ultimately having a negative effect on my daughter and my wife. I had it backwards. I felt that by others dropping the ball, it placed my business in a precarious position. I was also railing against the fact that I had done favors for some of these people, and when I needed one of them to pick up my daughter they were nowhere to be found.

After blowing off steam in all the wrong directions for an indeterminable amount of time, it suddenly dawned on me that the most valuable and important person in my life could be sitting there at the school, with a stranger, and feeling abandoned. That immediately shocked me into the reality of what was truly important, and that was my family, and most specifically in that moment, my daughter.

The only way you can show your vendors or employees what is important to you, is to demonstrate that with your behavior and your actions. You don't speak about your priorities, you live them. If you would leave your kids, you would certainly leave your vendors and employees in the lurch. It was as if God slapped me to say, "Wake up. I would never leave *you*." I drove the forty minutes to pick my daughter up from school, and brought her back to the job site with me.

Well, just a few years ago I had to make another critical decision about whether to go and visit a friend in the hospital or stay at work and oversee my business that day. I chose to pay a visit to my friend who was in the hospital, and here is why that was a pivotal decision. Shortly after that day, the roles were reversed when I found myself in the hospital.

I was visiting my daughter in Texarkana and suffered an acute episode with diverticulitis. My intestine pockets had ruptured and I was turning septic. I was told by the doctors, "Mr. Ali, you are not going to make it unless we do emergency surgery." I had mere hours. I called my mother and my minister, and I also called my business partner. When my daughter rushed to be by my side that day, my mind instantly traveled back to that day when I had to make the decision to leave work and pick her up from school, and I realized how critical putting family first really is. But here is what really surprised me. When I called my business partner to explain that I was in the hospital in dire condition and needed emergency, I said, "You stay at work and run the company. It's most important that you be there to take care of the business at hand."

When I opened my eyes after surgery my daughter's face was the first thing I saw next to my bed, but here is what surprised me most and I remember it like it was yesterday; my business partner's comments in my response to telling her to stay at work and run the business were, "You are more important than any business, and the people who work for us will understand. If they don't understand, that will be a shame because we may have to reevaluate those relationships." When the people who are important to you know they can depend on you and that you value them as people, they tend to do a better job and they tend to reciprocate, not necessarily when or how you want them to, but they always do it. And it may not even be who you helped, but it may be someone who was watching and it could be at a critical time when you need it. It has happened in my life over and over again.

This is the difference between real need and frivolity. When somebody in your life asks for your time and energy for something frivolous, that means they are not honoring their relationship with you, because they are not honoring what you hold most valuable. Conversely, if a loved one, friend, or business partner is in real need, then you must honor that relationship contract and put that human relationship before business or money. You must be wise enough to distinguish between the two, but when someone you care about is in real need, putting people before money is always a wise investment. And when making a decision to deviate from your original schedule or plans, please let your "Yes" be a yes, or your "No" be a no.

Many people will fall back on a contract, but I prefer to fall back on my word. Written contracts may have legal loopholes that favor me over the other party, but people will not trust you when you take advantage of those loopholes if it means going back on your word. When people can trust your word, you will actually get more good will and flexibility toward you as well. Everyone understands that from time to time things will happen, and grace and mercy is understood. Now, you do not have to subscribe to the same beliefs as me, but speaking for me, I am a Christian first, then a friend, and then a businessperson.

If you chase money or the next contract or deal, you will find that it will always be elusive and just out of your reach. And you will have a series of "almosts," which will be the story of your life. One of the key ingredients in financial and business success is figuring out how to solve people's problems to make their lives easier and more enjoyable. When it comes to business or your work environment, that is the key.

People first. Period.

Chapter 12

Interviews with Money Masters

"Mentor someone who's insight can become your foresight." -
Anonymous

Through my *MBA: Minority Business Access* podcast, I have had the immense privilege of sitting down with and interviewing some of the most innovative minds in business, finance, intellectual property protection, and entrepreneurship across a variety of industries.

The mission of my *MBA* podcast is to give minorities, people of color, and other folks starting out on their entrepreneurial, financial, or business path valuable insights that are normally what I would call "elite insider information." What do I mean by this? Very often, the professional, social, and familial circles you have access to will determine and define your ability to understand money, your ability to raise working capital, and your ability to properly structure a business. This will ultimately determine your financial destiny.

As an African American man who came up in a working class family, I know how challenging and demoralizing it was to climb this ladder on my own through a lot of wrong turns and trial and error, and how my lack of access to certain circles nearly kept me from achieving my goals. I managed to eventually cross paths with the right people who believed in me and my vision, and I was able to eventually transmute my mistakes into long term successes, but it was not without years of dead ends and a whole lot of pain.

The fact is, there is a better way, and my platform at SolomonRCAli.com as well as my *MBA: Minority Business Access* podcast, aims to democratize this inside information. On my podcast and in my business consulting practice, we cover:

- Establishing and Scaling Your Business the Right Way

- How to Increase Your Profits

- Obtaining Growth Capital

- Debt Funding vs Equity Funding vs Venture Capital Funding

- Establishing Effective Tax and Estate Planning

- Smart Investing with Due Diligence

- Safeguarding Intellectual Property

- Building Long Term Generational Wealth

Below are a few people I would like to acquaint you with who can share some invaluable, insider information that is typically only accessible to the wealthy and well-connected.

So, you want to build a brand. First, you will have to learn the indispensable skill of hiring the right team of people to surround yourself with and getting the most productivity out of each person you employ. Who are the right people to fill in the gaps in your own education and skillset to help you scale your business, build brand equity, and take things to the next level? Oh, and once you have built your brand, how can you strategically monetize all aspects of your brand?

Meet Amilya Antonetti

Amilya is the CEO of Genius Key, a company that helps to assess and implement people's highest growth using her company's interpersonal proprietary technology. Oprah calls Amiya "A visionary, and woman to watch in business!" Client Steve Harvey shares, "Amilya is a wealth of knowledge in business and relationships," and motivational speaker Zig Ziglar called Amilya, "A one of a kind, natural leader."

Amilya Antonetti is a highly sought-after human behavior, conflict resolution expert & Interim C Suite Executive. She has helped companies innovate, manage turnarounds, and set strategies for some of the most high-profile clients in the Music, Sports & Entertainment industries. Her national popularity spans a series of successes, from selling her 1st company in the late 1980s, to successfully founding Soapworks™ (one of the fastest growing, privately owned household product companies in North America). She eventually sold the company to a leading consumer, packaged goods company with annual sales of $200M.

Amilya has worked with businesses such as: Sharper Image, George Foreman Grill, Yummy Fashion, Ninja® Blender, Cold Stone Creamery, Happy Napper, Kiddie Gym, Listerine Strips, Dermafina, QVC Roadshow, NBA All Stars, gymGO, Eff Creative Group, Entrepreneur Elevator Pitch and Myos.

She has worked on the foundational implementations of IBM, Watson, and Blockchain in relation to healthcare, marijuana, precious gems, and crypto industries. She has innovated and developed new revenue streams for celebrities, including: Mike Tyson, Montel Williams and Billy Mays. Most recently, Amilya served as the Chief Digital Strategist & CMO for Steve Harvey and his business interests.

Throughout her career, Amilya has managed over 49,000 people in the USA and globally. Her ability to maximize Human Capital beyond biases, to focus on the holistic abilities of people, (from baby boomers, Gen X, Y, Z and the fast-approaching Generation Alpha), uniting people with advanced technologies, setting up organizations to succeed from within, using their greatest asset: their "people."

"74% of people who have unique abilities are in the wrong job."
- Amilya Antonetti

Solomon: Amilya, thank you so much for being here. I'm excited. Let's jump right into it. Tell us about Genius Key and what's going on?

Amilya: Genius Key is answering a problem that businesses have had for a long time. We're poised now for a big paradigm shift. Businesses have struggled for decades in being able to identify top talents, to bring that talent into their organization, to continue to develop them, to pair them with their highest best, and to reward them for something that is unique to them. We continue to struggle and go back to old tools, but as more technology and digital applications have come into our lives on a very personal level, top talent has a plethora of opportunities. If they can see that the company isn't set up to further develop them, they're not even interested anymore. And right now there is no system for this.

Solomon: Is that global or just domestically?

Amilya: It's global. If you take a look at the numbers, over 74% of people who have a unique ability are in the wrong job. They took the job that they could get, not the job that serves their highest best. If I want to work for your company and the only job that's open is a sales position, I'll apply for the sales position because you don't have the job I want. I don't qualify for it or I can't even get a seat at the table. I come in through the sales door. If I'm in sales, I will never get out of that lane. You'll never get the sales division to go, "She's an amazing COO."

We now have more independent contractors than ever before because top talent now has a choice. The same thing happens with efficiencies. In order to scale, businesses have to be able to get more and more efficient, but there isn't a "people operating system" that nails down efficiency. We're still measuring based on time and measuring the multiplier or the revenue. What causes a company, from the inside, to have that impact is energy in and energy out. The more efficiently you can use the energy of the collective group to hit those desired outcomes with the least number of resources, that's what creates that impact, but we have no way to measure it.

Solomon: You have me hanging on every word. Can you tell us a little bit about your industry? What does it mean, and where is it going?

Amilya: There are a couple of industries that have collided out of the belief of trying to make people more tactical. We heard a lot of things about trying to make humans more like technology. There are big conversations about what humans are going to do that technology can't do. We came out with project management systems to try to make humans more tactical. We have project management that's focusing on efficiencies, yet we're wondering why we have all these tools, but our people are not developing the way they should. Our people are not hungrier or going after the work they're properly paired for. It's because we have the wrong tool.

Solomon: Does that mean your industry is going to grow? What kind of companies are in your industry?

Amilya: There's a couple of them. You've got the human behavior or the personal development space that has notoriously been outside of the B2B world. It's been in individuals. When you say B2B, we're talking business to business.

A typical business, to date, has not incorporated personal development skills inside the organization. The closest we've got was emotional intelligence quotient. Because you can't measure it, people don't put a lot of stock into it, but it's there. It's in that space. We nibbled at it a little bit. We use a lot of personal assessments, but there wasn't an immediate, measurable, and impactful thing for a CEO to lean into that. It came in a little bit. We've got the personal development space.

We have the invasion of the digital, social and technology world, which continues to grow because that has a measurable impact on a business. You have these two worlds, personal development, software technology, the social impact, and the space of companies saying the only way we're going to be able to compete faster is with efficiencies, but we don't have efficient operating systems. We have the old and antiquated, "This is the way we run our businesses."

Solomon: Let me see if I understand this. You have three industries that have merged into one industry. You're about to disrupt all three at one time.

Amilya: A lot of businesses now have been sanctioned with having a sustainable mission. A lot of companies over the last couple of years have been saying, "You have to have a sustainable mission." Companies try to get their people to determine, "What is that sustainable mission going to be?" But that's like herding cats, so instead they gave them one. "We're going to focus on education or shoes," but there's no way to measure what is the motivation or what is the inner desire that your team has on what their impact is. Genius Key immediately measures their belief system and how that relates to our global economy. You can align a sustainable mission immediately based on your people's perspective and measure it.

Solomon: If I understand correctly, what you're saying is, not only will Genius Key disrupt the whole industry, three industries that have collapsed into one, but you guys will perhaps be the largest player within that industry.

Amilya: You haven't even thought about yet the gig economy. The top talent now has a choice. What COVID did was it gave us a year to say, "Do I want to participate in the behavior that I've been behaving for? Do I want to keep going for this gold watch?" When you say gig economy, some people might think that it's crypto. I think I know what you're talking about. You're talking about how companies will hire people to do the work going forward.

We have more independent contractors than ever before, because top talent has a choice. They don't want to come into the 5, 10, 15, 20-year career. Why don't they want to? It's because the inner operating systems of companies are broken. Look at you, for example. Everybody looks at somebody based on your last best or your last worst experience. Even though I may be the perfect candidate to do what the company has set out to do, let's say a company says, "This year, we are focused on disruptive innovation," there isn't a tool to measure, "Do your people have the innate ability to do what you're asking for?"

Solomon: Your company, Genius Key, is going to disrupt three industries in one. Because of COVID, it's going to turn

around. We're looking at something that changed society as a whole, and how companies and everyone will do business moving forward. Because of the need now for gig workers, you're not just at the right place at the right time, you're it.

Amilya: We're empowering the individual. What we're finding is that when individuals have these types of tools that connect the individual's genius to the work, itself, they take 70% more work than you could have ever given them, especially about behavior. If I gave you a list and I said, "Here are all the things that you love to do and you can have as many of them as you want. Here's the abundance of things that you hate to do." What lists are you picking from? It's things that I like.

Imagine if you could see everything that you love to do across the entire company, every single task that you love to do, and you could asset access it at your own pace. You do not have to wait for somebody to assign it. You can go through and go, "I want to do that." Would you not naturally take more? That's where the 70% increase in company productivity is coming from.

Solomon: As one that has always been an employer, I can only imagine my bottom line increasing tremendously because I'm getting more productivity out of each employee/team member. It's probably going to be more efficient and a higher quality of work because people are doing something that they're passionate about doing, not because I assigned them a task.

Amilya: Success does not happen unless you have the right people doing the right things. From the behavior aspect in a company, we see that people become happier. They become more engaged and more responsible. They now feel the trust factor because they're engaged. The limitation, they can pick anything they want, their curiosities, what they love to do, things that they've never done before, working with colleagues that they never thought they could work with before, and then immediately measuring those. The minute the task is finished, the system comes back and says, "From 1 to 5, measure all these things: time, focus, freedom, happiness, reward. How did this rate? You go through and you click. Let's say you gave it a 4 out of 5, and the system then goes, "Here's all the 4 out of 5 projects across the entire company that matches what you did." Now the system is getting smarter and learning what you love to do.

Solomon: It's going into artificial intelligence. How long have you been doing this?

Amilya: I've been doing human behavior for 35 years.

Solomon: It's safe to say you're a total expert. You know what you're doing. I also understand that your company is going public. You're going to have shareholders. What would that mean for your shareholders?

Amilya: For the shareholders, it's not only being able to have measurable results and not only within our company or ourselves, but an enormous amount of data that's never been seen before across all of the other companies, of how people and work have a relationship. A person's motivation isn't necessarily on the rise. A person's motivation is maybe just working with a colleague. It may be the curiosity. All of these other factors that we've never considered in the business, we've considered them in the personal development space. They are now inside the operating company of an organization. That organization cannot only reach into their own pool. They can reach into the gig economy to say, "I need to bring in somebody who's got this one unique key, for this project, for ten days." Now they can pick up on a whole plethora of people. It changes not just the project. It changes the entire feeling and emotion inside of the company. When you add an extra element that wasn't there before, change is vibrant.

Solomon: I have some principles that I love following before I will invest my money into a company. It's helped me to identify some key things, and that's management. Comparing management to the top five in the industry and everything of that nature. It's also looking at the industry itself and seeing if there's a growth opportunity within that industry, and what does that look like. In your industry, what you're talking about is you're about to disrupt it. We like to look for at least 3% to 5% growth within the industry.

Amilya: People are going to start looking for a genius company to go work for or to work with. They're not going to work for a company that doesn't have the infrastructure and the operating system to see, hear, recognize, and reward them in their empowerment. We're talking about employee empowerment in relation to the work, not just employee experience.

Solomon: One of the things I heard when you spoke before was it takes the bias out of it. If you are a woman or a minority, you sit in front of another human and they may

have some biases and not give you that opportunity. But Genius Key takes the bias out of the equation. It's not going to care if you're a woman, where you're from, if you're Black, or whatever. It's going to say, "This is the best person to do this job." That to me is phenomenal.

Amilya: That means probably more people will be working and doing the things that they love. Society should be better, because everyone's stress levels will be down. Why? Because they're not doing things they don't like. More importantly, your company is going to be phenomenal from a profit standpoint because everyone is doing the things that they're enjoying. They'll get it done faster. They'll get it done more efficiently and be happier for doing it. Overall, humanity will be better, even post-COVID.

***

Life, if done right, should become an endless loop of learning and teaching; learning some more, and teaching some more. We should always be mentees or mentors. Learning and then giving back are instrumental to professional and financial success, and personal success for that matter.

Meet Jeff Hoffman

Jeff Hoffman is an award-winning global entrepreneur, proven CEO, worldwide motivational speaker, bestselling author, Hollywood film producer, a producer of a Grammy Award winning jazz album, and executive producer of an Emmy Award winning television show. He is an Executive Producer and stars in the groundbreaking TV series *Going Public*, a show where viewers worldwide can invest in the startups that Jeff is mentoring on the air. In his career, he has been the founder of multiple startups, the CEO of both public and private companies, and he has served as a senior executive in many capacities. Jeff has been part of a number of well-known successful startups, including Priceline.com/Booking.com, uBid.com and more.

"The two most important days in your life are the day you're born and the day you figure out why?" – **Jeff Hoffman**

Solomon: What would be some advice that you've given to minorities in business?

Jeff: The first piece always starts with education. Education is not equally accessible around this country, but in a lot of cases, it's economically based, etc. But that's an excuse. I'm tough on you. I work with a lot ex-cons now and I'm tough on them. These are good people that made a bad decision. They're not bad people. They were in tough situations and made the only decision they thought they could, and now they want to turn their life around. We're tough on them. The education, if you can't get it, find it. We live in an internet age where you can take courses on Coursera and you can study TED Talks. The first step is to get educated anywhere, anytime, all the time, and continue to learn. That's the first piece of advice we give them.

The second piece is about building your network, and you build your network before you need it. I am an engineer. I'm not a finance guy. The list of things I don't know how to do is way longer than the list of stuff I do. What you've got to do is surround yourself with people smarter than you. We teach them the value of networking and how to find and reach out to people that are smarter than you, everywhere, and build that network around you. The third step is you've got some education, resources, people to go around you, now you've got to solve a real problem in the world.

Economic prosperity, independence and [financial] freedom comes from solving a problem that is valuable to somebody in the world. My first startup, when I was twenty-something, you used to have to wait in line to check-in at an airport at the ticket counter, and my first product was those kiosks that you check-in at in an airport. I solved a real problem. Every airport line in the kiosk, people didn't want to wait in line, and that enabled me to obtain economic freedom because I solved somebody's problem. That's the third thing we shared with them.

Solomon: That being said, Jeff, when starting a business and running your business, a lot of entrepreneurs, especially minorities, are under-capitalized. What do you suggest they do?

Jeff: That is a two-sided problem. A big part of that is reaching out to the other end. It's people that do things like you do. You give back so much and help so many people. We need more of the people, once they make it, to turn around, reach back, grab the hand of somebody that needs the help and pull them forward. First of all, we need more business angels. I actually like the fact that they use the term "angels," because sometimes they are. We need more successful people that came out of the situation that are minority role models who are willing to help. They need to reach back and help. That's the first step. Business angel networks are important. We go into communities like Ferguson. We went to Baltimore or wherever there was trouble. We went into a lot of these communities. I do this with Ray Lewis, the football player, who's a friend of mine. Sometimes Jim Brown comes. We've gone into these communities to try to fire up the community. We then ask the corporations and the companies to step up. People need to help their own. These are your people.

These are the entrepreneurs in your community. Help them start a business. That's one end. On the other end, part of the reason that they have trouble getting funding is they haven't been given the training on how to pitch this stuff. I sit through these pitches. We did one here in LA. We called it "Black Tech Day." We had all these minority entrepreneurs pitch businesses. I thought, "Has anybody ever taught you guys how to present your idea and how to pitch?" They said no. I said, "If we could get you more training on how to pitch an idea and how to write an investor deck, how to do all that stuff, your odds would go up with getting funded." There's a bunch of things we need to do at once. They will increase minority funding for a business.

Solomon: What you're doing is totally awesome, especially in the minority community. If a new entrepreneur in a minority community is starting, they could be male or female, what would you suggest other than

reading the book and building their network? What else would you suggest?

Jeff: One of the important things is finding mentorship. That's the other thing that you and I need to do. We need to encourage more people in every community to be mentors in their own community. A lot of people say, "I've never built a business. How can I be a mentor?" How about because you're an HR executive at a big company and you know everything about HR, and this entrepreneur doesn't know anything about hiring people? Almost everybody has some value that they could provide as a mentor. They don't think of themselves as mentors. What you and I have to do is tell them, "Your knowledge is valuable to this community. You need to mentor." What I tell these people is, you've got to find a mentor.

Mentors aren't going to ring your doorbell. You have got to reach out the way I found my first mentor. I showed up at a social event on a Saturday, he was going to it. I bought a ticket and he's like, "What are you doing here?" I said, "I'm just checking it out." We met at a social event because I couldn't get an appointment with his office. I found out he was going to this thing on a Saturday. I bought a ticket and showed up, wandered over, and met the guy. Go out and find a mentor. Find somebody that can help you. If you're on the other side of the equation, find a way to be a mentor. It's important to have someone to turn to.

Solomon: One of the things I remember when I started my first business, I was going to get a $1 million loan and I had to call the guy every day for six months. I would call him

and they were like, "We have nothing different to tell." I say, "Okay. I'm just calling to let you know I'm still here." After the sixth month, he said, "I'm going to do this loan for you. No problem. Anyone who calls me 180 days straight, he's going to pay me back".

Jeff: Persistence is so important. For them to see that in you, that's good advice to give these startups. You've got to persist.

Solomon: I have found that the world is very challenging. It's up and down. When you're in that low spot and business is not going well, everyone around you is telling you to abort it and do something else, what would you say?

Jeff: That is the reason you've got to find your tribe. First of all, all of us have been through failure. Nothing ever goes perfectly. Life is messy. That's God's plan. If everything went perfectly, it'd be a pretty boring life here if we didn't have the stuff to deal with. You have to believe you're never given more than you can handle. There is that belief as well. You're being tested for reasons so that you can come out stronger. What I mean by finding your tribe is, someone's already been through this. If someone came through the other side, you've got to find that person that can give you an honest assessment.

Meaning your buddies, your spouse, your mom is telling you it's a bad idea. In fact, they aren't qualified to say that. If I was a young entrepreneur and everything seemed to be going bad and I got a chance to talk to Solomon and you say, "It's fixable, here's what you need to do," I would believe in him. I would have connected with someone who's been there, who's done that, and who's advised by the same token. If you said to me, "Jeff, I'm not seeing it. Maybe you should spend your life's energy on something else," I would take that advice. Find those people, find the tribe, find the people who have been there, done that, and whose advice can help you make that decision. If those people tell you to keep going, then keep fighting.

Solomon: For my audience, how do they reach out to you and contact you?

Jeff: The social media I'm on the most is LinkedIn. I'm on there every day. I love connecting with people because in the end, the next great idea is going to come from someplace we never thought of. Sometimes people think because they have a low status in society that they're less important or less intelligent. No, intelligence is equally distributed across the whole planet. Opportunity is not. That's the problem you're fixing it. There are brilliant people. I got to tell you a quick, funny story.

I was dealing with a former drug dealer and he got out. He was trying to turn his life around. He wanted to start a tech company. He knew he made mistakes. He didn't want to make them again, so I was teaching him how to run a business. I said, "Let's talk about cashflow." He said, "I am all over that." I said, "Let's talk about building teams." He said, "I know how to do that." I said, "Let's talk about marketing." He said, "I already got that." I said, "You know who makes a good entrepreneur? Unfortunately or fortunately, drug dealers." He already knew how to do all that stuff.

He had a skillset. What he needed was someone to believe in him and someone to tell him that he didn't have to go back to the old way. We have to change the friends around him, but he's doing amazing now. People like you and I got to be out there pushing them. We've got to go out there encouraging them and finding people that can make a difference because they can. This is a guy that society wrote off because he was in federal prison. In fact, this is a guy who might be one of the world changers now if somebody believed in him.

Solomon: Lastly, can you tell us about your greatest success?

Jeff: I can. You know that saying that the two most important days in your life are the day you're born and the day you figure out why? Mine has nothing to do with business. I was blessed enough to have several of the companies I was part of become multi-billion-dollar companies. It's none of that, and be part of an IPO, it has nothing to do with any of that. We've been blessed enough that we won a Grammy in the music business and we won an Emmy for television. None of those things came anywhere close to the first time somebody encountered me. By the way, this was a 40-year-old Black man that was down on his luck. The world had dealt him every bad hand you could think of. He had every reason to give up and everybody wrote him off from society, and I spent a couple of days with him.

Years later, I was at a conference. A very well-dressed gentleman like you, very refined, came up and started talking and all of a sudden, he said, "You don't remember me, do you?" I said, "We met?" He goes, "Four years ago." I said, "I don't remember the event." He said, "I was on the street. I was down and out. I was thinking of committing suicide." He said he spent a couple of days with me and it literally turned his life around. He said, "You lit the spark that caused me to believe again. Now I own a business. I have employees, my kids are in college, I have a home now. If you didn't spend that time with me, I wouldn't be standing here." That was the coolest moment of my life, to find out that we can change somebody else's life by sharing our time with them.

***

Once you have followed this book's blueprint and you start accumulating some financial success and building your generational wealth, you will need to protect and insulate what you have worked so hard for. This is something that all wealthy people know and it is critically important, not just for you, but for generations that come after you.

Meet Kevin L. Day, JD, MBA

Kevin Day is an attorney specializing in asset protection and estate planning. He shares some key secrets surrounding this legal area, from how irrevocable trusts work, the right time to acquire asset protection, to what people can do at a bare minimum to mitigate the risks of lawsuits; in other words, the playbook of the wealthy that you are about to learn. Kevin L. Day is one of the leading estate planning and international asset protection planning attorneys in the United States.

In addition to his legal expertise, Mr. Day brings his extensive business knowledge as an MBA in International Business to his law practice. He is admitted to practice law in the California Supreme Court; U.S. Southern District Court, California; U.S. Court of Appeals, 9th Circuit; U.S. Central District Court, California; U.S. Court of International Trade; U.S. Tax Court, Washington D.C.; U.S. Court of Appeals, Federal Circuit; and United States Supreme Court. Mr. Day is a member of the California Bar Association, the Offshore Institute, the International Tax Planning Association and the American Bar Association's sub-section on Asset Protection.

Solomon: Kevin, it is so exciting to be here with you. I'm glad to have you here for this interview. Can you tell my readers a little bit about yourself?

Kevin: Solomon, I've known you for a while. Thank you for having me. I appreciate it and the privilege is all mine. There are many facets of me, but on the business side, I am a lawyer. My particular expertise is in lawsuit protection and privacy planning. We have lots of actors and ballplayers that want privacy. That is usually the drive, and lawsuit protection is good for them too. We have business owners that come to us and say, "I need lawsuit protection," and then lowering profile (aka privacy), and other things or concerns of their family. I do offshore trust, domestic trust, and privacy companies. My firm is about 28 people. We've got a litigation team. We've got three tax attorneys.

We do charitable trust, foundations, all the normal wills and trusts, and normal estate planning. Bridget Burns is the Head of our Lawsuit Protection and Privacy Department, and I've got one partner, Elizabeth Tresp.

Solomon: Kevin, you're the number one leading expert attorney on trust law. What does that mean? I know what it means for me.

Kevin: My firm is in the top two in the country. I came in at the very highest-level, right after the Hague Convention was signed by the U.S., where U.S. citizens could establish a trust under other U.S. law, and it would be the law of the land and recognized in the U.S. Essentially, we could do things with international trust that would not have been otherwise legal under U.S. law. Treaties, conventions, Presidential Decrees, they're higher than Federal Law.

The only thing that's above that is the U.S. Constitution. Then we started having copycat trust. I wrote a bunch of books in the early '90s right after Hague Convention was signed. I'd love to say I was particularly brilliant, but me and Arnold Goldstein each had a book. We became the leading speakers in the continuing ed arena all over the nation.

Solomon: You state that this trust law is higher than almost everything except the constitution.

Kevin: The Hague Convention on Trust that the U.S. government signed. You've got Municipal Law superseded by State Law, that is superseded by Federal Law. There are these treaties and conventions above that, and then the U.S. Constitution.

Solomon: Is that irrevocable trusts that we're talking about?

Kevin: Not just irrevocable, but if you're going to have a revocable trust, you don't have privacy because your name, "Kevin Day Trustee of the Day Family Trust" is made public. But with irrevocable trusts, you're under U.S. law removing U.S. Court Jurisdiction. By signing that, all 50 states, the IRS, and everybody recognizes it. It's not a black box. Every entrepreneur, no matter how much stuff they've got, should never let their checkbook go.

Solomon: Let me see if I understand this, if I can somewhat regurgitate what you said. Under U.S. State and Federal Law, an irrevocable trust is removed from the courts.

Kevin: If it's settled under a different country's law. That was the first time. Until 1987, if you wanted to lawsuit proof something and you put it into the Trust, you could not be the trustee or the beneficiary. You had to give up all ownership and control. That's fine if you're giving it to your heirs and your charities. If you're saying, "I still might want to spend a bunch of millions after I retire, I want to spend $1 million a year in Europe, and I don't want to give it all away," it does not belong to the United States until the Hague Convention. At that time, you could only do it if you did an Isle of Man Trust, Bahamas Trust, or Cook Island Trust, where their country said, "You have a lawsuit-proof trust even though you name yourself as a beneficiary." Legally, you can say, "I don't own all that stuff in that trust," but you still can get it all and have access to it all.

Solomon: I have an irrevocable trust. I have one that's in the state of Georgia, and then I have one that you guys set up for us. We have a few of them, so I don't own the trust. If someone had an irrevocable trust that was set up, do they have any ownership with that trust?

Kevin: They have *beneficial* ownership. The trust is lawsuit proof because in the Isle of Man, Cook Islands, or Montserrat, the irrevocability still allows for that. Before 1987, in the U.S., you had to give up both types of ownership, the legal title ownership and the beneficial use of all the assets. These other countries have evolved. Business owners have a right to lawsuit protect their assets, and they can still name themselves as the beneficiary and have all the use of their money and assets, but they need to put it into this trust. It's still your estate, it's still all yours to use, but if you get sued and somebody says, "You haven't written me a check yet," because they say, "Under penalty of perjury, you need to list everything that you own," you can legally say, "This is what I own, and I do not own these particular assets," because the law says an irrevocable trust is an ultimate owner. Having a beneficial interest isn't enough ownership for you to have to legally say that you own this company, that company, or that bank account.

Solomon: Legally, I would not have that ownership.

Kevin: No. But you do have the beneficial ownership to go, let's say, to a bank for financing or to have use of those assets.

Solomon: Kevin, I want to know a little bit about minimizing the risk for companies and families. What is the true benefit, and how do you minimize that risk for companies?

Kevin: It's the whole process of lawsuit protection. You think of minimizing risk, do you have a good policy and procedure you fall on? That's all the normal stuff, but that can't control a lawsuit or the outcome if you do get a lawsuit. That's the arena that we work in. The basics that people have to understand about lawsuit protection boils down to, if you [legally] own it, it can be taken, even if it's a deferred right. Somebody owes you some money, it doesn't start for five years. That judge is still going to go to that person and tell them, "Instead of it going to Kevin Day, you will be paying Mr. or Ms. Plaintiff here." They can do judicial foreclosures and all the rest of it. This is logical and it's good.

They didn't have all the good strategies and structures available to them. They go, "My wife and I own these different businesses. We own this real estate and we're going to be the lightning rods. Let's put the cash, portfolio, and something else that's high value in our children's names." They have a lower lawsuit profile. What happens if they get in a freak car accident, or they get a divorce? What the parents thought was part of their estate is now being taken. They did the best that they could do. You go to a corporate lawyer, a real estate lawyer, or a trust lawyer and you say, "I want lawsuit protection." What do they do? You've heard it a million times, "You have this many items. You need eight LLCs. That way, if this boiler blows up, they can't take your home or the other investments."

If you get sued personally, they're coming down and taking all of it. Even if the boiler blows up here and it doesn't get out of that box, you're still losing that apartment building or that rental. Our strategies of creating a separate legal owner recognized as a third party owner under the Law of Trust, give back the control to the client with an underlying privacy company in Nevada or Wyoming and then puts senior liens on the equity. You can't get a lawsuit because there was a horrible fire, and you will still have that home.

Solomon: When you say "senior liens," Kevin, are you talking about UCC-1? What are we talking about?

Kevin: There are two instruments to put senior liens on something, and one is a mortgage or deed for real property, and UCC-1s for everything else. Computers, freight trucks, warehouse stuff, and cash are UCC-1s *(UCC-1s are required for all business loans under the Uniform Commercial Code (UCC) and establish a relative priority over which specific assets may be seized, and in what order, while solidifying the collection pecking order in cases where there are multiple lenders to the same debtor)*. The first in time to the public record, not the contract. If I'm carrying back a note from you and then you get sued or you go to the bank and get financing, and then I go, "We signed a contract a year before, but I didn't tell the world that I had that right." Whoever puts the lien in the public record first will get every dime.

I need to presume that I have to tell a judge everything I've done and still work. We create and work with the client to create the proper consideration, which is a legal term, to make sure that it is a proper deal that this company and this company, even though both are part of your estate, they have enough legal independence that they are entitled. The law, the IRS code, and the corporation code says, "They have to have as formal a relationship as me and Bank of America would have. I'm not going to get any money from Bank of America unless they get a lien. Your little privacy piggy bank company or intellectual property company said, "I'm not going to give you this contact list or whatever it is. This is worth $3 million. I'm not going to give it to you unless you give me $3 million of collateral." You take something that you already have. You put it in your left pocket and the law requires you and gives you all these rights.

Solomon: Does the trustee have to disclose that I'm the beneficiary of my irrevocable trust?

Kevin: They could, under extreme circumstances, but what we found in real life where our clients were under duress is that 80% of the time, the other side doesn't even ask the right questions; they don't even think to ask. They don't even bark up that tree. Some have barked up that tree because they have been in a few places. Of course, if you have good money and interest from a particular finance source, why aren't you going again to that same trough? They might ask, "Do you own this company?" You can say it's tactical. We should be able to say, "This is what we did. We did it five years ago and you can't touch it."

I've not met a litigator that says, "I've seen this 100 times. I can bust through this." You haven't seen this once buddy or gal. They can, but their client spends $50,000 and trying to dig it out. You have to spend $50,000 explaining to the court and the other lawyer what the law is on these trusts. These guys were never trust lawyers or litigators. They didn't come from this field. They don't know it, but because it's a separate legal owner under the law, nobody owns a trust like nobody owns a human. Nobody owns you or me. This trust is stand alone.

Solomon: What you're saying is if I'm the beneficiary, I don't own the assets in the trust. Do I control them?

Kevin: You can't control it at the trust level because then you became a trustee and you also have beneficial ownership, so you've merged the two that make it lawsuit proof, but you can manage the underlying company. Ninety-nine percent of the time, we're creating irrevocable trusts that are dormant trusts. Inactive trust is like a Carnation grandchild or Kennedy grandchild. It has to go to the Bank of New York Trust Department and say, "I need a business class airline ticket for me and two of my close friends, please pay for it. I want a new house in Portland," or whatever it is. That's an active trust.

Solomon: You have been in business as long as you have been practicing law. I know you have many horror stories. Can you share 1 or 2 with us?

Kevin: I'm not naming names, but a real estate owner bought an existing apartment complex. It was eighteen doors. He came on the scene and a tenant said, "We want some lights in the back

because our kids can't play. It's dark when they get home at night."
He granted them that, but he went beyond that and had the office
manager make a little half-court basketball court. He was great, a
good guy. A nice guy, nice gal doesn't mean anything in a lawsuit.
Unfortunately, the manager hired an unlicensed handyman and a
twelve-year-old kid grabbed hold of the chain-link fence and got
electrocuted to death. He was a good guy, being a good landlord
going out of his way to be better for his tenants, but there was a big
lawsuit and a lot of equity lost. It didn't have to happen. He didn't
have the irrevocable trust to protect him. He had been talking to
us about it and he never got off the dime, or like some people,
they got some of the structure but they didn't connect all the dots
and complete it.

**Solomon: It reminds me of years ago when I lost my
nursing home businesses. I kept saying over and over,
"I've got to finish this. I've got to tie it and transfer the
ownership." I kept procrastinating and I never did it. I found
a new building. I needed to pay attention to that and buy
another one. All of a sudden, I had regulatory problems. I
remember being told that if I had done everything I was
supposed to do and finished that process, the buildings
would have been transferred over to the trust, the trust
could have continued to collect rents on the buildings and I
would have been okay. It was tragic because I was at a point
in my life, I lost $118 million. We had over 500 employees
and everything. We had 13 nursing homes, 8 assisted living
facilities, and it was crazy. I was going to kill myself and do**

all kinds of things. Losing $180 million is tough to swallow. I knew it was my fault. I couldn't blame anyone else, because I knew that I should have finished it, not procrastinated, and placed everything in that trust. If I'd done that, I would have still had income.

Kevin: You wouldn't have to start all over again and had to have brought yourself back up.

Solomon: How many people do what I did out of either procrastination or ignorance?

Kevin: Out of 100 people, I hate to say it, there are about 20 of them out of 100. That's a lot, I think. When they've spent good money, they've done little parts but didn't get one last piece that we needed back to do a document. We hound. We pester entrepreneurs. They're entrepreneurs because they like the next thing and they're balancing.

Solomon: They're so focused on the money coming in. It's like, "I'll get to that."

Kevin: Even in an MBA program, I've got an MBA, they never teach you about financial structuring. When I started my firm, I literally started with $500 in my bank account. Within a year, I was still eating law school student steamed rice and collecting a couple of dollars so I could eat at McDonald's. Within six months, I had four attorneys that had offices and employees coming to me to work. They started working for me. I had a vision and it worked out. Going back, it's all about how to make money, reach more people, make a better widget, and come up with a formula that's going to make you and other people satisfied. Nobody says, "Let's pay attention to keeping what you've worked so many years to build."

What I've found with everybody, if you get up to about $3 million to $3.5 million, most of your creature comforts are taken care of, and now you have disposable income. Now there's enough money where the money starts making money. They're not pushing the ball so hard for every single dollar. They've made enough. Once they feel that money can make money for them instead of them pushing the ball, they go, "I never want to start over again."

Solomon: When is the best time for an entrepreneur to start this process?

Kevin: The best time to do it is before you get sued. We don't have a crystal ball that we can figure that stuff out. The academic answer is you do it simultaneously when you start your business. The only way to attack an irrevocable structure is to allege and prove fraudulent conveyance, that you had known of debts to existing creditors and you were setting this up to not have to pay them or whatever. If you enter into a contract with somebody three months later, that's impossible to be a fraudulent conveyance.

Solomon: For my audience, I want to go back and recap that. The best time to establish the trust and to protect their assets is at the time that they start their business. That's when they need to call you.

Kevin: It's hard and we understand that, because entrepreneurs usually scrape all this money together for this new project and they need that money. They need to buy new business cards, a new logo, a website, marketing, and all that stuff. "What's lawsuit protection? I can't afford it." What we can do is we call it Road Mapping. It's to try to see what is the perfect structure that if money was no object, what would we put in place? Let's get economically real. What should we start to do first?

You want to know where you're going and then you can start budgeting for it. Unfortunately, the trust, which is the most solid lawsuit protection aspect that you can have in this country or in Europe, is not entrepreneur friendly. You have to have an underlying company. If somebody is road mapping, nobody wants to go ask a trustee for stuff. Nobody is going to put the checkbook in their trustee's name. We start with the privacy company. When we can budget for it, we want to make sure a company that doesn't have the people's name on it, it can start licensing intellectual property or loaning back.

The best time to establish the trust and protect assets is the moment you start your business.

It's money from your left pocket but if you're using legal constructs, that's what you need to do. There are separate legal people. What it comes down to is, if somebody barks up that tree and says, "Do you own Golden Mountain Funding?" You're able to say "no," because it's in the trust.

Solomon: I know the answer to this, but I'm going to ask this question. If I'm the settlor of the trust, is that ownership?

Kevin: No. A settlor means you settled it, you pushed it all into motion. You might be creating an irrevocable trust for your children and grandchildren, a dynasty trust, that will go on for generations where you're not the trustee or the beneficiary. You're a settlor. You can set up a trust where you're naming yourself as a beneficiary and you're still the settlor. Being a settlor is the giving away process and the formation process, no ownership.

Solomon: Trust Law is so specialized. Why do so many attorneys not know or understand irrevocable trust? What I'm trying to get at, Kevin, is they can't go to any attorney or someone that does wills for a living trust. They need to come to a specialist like yourself.

Kevin: For this purpose, yes, and I don't mean it in a derogatory way, There are a lot of estate planners and all they do is wills and trusts. It's important because they do a lot, they drive down the costs, and you can avoid probate which saves your family $50,000. Instead, you could have spent $2,000, $2,500 to have a trust and then you won't need a lawyer to go to probate court. It's a no brainer. We're talking and losing 4% to 6% of your estate by going through probate.

Solomon: Kevin, I had a friend, she was telling me about a trust that she had out of Charlotte, but it wasn't an irrevocable trust. I said, "That doesn't sound quite right. That doesn't sound like what I have." The attorney told her, "In North Carolina, you don't have to worry about anyone ever taking your home, because they can't." I said, "That doesn't sound right."

Kevin: Everybody has heard of this thing called "Homestead Law." If my house is homesteaded, I get to keep it. In the old days, that's what a homestead was. You wouldn't lose your property. Every state has eroded that law except for Texas and Florida. OJ Simpson had a trust in Isle of Man, that wasn't even touched. He had his pensions that were Arista protected and he tried to sell as much as possible. He bought the biggest value that was in the confined space, that was fully homesteaded in Florida. Texas had such big ranches there.

It's a home of homestead. You think of the ranches, that's the homestead. You had 100% homestead for a guy that had a skyscraper. I figured sixteen stories, he owned the penthouse and everything else was rentals. The homestead covered that because his home was on that property. They changed statutorily. They said, "This is not what the law was intended for." In California, what they do is they still judicially foreclose on your home, and the homestead if you have filed it with the court, you can get $67,000 or $100,000 so you're not a ward of the state and you can go pay rent for an apartment. They're still taking your home. That's what most of all the other states, except for Texas and Florida, do. You get a chunk of money so you don't have to be a ward of the state and you have some rental money, but without an irrevocable trust, you're losing your home.

Irrevocable Trust is the only instrument that can lawsuit proof your business assets, accounts receivable, and your home assets. Most of the other things are either protecting your home, protecting your business, or shielding parts of the business from other parts. This third party outside interaction, an asset is an asset if there isn't any equity in it. If I get a judgment against you and I see Bank of America has 50% or 80% and I go, "Take your lien off. I have a judgment." They say, "That's why I'm there. I get every cent." If there's no equity there, there's nothing to take.

Solomon: Kevin, I have a lot of clients that I consult with on their stocks, to the various companies that I invest in and am taking public. I always tell them, "You need to go see Kevin's law firm. He's the best at what he does." Some people say, "It's too expensive." I say, "But try losing everything you have, and then you'll find out how inexpensive he truly is." They do stocks, bonds, promissory notes, and things like that. And they have asked me, "Does that work? I thought trust law was only for real estate." I said, "No, he was working for me." Can you speak to that, protection for the stocks, the bonds, and convertible notes, that people owe?

Kevin: As a lawsuit protection attorney, our main thing when we start working with a client is an oversimplification, but we say, "Is this high liability, but not very valuable? Is this zero or near zero liability like cash, portfolio, and notes? There's not much viability there, or is this high value and high risk? It creates the main cashflow into the family but it's higher risk. What do we put in the lawsuit protection side? What do we put on the standard normal living trust side? If a client's going to get sued anyway, they're the lightning rod, we're not going to put something high liability with the cash and portfolio or notes, or anything like that.

We have people that have gold and silver, for example. We have a client here that has an incredible real art collection, like in a museum. We make sure, and we do all the documentation, so we can show that it's owned by this legally third party, part of their estate plan, but there's a contract back that they are the one to be the custodians of [their art], not put it in a closet and get black mold on it. It's on their walls, but they're getting paid to take care of them. If a creditor comes in, they can take furniture and everything else out, not foreclose on the home.

Solomon: Thank you for sharing your knowledge and your expertise. How can everyone reach you?

Kevin: My phone number is (858) 755-6672 or <u>Kevin@TrespDay.com</u>. Either one will reach me.

***

Everything starts with the power of belief. Belief in one's own vision can provide the fuel necessary to sustain the journey and ultimately move mountains in your life, in your health, in your relationships, in your career, and in your finances.

***

Meet Les Brown

Les Brown is a dynamic personality and one of the world's most renowned and highly-sought-after motivational speakers. Les is a highly-sought-after resource in business and professional circles for Fortune 500 CEOs, small business owners, and non-profit and community leaders from all sectors of society looking to expand opportunity. As a premier Keynote Speaker and leading authority on achievement for audiences as large as 80,000—Les Brown energizes people to meet the challenges of the world around them.

For three decades he has not only studied the science of achievement, he's mastered it by interviewing hundreds of successful business leaders and collaborating with them in the boardroom, translating theory into bottom-line results for his clients.

Solomon: Welcome, . Thank you for doing this interview. I won't do you justice in trying to say who Les Brown is. I'm going to allow you to say who Les Brown is to our readers.

Les: I speak for corporations, small businesses and Fortune 500 companies. I've spoken in over 51 countries. When I started out, it was unusual to see an African American speaking to the general population in this area and space, and teaching them how to make a point and make a sale. I decided to do this because of a defining moment in my life. I met a high school teacher who interrupted my vision of myself. I was born in a poor section of Miami, Florida called Liberty City, in an abandoned building on a floor, with a twin brother. We were adopted by Mrs. Mamie Brown. I used to have a talk show and I would always end it by saying, "This has been Mrs. Mamie Brown's baby boy."

When I was in the fifth grade, I was labeled educable mentally retarded. I was put back from the fifth grade to the fourth grade, and I failed again when I was in eighth grade. I had this high school teacher who had a personality similar to yours, because I think the vision that you have and what you have put together is to give entrepreneurs and business people a larger vision of themselves, beyond their [previous] mental conditioning. And you're helping them to get the tools and strategies they need that will allow them to have breakthrough experiences in business and go to the next level.

This gentleman, he helped to create a different experience of how I saw myself, and how we live our lives as a result of the story we believe about ourselves. When I was labeled educable mentally retarded, faith comes by hearing and hearing. If you hear something enough, even if it's a lie, you eventually begin to believe it. This defining moment when I met Mr. LeRoy Washington, he was a speech and drama teacher, and he asked me to do something. I told him I couldn't do it. He insisted, and to make a long story short, the other students started laughing and saying, "He's Leslie. He's got a twin brother, Wesley. Wesley is smart. He's DT." "DT" as in "the dumb twin." I said, "I am, sir." He then came to me from his desk and he said to me, "Don't you ever say that again. Someone's opinion of you does not have to become your reality." At that moment, he interrupted how I saw myself.

Solomon: A lot of minorities are starting to go into business. They take what little monies and resources they have, whether it's from their 401(k)s, pension or equity in

their homes. What would your words of wisdom be for them?

Les: The primary ability for them succeeding, in addition to them mastering the knowledge and skill in their area, is mental resolve.

Solomon: What does that mean?

Les: Over 90% of businesses fail their first year, so you want to fail your way to success. Walt Disney filed bankruptcy seven times and had two nervous breakdowns. You're going to fail your way to success.

Solomon: That is one of the things I normally say. People want to go in business and they think they get a few business cards, open a website, things like that, and that's it. I say, It's a lot tougher than that. It's going to get lean.

Les: Ask for help, not because you are weak, but because you want to remain strong. In the times that you're prosperous, you put it in your pocket. Those lean times are character-building experiences and you learn things about yourself and how serious you are. I remember there was a lady in Detroit, Martha Jean "The Queen."

She had a radio show. She had a speech that was her signature message, "Do you really want to win?" That winning comes at a price. That winning requires sacrifice. That winning requires that you be willing to do the things that others won't do, in order to have the things tomorrow that others won't have. I remember when I started out, they used to tell me, "There's no way that you'd be successful as a speaker and speaking to corporations. There's nobody that looks like you. That's not going to happen. You have the complexion of rejection."

Solomon: My mother taught me that opinions are like behinds. Everybody's got one. I remember I paid a guy to give me some pointers of what it took for him to become the first African-American vice president of Ohioville. He spent a whole day with me. I paid him for his time and then he told me afterward that he wouldn't hire me. I said, "Why?" He said, "Because I know you and I can't justify it. You don't have any college education.

Les: Because you didn't have a college education, he would not hire you.

Solomon: He could not justify it, making the allocation to pay me. I don't hold a college degree and I work in an industry taking companies public and raising millions of dollars for companies that are going from private to public, or who need access to capital. Everyone thinks getting capital is easy. When I was down and out, years ago, I went to one of your books back in the day. In my spirit, Les Brown's books and audio, it was in my head so I got myself up. When you're down and out, you have no faith, everything is lost, everybody is telling you to give up and go get a job somewhere, what does Les Brown say?

Les: I was engaged to someone that I loved very much and she invited me to go to lunch with her, and she invited a friend named Roselyn. Roselyn asked me, "What do you do, young man?" I said, "I'm a motivational speaker." She asked, "Who do you speak for?" I said, "No one yet. I will be speaking for major corporations all over the country, and around the world." She asked, "What college did you attend?" I said, "I have no college education. In fact, I was labeled as educable mentally retarded and put back from the fifth grade to the fourth grade, and I think that's going to give me an advantage when I tell my story." She then said to my fiancée, "Mildred, can we go to the restroom for a moment?" They stayed in the restroom for a long time and when they came back, her friend Roselyn said, "Bye, Mr. Motivator," and Mildred's eyes were red. I could tell she was crying. I said, "What's going on?" Roselyn, referring to me, said, "You should not marry him." I said, "Why?" Mildred then said, "She is a psychiatrist and she said you're suffering from delusions of grandeur." I said, "Is that a bad thing?" She said, "Yes, you are crazy." She broke off the engagement.

Solomon: You must have been devastated.

Les: I was devastated. She said she would be unevenly yoked. She was an ophthalmologist and there I was with no college education and sleeping in my office in downtown Detroit and hiding in the closet when the janitorial staff came in to clean up. Let me tell you what happened. I spoke at a place called The Church of Today. I did a six-week series, and the sixth weeks, because of my commitment and not giving up, news reporters came out to interview me to find out what was it that I was doing that brought over 2,000 to 3,000 people out to hear me do this series called *Choosing Your Future*. One of the King brothers, Michael King *(of Kingworld Entertainment)*, saw the interview and he called me the next day and said, "I'm looking for someone to be a Black Jerry Springer." I said, "I'm not your guy," and hung up.

Solomon: You passed up an opportunity that wasn't for you.

Les: I said, "That's not me," so he called back and said, "I'm going to send you something and you are to call me." I said, "Don't lose any sleep over it." Three days later, I heard my secretary said, "This can't be real." I said, "What's wrong?" She came in and she showed me a check and a contract and the check was for $2.5 million. He offered me $5 million to do a talk show and they made a $2.5 million deposit. I was blown away. I'll tell you, this thing called life is interesting because what are the chances that he would be watching me do that television interview that day. I was being interviewed and it caught his attention. I encourage you to make the word "No" and rejection your vitamin. There's a scripture that says, "Commit thy works unto the Lord and thy thoughts shall be established. In all thy ways, acknowledge him and he shall direct thy path."

The keyword there is commit, the difference between commitment and involvement in the dream. The next time you have bacon and eggs, look at it. The chicken was involved, but the pig was committed. He had to give it all up and why? I had given it all up. I burned the bridges. I was no way thinking about going back to working for someone else. I'm not mentally fit to do that. I was determined that I was going to make my mark in this area of speaking. People say, "There's no way you can do that. There are over 3,000 speakers. There's no way that you can make yourself stand out." I did, because I was willing to commit myself to do the work.

Solomon: I want my audience to understand what Les is saying. I've had more failures in business than I have had successes, but my successes trump everything, collectively. The experience and the knowledge and the wisdom that we get and learn to go through a struggle, going through a difficult time must not be discounted. It must be placed in the credited column, because you're going to be able to spring off of that. Within my portfolio of businesses, I've got the fifth-largest energy company in the United States. That's a minority-owned energy company. You know about the technology and everything that we control. If I hadn't heard one of the greatest motivational speakers in the world, Les Brown, I might not be here now.

Les: You've got to monitor what you say to yourself. Studies indicate that over 85% of our self-talk is negative. There was a guy who was awarded the Nobel Peace Prize and part of what he won it for was that he said, "When something happens to you of an adverse nature, do not listen to your first thought when that happens." He said, "Let the time pass before you look at it and make a decision." When you make a decision based upon appearances, that would be the wrong decision. I submit to you that when something happens to you, that you have to stop, take a breath, look at it and put it into perspective. At that moment you need to ask, "What is it that I don't know now?" I used to be a state legislator in Columbus, Ohio from the 29th House District.

When I won an argument on a piece of legislation on the House of the Ohio Legislature, I won because of what I knew. If I lost that debate around that legislation, I would have lost because of what I did not know, and that would cause me to go back to the drawing board. Einstein said, "The thinking that has brought me this far has created some problems that another way of thinking can solve." Part of what I encourage people to do is ask for help, not because you are weak, but because you want to remain strong. Ask for help and don't stop until you get it. Sometimes you need another perspective to look at it and to let you know, "Here are some other options that you have." Many times, you can't read the label if you're locked in the box. You are able to get some other thinking and some fresh eyes.

The other thing is you've got to be willing to be persistent. Og Mandino wrote [the book]. He is a good friend of mine. He said, "I will persist until I succeed," so even a broken clock is right twice a day. I kept on knocking. A guy told me that there was no way that I was going to make it. His wife asked him, as they looked at me getting into my car to drive away, she asked, "Do you think he's going to listen to you?" He said, "No, because he doesn't know enough to know he can't do it."

Solomon: I think that was me. I think I didn't know enough to know this probably won't work, or maybe I should stop. I was dumb and foolish enough to keep barreling right on through, and I ended up on the other side.

Les: You don't know enough about yourself to be cynical. I think you have to be intelligently ignorant. We have the ability to do more, but because we live in a culture where we've been told more about our limitations than our potential, most of us surrender and we have a limited vision of ourselves. You can't fit a big dream into a small mind. That's why mental resolve is important, because as you begin to expand your awareness of yourself, you expand your awareness of what you can do. The Laws of Aerodynamics always existed, but because we did not know about it, we were not aware of the Laws of Aerodynamics. We rode the backs of animals. As we expanded our vision, we began to look for other ways to transport bodies around the world and out into space.

Self-awareness, taking a personal inventory of yourself, constantly studying to expand your knowledge and your experiences. Helen Keller said, "Life is either a daring adventure or it's boring." Upgrade your relationships. Dennis Kimbro said, "If you're the smartest one in your group, you've got to get a new group." I sat on a board with Bishop TD Jakes and he came in and said, "The meeting is now open. Listen to me clearly, as soon as I know as much as all of you around this table, you're fired." What was he saying to us? He has us there because there was something we knew that he did not know. As soon as he discovers that his knowledge is comparable to what each of us brought to the table, he would get us out of the room and bring in some people that he had more to learn from.

Solomon: What you said is powerful. They were smarter than him. He recognized that he had to surround himself

with people who were smarter than he was. But the moment he obtained all that knowledge that they had, he knew he had to graduate and get a new group.

Les: And what Alvin Toffler said, "We must learn, unlearn, and relearn," because this is the era of what he called the three Cs: accelerated change, overwhelming complexity, and tremendous competition. As we speak, I can have this interview with you with holograms and do it in 50 different countries. That technology is available because technology eclipsed geography. We have to run to stand still and stay on the cutting-edge because this is where we are. Artificial intelligence is replacing over 20,000 jobs a month.

Solomon: I hear all the time people from my audience say, "I'm Black. Everything's against me." They may say, "I've been arrested or went to prison. I can't get a job," or something of that nature. "No one will give me an opportunity." To those people, what do you say?

Les: There are three things that would allow you to make it. Number one is mental resolve. Two is increasing your skillset in some areas that are aligned with your passion. Three is creating collaborative achievement-driven and supportive relationships. Let's deal with the issue of, "I have a record." Don King who became a dominant promoter in the boxing world stabbed a man to death in broad daylight in Cleveland, Ohio, and went to prison for manslaughter. While he was there, he studied the boxing industry, he came out and decided that he was going to become a promoter.

Solomon: What you're saying is Don King took the time to do the work to become professional and an expert in the boxing industry.

Les: You have to find something that you're going to master, something that becomes your magnificent obsession. I don't get paid $70,000 an hour to speak. I get paid $70,000 an hour for the value I bring to that hour, for the experience that I'm able to orchestrate that will transform that audience, individually and collectively. The reason that I'm being flown to Dubai with seven of my staff, first-class and paid $225,000 is because of the experience that I could orchestrate that will impact their bottom line. That's the name of the game. Oliver Wendell Holmes said, "Once a man or a woman's mind has been expanded with idea or concept or experience, it can never be satisfied with going back to where it was." As small business owners, we have to create an experience with our customers to increase repeat business and referral business.

Solomon: One of the problems that I've noticed with minority businesses is that they don't want to spend the money in the right places, to purchase the right resources that will help them to graduate and make that leap. Can you speak to that a little bit?

Les: I spent years going to seminars and workshops, and reading a minimum of 2 to 3 books a month, and thousands of them. You want to be current. Things are changing fast. You have to run to stand still. By the third year of college, the curriculum that you have studied is already obsolete. Things are changing rapidly. I'll be able to leave a business for my children that my children, my grandchildren, and my great-grandchildren would be able to see me through a hologram teaching the class, and in my voice. The information will then be upgraded to match that day in the data that's available on that particular day. I'll be teaching from the grave. That is the time that we're living in. Tony Robbins, people have seen a hologram with him and other speakers, now, training in several cities simultaneously. They did this test with 2Pac and Michael Jackson. The game has changed in all of our industries. You expand, or you're expendable. This is no time to sit on your laurels. There's a book called . You can't be average. You've got to find something that's you, something that is your magnificent obsession. I was born to speak. I talk in my sleep.

Solomon: You were born to speak and I was born to finance companies, put deals together and see what other people can't see. A lot of people say, "That company won't work. Don't put money into that. That's not good." I'm like, "No, I think we've got something here," and it always works out. I don't know if it's the many years of experience or if all the failures that I had allows me to put the dots together quickly for the quick successes from all that hard work. What do you say?

Les: I think that hard work is important. I don't think that billionaires are born. I think they're nurtured and they're developed. If my birth parents came in here, I would not know either one. No one could have convinced me by giving a 90-minute presentation at the seminar of the century with T.

Harv Eker who wrote , that I would be able to earn $410,000 in 90 minutes. I had no idea that was available for me. There are things that we can do that we don't know that we can do. It is important what you're doing, you're opening up people's minds saying, "We have access." You can point to the problems that we face of racism and discrimination, or you can find a way to win and that's what you're doing. You are giving people the tools that they need, access, how to get into the game and win. I remember Jackie Robinson said, "Don't make it a level playing field. Let me on the field and I will level that myself." I say, "Just give me the mic." I told my kids when I die, don't let them embalm me for three days. Sneak in the morgue and put a microphone in my hand. If I don't grab it and say, "You've got to be hungry," you could call your brothers and sisters and say, "He's gone now."

Solomon: Tell us the name and the title of your [latest] book.

Les: It's called *You Gotta Be Hungry*. If you have the complexion of connection, you can have a burning desire.

I know a thing or two because I have seen a thing or two. It's been exciting. I used to think people in their 40s are old, but now that I'm 75, I believe I was a waiter at the Last Supper. When you are doing what you love to do, there's a joy that comes with it that passes all human understanding. I don't get paid for the speeches. I get paid to get on an airplane. That's what I tell them, to get on another airplane and I look forward to it. I never ever get tired of what I do. I was taught and I do believe this via Mr. Washington, that inspiration, motivation and encouragement are perfumes you can't sprinkle on others without getting a few drops on yourself.

If the audience walks away with 10% of what I provide for them in that experience, then they got something. I want to impact people and live a life that will outlive me because of the impact that I'm able to make with the people that I train and influence, and the people they train, influence and make their mark with. Oliver Wendell Holmes said that we should be ashamed to die until we've made some major contributions to humankind.

Solomon: I know you have a training program that teaches and trains speakers. Can you tell us a little bit about it?

Les: I work with a select few people. I don't work with everybody. We do a vetting process, but for those of you that are interested, they can email me at <u>LesBrown77@Gmail.com</u>. What we do is we conduct an in-depth interview to extract your story in those special moments, then show you how to organize that and develop a master keynote [speech] that allows you to go national and international. I've earned over $65 million in this area since I've been doing it.

Solomon: I would like to thank you for doing this interview.

Les: I want to thank you for interviewing me. Out of 51 years, I probably have been interviewed by someone that looks like me, maybe eight times. Ninety-nine percent of my clients are white. I'm not complaining. I feel like Jesus, "Whosoever will, let him go. He who has fear, led him here." What I'm saying is that I'm so appreciative of you, I have to contain myself being able to talk to you and to be on this program and have this moment with you. I hope your audience gets some value out of it.

CHAPTER 13

—·—

STRUCTURING YOUR BUSINESS

"Be clear about your goal but be flexible about the process of achieving it." – Brian Tracy

There is a lot to unpack here so I am going to touch on a few business topics that you will need to be aware of if you are a business owner or entrepreneur with the big picture in mind. By now we have discussed the history and psychology associated with people of color losing with money for far too long. We have discussed bad money habits in detail, where they come from and how to break those habits for a brighter financial destiny for you and future generations to come. We have covered how to respect, save, and invest money, and how to avoid unproductive debt. We went through some smart strategies for building a net worth and creative ways to position yourself as a business owner, property owner, and financial head of your family unit.

While many of you reading this book receive salaried wages and a W2 from an employer, some of you are in business for yourselves as either solo entrepreneurs or small business owners. Some of you might be aspiring business owners looking for insight to point

337

you in the right direction. In this chapter we are going to delve into aspects of business that you may not be aware of, but that you can either put to use, or simply keep in your back pocket as knowledge for a future opportunity.

For starters, let's talk legal entities. There are a few types of legal entities in business that offer you, as the business owner, varying degrees of protection from personal liability. There are corporations, which are classified as either C Corporations or S Corporations. There are also LLCs or Limited Liability Companies. If you are going to register a new business, you are going to have to determine which one of these is the best fit for your business. You can make this decision with the help of an attorney and/or Certified Public Accountant (CPA). If you elect to set up your company through an online legal processing service like LegalZoom, please get advice from your own networking circle and do your research online. Please note that DIY legal document processing platforms like LegalZoom and others are not attorneys, and therefore they cannot offer you any legal advice.

Limited Liability Companies – LLCs

An LLC provides a great deal of flexibility, does not require a board of directors, and you as the owner are not personally responsible or "liable" for any business liabilities. Your taxation structure is somewhat flexible in terms of when you pay taxes for your business. With a Limited Liability Company you cannot go public. If you have no intention of ever taking your company public and you plan to operate as a relatively small or medium sized enterprise, an LLC might be the right legal entity for your business.

S Corporations

S Corporations are better for smaller corporations with fewer shareholders. Your tax structure also allows you to write off a fair amount of business expenses, lowering your overall tax burden. Unlike with a C Corporation, you are taxed only once and only shareholders pay on profits received. There are ongoing filings and fees in order to stay compliant, stricter guidelines, and all shareholders must be U.S. citizens or U.S. residents.

C Corporations

C Corporations are generally reserved for larger corporations with greater revenue, who have their sights set on going public. With a C Corp, you can have unlimited shareholders which would eventually include your investors, should your company go public. Owners of the C Corp can get preferred stock prior to stock being accessible to outside investors. As with LLCs and S Corps, you are not personally on the hook for any of the company's liabilities. However, with a C Corp, be prepared to be taxed twice and to fill out a lot of paperwork in order to remain compliant.

Sit down with an advisor and do your own homework before you proceed with the registration of your company. When registering a company name, many people do some market research to ensure that they are not infringing on a direct competitor's copyright (what you see visually) or trademark (a company's name). It is also important to do your due diligence to be sure that you choose a name that will be easily identifiable within your industry, and something that will resonate with your target demographic.

Ask yourself: Who will your customers be? How do you intend to get paid? What problem are you solving for people, or how are you disrupting the market in your industry? What do you want people to associate with your business?

These key questions will help you in determining a name.

How will you determine if someone is credit-worthy or not? If you chose to process payments directly, by credit or debit card, by what means will you do that? Will you use a third party vendor like PayPal, or will you process your credit card transactions directly through your bank?

Lastly, is there a set industry standard for payment terms in your industry, and if there is, are you able to break that mold without turning off your customers should you choose to do things differently?

Speaking of getting paid, I want you to really think about who will be paying you, why they will be paying you, and how they will be paying you. Will you be paid in cash? On credit? With 30 or 60 day terms? Prior to service or after service is completed? The way you pay your corporate taxes will be largely determined by how you structure your business, as we spoke of above. And when in doubt, consult with an attorney and a CPA.

Let's talk capital. I know I have repeated myself throughout this book, but there are certain steadfast rules I want you to walk away with when you are finished reading this book. Most businesses fail because of a lack of capital. If you follow me for just a moment, think of a nice brand new car. Maybe a shiny red Corvette that you have just purchased. The Corvette represents your legal entity (the business). Now you need to place gas in that Corvette, yet you have no more money or resources to place gas in your nice brand new shiny red Corvette. And that doesn't even begin to mention insurance, regular maintenance, and repairs.

This lack of foresight is why over 85% to 90% of new businesses go out of business within the first five to seven years. They run out of money and they have no way of accessing additional capital.

Many of you have thought that if you got a big contract, you would be able to access capital. In your excitement, you have overlooked some fundamental things. Just like that nice, beautiful red Corvette, when you bought it, you spent your money on purchasing it, not realizing that it was going to cost so much in insurance, maintenance, gas, and repairs. If you remember, we also spoke about this using the analogy of a home purchase in a previous chapter. A home is great, but what about homeowners insurance, HOA fees, property taxes, lawn care, roof and air conditioning unit maintenance... the list goes on.

As with all major undertakings, businesses need working capital.

As you are now well aware, patented technology is primarily what my team and I leveraged to grow our business enterprise and our personal wealth, so let's start there. While we cannot eliminate the competition, we can certainly do our best to keep them from encroaching on our intellectual property and branding, with the use of trademarks and patents.

Trademarks

Obtaining a trademark can take anywhere from a month to one hundred and twenty days, which is considered a fairly quick turnaround process that is proceeded by an investigation to ensure that your desired trademark is available. Trademarks are a pretty simple proposition. In fact, many of you may already hold one or more trademarks if you have a business. If you do not, you should consider obtaining a trademark to protect your position in the marketplace. Trademarks essentially protect your product or service's brand position so that no one can poach what makes your branding unique and distinguishable from your competition within your industry. Trademarks are managed and obtained through the United States Patent and Trademark Office (uspto.gov) or "USPTO." Here is the USPTO's definition of a registered trademark:

"A trademark can be any word, phrase, symbol, design, or a combination of these things that identifies your goods or services. It's how customers recognize you in the marketplace and distinguish you from your competitors.

The word "trademark" can refer to both trademarks and service marks. A trademark is used for goods, while a service mark is used for services."

A trademark:

- Identifies the source of your goods or services.

- Provides legal protection for your brand.

- Helps you guard against counterfeiting and fraud.

It is also important to note:

"You're not required to register your trademark. However, a registered trademark provides broader rights and protections than an unregistered one."

Patents

Patents protect intellectual properties. How something is designed, how it works, the mechanics involved, etc.

Determining if Your Idea is Patentable

There are some key questions regarding patents that must be answered before moving forward. The questions below will establish your patent viability:

Does my idea meet a specific demand?

Does my idea solve a current or emerging problem?

Is my idea in line with where my industry is going?

After answering the above questions, onboarding a seasoned patent attorney who can act on your behalf to do proper research, filings, and acquire a patent from the U.S. Patent Office would be your next step. There are different classifications of patents, including but not limited to:

Provisional Patents – According to Investopedia, "a provisional patent offers twelve months of protection for a new invention before a patent application is filed." It provides an umbrella of temporary protection from your invention being copied.

Utility Patents – according to Cornell Law School's definition, "a utility patent protects the way an article is used and works.

Design Patents - according to the USPTO, a design patent protects the way an article looks.

The process for obtaining a patent is more complex than the process for obtaining a trademark, and can take anywhere up to one or two years to get approved, sometimes even longer. Many times other people may have similar patents or pending patents. It could easily cost upwards of $1 Million or more to engage a firm and begin the process of preparing to defend a patent.

Cost of a patent. For my part, my team has created a company that sits in the middle, between an inventor and a licensee, doing patent development. Our "middleman" company would do the official writing of the patent and then consult with the law firm who would then file the patent application for us. There are a lot of companies out there who will help you write and get a patent, but if you need to use the patent as protection in your industry and you plan to monetize your patent, you need a more sophisticated representation. As you are probably realizing by what is involved monetarily in getting a patent, large corporations run the show and they are about making sure the small inventor does not poke their head up and get any air. Yes, the world of patents and all of its red tape and high costs are designed to keep the independent inventor locked out.

And before you can even ask the question, yes, it does discourage innovation that isn't born out of a large corporations. There are not a lot of patent law firms to help the little guy, as their high fee structures are all about engaging the business of large corporations. Therefore, your best bet is to have someone in the middle to write the patent and do most of the legwork before a patent attorney files the patent application for you.

The number one rule in the world of patents is: if you can't defend it, it's not yours. We are not talking morals and ethics. We are talking capitalism and large corporations. They will only play ball with you if given no other choice.

Can you find a patent attorney to defend your patent on contingency? Yes, but it is not the norm. Your patent portfolio would have to be so strong that when they take a look at it, they would be willing to defend it on contingency. Sometimes, if your idea is out of this world, a law firm might take you on contingency, but know that they are going to want at least 30-40% because they would be positioning themselves as your partner.

To defend a patent is extremely difficult. Like anything else in the law, you can go in thinking you are 100% right and come out of court and be wrong. Most inventors run out of money and that is where a company like ours EyeTalk365 comes into play. EyeTalk365 is a patent farm, meaning that it consists of patent researchers, graphic designers, marketing people, mechanical people. The purpose of the farm is to seek out bold new opportunities, implements and defend them if need be. We are always researching old patent technology, researching patents on our clients' behalf and seeing where we can profit from it all. All of this holds down the costs associated with working directly with patent attorneys. We come in and help fund it, grow it and build it out. We are essentially funding the build out of a full portfolio of patents, because a few patents doesn't cut it. We then use our attorneys and experts to pursue a patent when we feel it is viable and potentially profitable for us.

Your attorney should be able to advise you on which type of patent to use. Another important patent classification to take note of is a "closed" patent versus an "open" patent. If your plan is to be able to augment an existing patent in the near future, you will want to file for an open patent. If you choose to file for a closed patent, you will not be able to add to that specific patent simply by filing a claim. You will have to acquire other patents through a legal acquisition process in the case of a closed patent, in order to add to the original patent. A patent attorney can advise on whether an open or closed patent is the right decision for your idea or invention.

But Solomon, this was all very complex and discouraging. No, let's turn that around and say it is empowering. Knowledge is power and helps you to move with your eyes wide open and the right resources and/or people in place so that you do not have to stumble and fall countless times on your road to success. You have been given an insider's look into the world of patents and an invaluable peak into how my team and I have managed to circumvent many of the intellectual property and financial roadblocks that too many green inventors encounter.

Know Your Path to Monetization

A solid strategy for monetization equals potential profitability. Patents can be licensed, sold, or directly brought to market. In certain cases, parties that infringe upon your existing patent can be converted into licensees. The best-case scenario is a licensee whose sole job it is to monetize your patent on your behalf. Our company EyeTalk365, our intermediary company that I spoke of above, their job was to go out and monetize our existing patents. EyeTalk365 struck a deal with Ring smart home doorbells to license our technology which was then bought over by Amazon. Amazon purchased Ring and that is how Amazon got our patented technology.

Options for Choosing a Patent Attorney or Going it Alone

The most seamless way to file patents correctly is to have an experienced patent attorney assist you in the entire process. The most effective way to find the right patent attorney is through your personal or professional network. Seek referrals for an attorney if one is not directly available to you. The most important element is an attorney that has relevant experience and a proven track record in delivering results. Ultimately, you get what you pay for. Avoid paying any fees upfront until you have an idea of the track record of the professional that you are using and expect to be hit with a retainer fee. Beware of professional stall tactics which elicit fees before anything tangible is delivered.

Alternatively, you can search or you can search the website which provides some step-by-step "How To" information for those who choose to apply for their patent directly through the United States Patent and Trademark Office.

Bringing Large Companies to the Table (Negotiating Your Royalty Deal)

A patent provides a means to protect your intellectual property. Establish a strategy for licensing your IP (intellectual property). Your attorney's goal is to establish barriers to entry, wherever your intellectual property is being infringed upon. The end game is to establish licensing relationships, whereby other parties pay for the right to use your patent/intellectual property. This party or parties would be serving as a licensee of your technology/intellectual property. Not for the faint of heart, many licensing agreements are born out of litigation or the assertion to litigate. Your patent attorney will act against anyone that may be infringing upon your intellectual property rights. Once this precedent is established, your attorney should be ready to initiate litigation proceedings to bring anyone to the table that might be infringing on your technology. One possible outcome of litigation is that the infringing party or parties would then negotiate to legally use your technology by licensing it. Licensing means royalty income streams. Remember our discussion on passive income. This would be one very effective method of establishing passive income.

Licensing Your Patent and Collecting Royalties

Your team, including a knowledgeable patent attorney, will not only create a revenue stream, but they will also ensure that there is an on-going process of adding additional intellectual property to the original patent, creating a perpetual licensing income stream. This methodology not only adds value to the original patent but creates opportunities for licensing to additional companies. Companies approached may be multibillion dollar behemoths. Only by following the methodology above, can a company blunt effort by other companies to take their technology and can proceed forward to prosper in the ultra-competitive world of patents.

If using an open patent, then additional intellectual property can be added using claims to add more intellectual property to the patent. Other ways that patents can be added to your financial portfolio is through acquisition - in plain English, buying up other people's patents. This is typically a way of adding additional intellectual property to a patent portfolio (collection of multiple patents). This is the primary methodology that is utilized when dealing with a closed patent. A technology belonging to a third party is identified, they are contacted, an agreement is then made for the acquisition of the stated patent.

How Can Startups Use This As Part of Their Business Strategy?

The preliminary business strategy must be based upon addressing a need or solving a problem. This provides a place for this product within the current market. It also addresses a potential need that might arise as the marketplace evolves. The information above will guide how you take the technology to market, monetize it, or even deal with aggressive competitors within the market space. Building the right team is necessary to allow you to capitalize on patents. Most importantly, within the business strategy, is a focus on team building, which will allow for the completion of all components associated with securing and monetizing your patent(s).

Patents and A.I. Technology

A.I. (artificial intelligence) allows for more information to be gathered for your end customer. More information can be gathered to create a truly personalized experience that meets the needs of the individual consumer. More devices will inevitably be connected to the internet that feed information to the A.I. on user preferences, needs, and wants (Samsung, for example, allows you to connect with 250 devices). Along with the A.I., expect faster access to the internet and more information gathered over a shorter period of time. Based on increased information, the technology will be able to anticipate what you need. The technology becomes an extension of the individuals' needs, wants, and expectations.

Taking Your Company Public

There are myriad myths about taking a company public versus keeping your company private. Most of the misconceptions associated with public companies are perpetuated by people who have not realized a certain level of success within their business. Let me start at the beginning.

Here's the reason I always felt the need to have a publicly traded company. As a minority in this country, I am always looking for a way to circumvent the word "No," rather than feeling defeated by it. I believe that taking a company public can be an effective and quite powerful tool for gaining substantial working capital for a company when more traditional methods of raising capital are not feasible.

Approaching banks and asking for business loans or lines of credit may require you to have three years of personal financial records in order, as well as three years of business financial records in order. Banks want to see proof that you are capable of successfully paying any existing debt on your books, as well as new debt that would be accrued with a business loan or new line of credit.

The majority of businesses are not in a position to be able to provide this kind of information because they are simply too new, or perhaps, because nobody ever took the time to really sit them down and teach them how to organize their financials to suit the criteria of most banks. Many times, I have found that the banks are looking for certain types of collateral for the investment they would be making. Keep in mind that a bank's investment is in the form of a loan that must be paid back with interest. What I have also experienced is that probably about eighty percent of the time, banks tell you "No." If you are a minority, you can take that percentage and increase it.

Banks will have various reasons for telling you no, which would be a whole book in and of itself, so let's move forward. Suffice to say, they simply feel that the risk is too high. I am sure you have heard the old saying that banks only lend money to people who do not need it, or some variation of that statement. That can be disheartening.

Banks are in business to make money. They are not in the business of loaning out their money to people who do not have the financial skills, collateral, or established track record to repay it. They are not in the business of funding your or my dreams. Yes, they do lean toward profiling people with unconscious bias when making their money lending decisions. These are the facts. With all of that being said, I have found that if you take your company public, you have a better shot at raising the capital you need to grow, innovate, and compete in crowded markets. However, keep in mind that this option is best suited for companies already producing seven figures in annual gross revenue. We will get to options for small businesses later on in this chapter.

Why do I need to raise capital? Why can't I just bootstrap my business?

A business absent of funding will remain a hand-to-mouth business. If your business is to grow and potentially become the wealth generating machine that you want it to be, you will eventually need growth capital to cover operating costs, innovate, dominate market share, and to cover future expansion plans. I have also found that growth capital provides you with the funds your business may need to ride out the storms when things are slowed down, or when things go wrong.

Never was there a better example than online retail juggernaut, Amazon. Amazon was publicly traded and had been losing money for many, many years before they turned a corner to financial stability and eventual profitability. That same company as a privately held company would not have been able to survive without the additional capital that being a publicly traded company provided. Typically, all banks would have told them "No," because of their financial condition and their poor track record of losing money and chronically being "in the red," as they say. There would not have been a place for the bank to position its money with Amazon. With that being said, that would have left Amazon with the options of approaching private equity or venture capital investors.

Many privately held companies will approach and pitch private equity or VC (venture capital) investors when they feel they have a strong and competitive business plan. For this type of investment, if you are lucky enough to get in the door and be able to pitch these types of investors, you will likely be confronted with automatic racial, cultural, and gender bias that you will have to try to overcome. It is possible, but it will not be easy. I have heard time and time again from people who have successfully raised this kind of funding that it is a "white boys' club." Yes, you read that correctly. I promised to give it to you straight, and that is exactly what I am doing. White men are automatically met with a bit more enthusiasm when pitching VC and private equity investors, while women, men of color, and even people of minority religions are often looked upon with skepticism in investor circles. Can a minority raise rounds of VC or private equity funding? Yes, it is possible, but you are fighting an uphill battle and you'd better have some solid advisors and strong introductions on your side, not to mention an airtight pitch presentation. This is because you will not be given the benefit of the doubt when trying to penetrate this club.

If you choose to go this route, working with an expert who can mentor you, help you prepare your presentation, and guide you in giving an airtight pitch is an absolute must. Do not go it alone. There is no room for error, particularly if you are female and/or a person of color. Even after dotting your i's and crossing your t's, you will face an arduous uphill battle and collect quite a lot of "No's" on your journey toward attempting to secure this type of funding. If you do get an initial "Yes," you will then be put through an exhaustive process called "Due Diligence," where your personal, professional, and financial background will be thoroughly vetted and scrutinized. This process is not for the faint of heart or for an unguided novice. Most companies who succeed in this quest either have the backing of a well-respected accelerator/incubator program, or a well-established mentor guiding their path and making strategic introductions on their behalf.

If all of the above is in your favor, sometimes VC or Private Equity investors, if they believe that you have a good management team, a solid business plan, and a truly disruptive and game changing business, will jump in and ride that wave with you. However, you will no longer be calling all the shots, as those types of investors most often have one of two things in mind. They will either want you to grow at breakneck speed to eat up market share and crowd out your competitors to eventually be bought out (acquisition by a larger company that views you as a threat), or they will eventually want to take your company public. Either way, there is a good chance that going public could be in the cards down the line.

For investors, the holy grail is a clear exit strategy where they can cash out on their investment with a considerable profit.

When your company goes public, that is one avenue that provides an exit strategy for your investors. Normally they can exit out between ten and a hundred times their initial investment, depending on the company and the volatility of your stock or your shares. In other words, depending on how well your story is told, how well your management team is doing, and what the impact is on your respective industry, your VC or private equity investors can reap huge monetary rewards. And let's not forget, you will also reap huge monetary rewards, as the founder of that company who retains a sizable amount of shares which would typically be between 20% and 30% once the equity pot is divided among your investors.

Conversely, you can invest your own hard-earned money into your business, and it can fail because you do not have access to additional capital to ride out the ebbs and flows that are common to all businesses. Preferably, you could be smart and draft out the correct business plan, with the right advisor assisting you, from the outset. I have always said, when you start out in business, you should first seek out and gauge your ability to obtain working capital. Think of it as the fuel you put in your car. Emergencies are going to happen. Slow-downs are going to happen. Initial missteps are going to happen. You always want to strive for the best, but be prepared for the worst. Being a public company provides capital that you may need at a moment's notice, or to innovate in order to keep pace or outpace your competition.

This is what I have found to be true throughout my thirty-five years as an entrepreneur and businessman. You see, there have been many times when I needed additional capital and banks have told me "No." My family and friends had no more money to give, as I had already gone to them and exhausted their resources. I had no more to give since I had given all I had by refinancing properties and exhausting my own resources. In my younger years, I made these common mistakes, and I hope you will take this information and advice to heart to avoid those common mistakes.

Always. Have. Access. To. Additional. Capital.

If you or anyone you know is in business, stop, and make sure you have access to additional capital, because a rainy day will come. It is said that it rains on the just as well as the unjust – a statement everyone can relate to. You can do everything right. You can have the sharpest and brightest minds working for you and with you, only to have a hiccup that has nothing to do with you or your company, or even your industry for that matter. Just look at the COVID-19 pandemic and all of the economic and supply chain fallout it has created that we are still feeling. Shit happens and it's not always fair or just, but we still need to be prepared. Do you know why more white-owned companies were prepared to ride out our global pandemic than minority-owned companies were? More white-owned companies were flush with working capital.

Some statistics that should (hopefully) act as a wake-up call to the importance of capital.

According to a January 26, 2021 Crunchbase article titled, Black-Owned Businesses Are Still Struggling to Find Investors:

"In 2020 alone, 41 percent of Black-owned businesses have been forced to permanently close their doors, compared to less than 20 percent of white-owned businesses."

A February 23, 2021 CBS News article states, "An H&R Block survey of almost 3,000 small businesses found that 53% of Black business owners saw their revenue drop by half, compared to 37% of white [business] owners, since the pandemic started. Black business owners also had more trouble establishing an online presence for their company and were more likely to have customers submit late payments."

A recent Mashable article about importance of supporting Black-owned businesses and the direct correlation between successful Black-owned businesses and establishing financially sound Black American communities states, "According to a [recent] report from Business Insider in February of [2021], only four of the current Fortune 500 CEOs are Black. None of those four are Black women, either, who face an even larger set of challenges in the workplace than their white counterparts."

Getting back to the point at hand, how do you overcome, adapt, and navigate unexpected business obstacles that you had not planned for?

For me, personally, having my companies be public companies has helped tremendously, both as an effective way to circumvent a slanted financial system and to sustain and grow companies under even the most challenging of circumstances. When you are public, you can place out additional shares to individuals at discounted prices. You can place out additional shares to individuals who are looking to own a piece of your company and who are wanting to be shareholders. They may not have been able to afford to invest with you as a credited investor, like private equity and VC investors/companies, however, they can support your stock by buying it off the open market or through buying additional shares from other people that currently hold shares of your company.

This is a wonderful thing if used correctly. Being a public company is, of course, not easy, as nothing worthwhile is easy. It is extremely regulated, because the government oversees and regulates publicly traded companies and their activities in order to protect all United States citizens, and all potential investors' money. When you understand this, you will also begin to understand that the accounting procedures that a public company goes through also do tend to have more credibility than that of a private company. You will certainly learn what you are made of through this process, and your confidence in business will grow exponentially. You will learn some of the greatest things about your management team. You will learn some of the greatest things about your followers.

Being public is indeed costly, in that it will cost you more money to be public than it would to be a privately held company. Here is where you will want to think about this option very carefully. Being public could cost you anywhere from two hundred thousand dollars to one million dollars per year, depending on the complexity of your business. Much of these expenses are by way of people you will need to hire on your company's behalf, including but not limited to: financial, legal, consulting, IR firms (investor relations), and other people who must be involved to help you tell your company's story.

To tell your story correctly you need advisors as well as a board of directors. You will need these people to help guide you, not just in running your day-to-day business operations, but to help you navigate a public market. As you have heard me directly mention as well as elude to in previous chapters, and a statement that my wife used to say:

"Being in business is more than a notion." She is correct. Being in business is tough. Now, when you add being public to the equation, that makes it even tougher. Running a public company is not like running a private company. Most significantly, there is more transparency in running a public company. You cannot hide behind smoke and mirrors or a false narrative.

More times than not, all of this compliance can make people question whether it was the right decision to bring their company public. I will say this: in most cases you will have made the right decision, in my opinion, on bringing your company public. This is especially true if you want to make an impact on your industry, and if you are looking to lead and manage a team of people.

One of the unique things about being public is the exit strategy it provides to its founders. This type of business provides you with an opportunity to exit, to pay off personal bills, to pay for your children's college tuition, to pay off your home, or to plan for your retirement.

Having a Public Company Requires Transparency

We spoke about transparency and government regulations, which is not necessarily a bad thing, as it teaches you compliance and keeps you organized. Being public does come with increased disclosure requirements. Sharing information with everyone about what your business is doing and how your business is doing is not always fun. The SEC does require that you disclose everything; the good, the bad, and the ugly.

Taking people's money in exchange for shares in your company is a huge responsibility, and therefore, it is not unreasonable for the government to require such transparency from you. You are becoming a steward over other people's money. In previous chapters, we discussed effective methods for becoming a good steward of your own money. It goes without saying that you cannot be an effective steward over other people's money until your own financial house is in order, just like you cannot go from kindergarten directly to college. This book takes you on a financial journey and you must take heed to each step of the journey within these chapters. By the time you are theoretically ready for this step, you will have already mastered the previous steps outlined in this book. Of course, it is perfectly fine and encouraged to read the entire book all the way through to gain the entire scope of what we are trying to accomplish together, and to get your head in the game. But please go back to the beginning and use this book as an actionable and interactive workbook to be applied step-by-step.

As a publicly held company, you are responsible to go out and do a job, a job that your investors may not have the time or the ability to do. They want to be a part of what it is that you are doing because they believe in your industry, they believe in your company's ability to dominate that industry, and they believe in you and your management team. This is why transparency and accountability are so important. Your investors or shareholders will appreciate it.

Understanding that you are no longer the sole owner of your company.

When a company goes public, they set aside a certain amount of shares to sell. If, as a private company, the stock was worth $1 per share and all of the owners and employees participate in this venture and own shares of stock, when the company goes public your employees do have the opportunity to sell some of the stock they own. The company might go public at $5 a share, and if 15 million public shares are sold, this theoretically means that the company is going to raise $75 million. This capital can be used to help fund operations, marketing, product or service development, and acquisitions. It also creates an exit strategy for management, employees and for the founders and initial investors. They can all gain huge profitability for having the foresight to invest in a company in its early stages.

However, as a founder or owner of a company, once your company goes public you are simply a shareholder in your company. You are technically no longer the "owner." Each stockholder owns a piece of your company, and depending upon how much stock each investor owns, determines whether they are classified as a minority or majority stockholder.

Someone can buy 5 percent or 10 percent of your business' stock and become what is known as an affiliate, whereby they are considered a larger shareholder. A majority shareholder owns 51 percent or more. Most founders do not own 51% or a controlling share of their company anymore, but are willing to sell majority shares in exchange for each share they do own being worth much more than 100 percent of their company was worth prior to selling shares of their company.

As the old saying goes, it is better to own 20 percent of something than 100 percent of nothing. There are some rare exceptions to this non-majority stake rule in the case of companies like Ford, Exxon Mobil, and Amazon, where the founders do own a majority stake in their companies.

Mistakes happen, and they have the potential to make you better.

Making mistakes is not a bad thing. Making mistakes is how we all learn and grow. If you have a glowing track record with no mistakes behind you, I have to say, I do not want to be there the day you fail for the first time, because you will not have the necessary coping skills to get through it.

A person who has not been tested, or a management team or company that has not been tested may not survive when they are tested at an inopportune moment. Going through the valley teaches you a lot more than riding high and winning the games. The games that we win are great, but it's easy to accept victory. It's hard to accept defeat. It's how you bounce back that counts. So tell the whole story. Tell about your failures. Let the shareholders know why you did not make the projections, discuss what made you fall short, and what you could have done better. Perhaps the best example of this is our country's most successful investor, Warren Buffet, and his team. Within his own company, Berkshire Hathaway, Warren Buffet does not shy away from the whole story and he does not evade owning up to mistakes or failures. None of us want to see a company we invest in fail or fall short of meeting its goals, but trust me, it happens. And it is not the end of the road. It is only the beginning, depending on what is learned from it.

If a company has learned the lessons from its trials and tribulations, it will go on to be a much better and stronger company. However, if they do not learn the lessons, their company will eventually fail.

Another advantage of being public, aside from a viable and profitable exit strategy, is your ability to hire and retain the best talent by way of having the funds to create a solid company culture, bonus structures, and other incentives for your employees. In other words, it helps you to attract and keep better employees that you would normally not be able to afford to pay.

Quality talent can come and work for you for an equitable salary, in addition to stock, and owning a part of the company. It is a magnificent thing when it comes together this way. It helps you to draw from a top tier talent pool. But please keep in mind, the disadvantage is that other management teams are looking at what you are doing. They are taking your public filings and they are going through them with a fine-tooth comb. They are seeing if they are missing anything within their own company. They are trying to take your secret sauce. So again, I must say being public may not be for everyone. As with anything else, there is an upside and a downside, but I want to provide you with alternative avenues to just knocking on more traditional doors that do not seem to be opening. I want to provide you with options.

From the perspective of a private equity investor

Going public was the right move for me, and something that I strongly suggest to many businesses that I consult with whom I feel are ready for this powerful step; especially when I believe that they have a strong story, a good management team, and the potential to grow by at least triple digits. I analyze the industry, itself, and realize that the industry will be growing by between three to seven percent. That is when I know the company has the right stuff and the makings of a successful public company with which I want to invest my time and money.

As an investor, when I compare a company's management team to that of other management teams and give them a letter grade to see how they would fare, I analyze what their shortcomings are. What are their strengths? Can they do this? Have they done it before? I still must caution anyone thinking about taking their company public, because while the benefits can be immense, the challenges are as well. To take a company public, you must be able to pay for the financial reporting documents, the audit fees, the investor relations department, the accounting oversight committees, the necessary attorneys, the board of directors that will be required to help you govern, and the additional board that will be required (for example: if your company is listed on the NASDAQ, more than one board may be required).

Smaller businesses may find it extremely difficult to afford going public because of the lack of resources currently at their disposal, and that is okay for now, because you are being armed with valuable information that you can draw from in the future. Smaller companies may also find that it is unnecessary to go public or question themselves by saying, "How can I even afford to go public? I do not have any money currently to run operations as it is. I cannot see the benefits of going public at this time."

If you are a startup or small business generating $500,000 or less in yearly revenue, then you are correct. This is not an option for you at this time, and we will discuss another option below. However, if you are generating $1 Million or more in annual gross revenue, but struggling to expand and scale your company, or keep pace with your competition, my only answer to that is, you may not be in business long anyway. This method assures you a way of getting more capital while also providing a way to be able to exit after stockholders have made their investment in your business in the years to come.

If you choose to explore the option of taking your company public, the first step would be seeking the advice of a seasoned mentor or professional consultant who specializes in this type of business structure. Please heed the advice beautifully outlined by Investopedia.com, below.

"Public companies are also faced with the added pressure of the stock market, which may cause them to focus more on short-term results rather than long-term growth. The actions of the company's management also become increasingly scrutinized as investors constantly look for rising profits. This may lead management to use somewhat questionable practices to boost earnings. Before deciding whether to go public, companies must evaluate all the potential advantages and disadvantages that will arise. This usually happens during the underwriting process, as the company works with an investment bank to weigh the pros and cons of a public offering, to determine if it is in the best interest of the company for that time period."

In searching for a concise and accurate explanation, I will again defer to Investopedia.com:

"Going public refers to a private company's initial public offering IPO, thus becoming a publicly traded and owned entity. Businesses usually go public to raise capital in hopes of expanding. Additionally, venture capitalists may use IPOs as an exit strategy, a way of getting out of their investment in a company.

Going public increases prestige and helps a company raise capital to invest in future operations, expansion, or acquisitions. However, going public diversifies ownership, imposes restrictions on management, and opens the company up to regulatory constraints.

[When] listing a company, the IPO process begins with contacting an investment bank and making certain decisions such as the number and price of the shares that will be issued. Investment banks take on the task of underwriting or becoming owners of the shares, and assuming legal responsibility for them.

The goal of the underwriter is to sell the shares to the public for more than what was paid to the original owners of the company."

Not all public companies are on the same platforms

Not all publicly traded companies are created equally. For starters, there are different methods for bringing a company public. Most of you have probably heard the term "IPO" or Initial Public Offering. This is the more popular, and much more costly method by which to take your company public

To make it simple, here is Investopedia's definition of an IPO:

"An initial public offering (IPO) refers to the process of offering shares of a private corporation to the public in a new stock issuance. AN IPO allows a company to raise capital from public investors. The transition from a private to a public company can be an important time for private investors to fully realize gains from their investment as it typically includes a share premium for current private investors. Meanwhile, it also allows public investors to participate in the offering."

IPO – Initial Public Offering

An IPO is the more common and also more expensive method for taking a company public. What makes the process so costly is the underwriting process that investment banking firms take you through in preparation of your public offering. These costs can range anywhere from a $1 Million nonrefundable retainer up to $10 million, or more. This price does not even include their other fees. First, they will investigate your industry and then they will investigate your company. Then they try to see if there is a market for your IPO, and if there is interest in your stock by Wall Street and by the public.

DPO – Direct Public Offering

With a DPO or Direct Public Offering your company takes on this process independently by hiring a specialized and experienced consultant to guide you through this detailed process. You would also hire a finance person to help arrange the necessary financing. This method brings the cost down considerably. Your company may spend somewhere between 250K and 500K, as well as giving up some of the ownership equity in your company.

When a company is looking to go public through a DPO, after hiring a good consultant and finance person, you will need to onboard a good marketing and branding person. These things will be critical to the implementation of a Direct Public Offering. Your management team, starting with your CEO, will need to read up on the capital markets to have a better understanding of how to be most effective in this public space. Your marketing team is in charge of keeping your company's name in the public consciousness, making the public aware of your stock offering. They can help in creating a strong buzz for your stock so that investors know about your stock and can ask their stock brokers to purchase your stock, or they can purchase it directly through an online stock purchasing platform.

Oftentimes management teams do not realize that when you take your business to the public market you are running two different companies. One is the day-to-day operation of your business, whether you are selling products or providing a service. You are trying to ensure that the company is, and remains, profitable and that it has the ability to grow and scale. The second part is the managing of the public company, itself. Managing your stock price and shareholders' expectations is a significant responsibility and cannot be neglected. You must also stay apprised of and keep up with all of your regulatory responsibilities as a public company. You must keep a good securities attorney on retainer as well as a good CPA (certified public accountant). You have quarterly reports that must be submitted to the SEC, as well as an annual report. This typically drives up the cost above your typical business operations.

Can My Direct Public Offering Get Onto Stock Exchanges?

One interesting thing that many people do not realize is that even with DPO – Direct Public Offering you can be on the New York Stock Exchange (NYSE) and the NASDAQ, in addition to the OTC exchange. Normally, to get on the larger platforms your company may have to have revenue of a certain amount. To get onto the NYSE you would likely need annual gross revenue of over half a billion. Yes, over half a billion. Again, we are learning and gathering information that may be of use to you either as a future candidate of a publicly traded company, or perhaps, as a future investor in public companies. Although it is not necessary, it is extremely helpful to reach this annual revenue threshold. Typically, they like to see companies that have a 20% to 30% profit margin. With NASDAQ, you are likely looking at gross annual revenue of $50M or up. What remains the same is investors in the street like to see companies with 20% or better profit margins.

I know what some of you are thinking. There are some companies that go public that actually have a negative profit margin, like Amazon, for example. They were brought public when they were losing money. This is a rare occurrence. I believe what made Amazon the exception to the rule was their scalability and their dominance over the online retail market. People thought they were the only candidate who could accomplish becoming such an online retail behemoth. And like most businesses, they ended up becoming something very different than what they originally started out as, which was simply an online book retailer.

The OTC (Over the Counter) stocks are generally looked at as less favorable, less prestigious and less effective than the NYSE or NASDAQ. However, it is important to note that the OTC Market has changed considerably over the years since the SEC has done an overhaul in their regulations. OTC has a tier that is pretty much on par with the lower tier of the NASDAQ, called OTCQX.

Pink Sheet stocks, although not talked about as much these days, is still an excellent place for new companies to begin on their publicly traded journey, because of the cost factor to get on that exchange. You can probably get there for $150-$250K. A lot of times people associate Pinks and OTC companies with penny stocks. The true definition of a penny stock is a stock that trades at under $5.00 per share. That being said, many of you have seen stocks on NASDAQ and NYSE that also trade at under $5.00 per share.

Make no mistake, a lot of these so-called penny stocks have made people quite wealthy. Some are large companies that have chosen a lower profile in the stock market for various reasons. Although I am not an insider in the workings of these companies, based on my decades of experience I can infer that some of these brands were not interested in being on NYSE or NASDAQ because of less stringent structural requirements and affordability on the OTC. They may have made the executive decision that the higher profile platforms are too costly and time consuming if their company has a lot of other moving parts taking priority.

Additionally, they may not want to deal with the accounting work involved with the larger trading platforms. Some management teams simply do not want to focus a lot of their energy on the public part of their company; it's just not where their main interests lie. Some of these stocks could trade at as much as $50 on the OTC, though some might trade at just a few dollars. I believe the OTC is a good springboard for less experienced public companies to cut their teeth. The smaller trading platforms can also be an effective springboard that can launch your company onto larger platforms as you grow and your shareholders expand.

Your company may not be in the market to raise hundreds of millions or billions of dollars. Your company may only be looking to raise a few million dollars to help with purchasing necessary equipment, innovating new products, and bringing them to market; or to make new hires or acquisitions. For these instances, the OTC market could be the right avenue for you.

Whichever method you choose, you do need to bring in strong advisors, people who have the background and the necessary experience to help you get there, and who can help keep your costs relatively low. Here are some of the requirements:

For many people, taking a company public is the ultimate dream landmark of success, one that is accompanied by a large potential payout. However, before an IPO or a DPO can even be discussed, a company must meet certain requirements laid out by underwriters. The company must have predictable and consistent revenue.

Many of you, after reading this section, are thinking that this is not even close to where you are at, and that is understandable. Let me be clear. This book is meant to provide a broad overview and an introduction to making better financial choices and toward becoming financially literate and confident. If your biggest takeaway from this book is that you begin to think differently about money, and you start to dream bigger dreams or become inspired to steer your financial ship in a better direction, it has done its job. With that being said, let's address businesses that are stable and profitable and in need of funding, but are not yet ready to explore the idea of going public.

Small Business Funding Outside-the-Box

Even if a company is only doing a few hundred thousand to a few million dollars in annual gross revenue, or even with no sales, but just an airtight concept to run with, it is possible to explore the OTC market as an avenue for going public. For this to be a consideration, a company must have a solid growth plan. You must show people where you are going with a clear position in the marketplace and detailed roadmap for scaling and expanding your business. There is no specific step-by-step I can offer you in this instance, because it would be uniquely tailored to your company. Many companies out there do not have the right structure, which creates a house built on sand scenario. If nothing else, please consult with those who are seasoned in structuring your type of business and make sure your business is structured properly. I'm talking how you choose to incorporate, how you pay your taxes, where and how you bank, how you get paid, your customer service, production, and so forth.

As a consultant for businesses, I completely dissect every aspect of a client's business, especially when I am considering coming on board as a potential investor. I help companies clean up and structure their business properly to prepare them to be good candidates for accessing capital.

A Friends and Family Offering

This could get tricky as many people feel some discomfort with approaching friends and family for funding. However, it is a viable option and one that can have some success if your ducks are in a row. What you are literally doing is creating a public offering that is exclusive to friends and family aka your personal network. You are offering them a chance to purchase equity shares in your company.

What I would suggest is a well written business plan describing your industry, your business, how your business fits within your industry, how you plan to grow and compete in the market, how your management team compares to other management teams, whether or not your industry is a growth industry or an emerging industry, and your potential to grow year by year by at least 3-5%. You must also be transparent about everything that can go wrong and how you plan to navigate those hiccups and course correct.

You will also need an experienced attorney to draw up an offering document which explicitly states the price of shares in your company, what you expect and what your stakeholders can expect from you and your company. Friends and family does not mean that we don't do things legally and properly so that all parties are protected and expectations are set.

Though you would not be on any public trading platforms, you are essentially serving the same purpose by opening up your business and offering shares to a controlled circle of people in exchange for an infusion of capital into your business.

Lastly, but not least importantly, you will need to provide a clear exit strategy to your stakeholder should their risk tolerance cease or should they wish to cash out their investment or cut their losses. Every investor needs a clear path toward an exit strategy. This allows your investors to decide how long they wish to be invested in your company.

Being a publicly traded company does not mean you are automatically going to be more successful as a business operator and that you are going to somehow be better at your job. You still have to run your business and be a good captain of your ship. It also does not mean that you can automatically stick your hand into the cookie jar and take more personal money right off the bat. If you are fortunate enough to raise capital through the selling of shares of your business, you will have more working capital to grow your business which can eventually lead to a larger salary, but does not necessarily need to lead to a larger salary in the short term. Money is a tool. How you use that tool is up to you.

CONCLUSION

A lot of people have asked me about how I made my comeback after my maintenance company and nursing home businesses failed and I lost millions of dollars and all of my worldly possessions. Although I have candidly shared my journey throughout these chapters, I would like to sum up this book by saying that it was when I realized how to use my unique talents to make people's lives better that long term success and wealth manifested in my life. True success comes when you can use your unique talents and gifts and provide people with a product or service that enhances the quality of their lives. Whether it is a skill or piece of knowledge you obtained through formal higher education at a university, a skill you picked up at a trade school, something that was passed down through your family line, or even a unique skill that you taught yourself, it really doesn't matter. Tapping into that unique skillset or talent and using it to make people's lives better is the secret sauce for achieving success. Implementing some of the financial skills we have gone over throughout this book will then help you turn that success into long-term, generational wealth. Imagine doing something every day that serves your higher calling, puts your God given talents to work, makes other people's lives better, and helps you create wealth.

For me, it was an innate knack for putting the right people together, raising money and putting deals together. Now don't get me wrong and make no mistake. In life, you will fail as much as you succeed if you are doing something right. Why? Because in order to achieve success, you must take calculated risks. I have had more deals fail than I have had be successful or completed. I have had many deals fall through, but I have successfully negotiated and completed more than a hundred deals. But here is the bottom line: I am servicing my unique gifts, helping people realize their business and financial dreams, and I have become wealthy doing it. That is what I want for you, no matter what path you choose to walk.

Another last thought I would like to leave you with is the way I structure these deals.

After I lost everything, my confidence was shot. I lost sight of my own gifts and began to doubt. I am sure many of you can relate to having a low moment when you begin to doubt your God given gifts and talents. You may have even turned your back on them to avoid future pain or rejection, like I did. I went to work on barges, doing manual labor and feeling angry with the world. Now, don't get me wrong. If you do manual labor or work with your hands and that is your calling, then I applaud you because you are doing what you have been called to do. And there is absolutely no shame in a hard day's work. However, my gifts lied in my ability to negotiate deals, and therefore I was not living my truth. If you are currently going through something similar, know that I have been there and I am here to tell you, do not turn your back on your gifts and talents. Rest for a season if you must, process what you have learned, be flexible in your approach, dust yourself off, and build your second act. My mother has always said, "Give away what it is that you need most. If you provide service to someone else and help them achieve what they are trying to achieve, your heavenly Father will help you to achieve what you are trying to achieve."

People had been asking me for months to help them raise money for various business ventures, and I would continuously turn them down because at that time I was holding on to this erroneous belief that if you fail in business once, you need to punish yourself for the rest of your life. I was punishing myself by not using my gifts. Finally, a very persistent friend who would not take no for an answer continued to pester me until I finally relented and agreed to help him raise money for his business.

With my help, he raised one million dollars in the form of credit lines to start his business, but here is the kicker. No sooner did he get the money, he started buying himself new suits and other personal luxuries, saying he needed to "look the part." When I said, "Hey, you can't do that. It is an improper use of those funds, he replied, "Hey, I got this." I was extremely unnerved by his behavior and eventually made the decision to end that relationship. As expected, this gentleman eventually went out of business. Why? He was squandering his gifts, squandering and misusing valuable resources that had been entrusted to him by various professionals, and he was not focused on making people's lives better; only his own. Even if you think no one is watching, God is watching, the universe is watching, and yes, your customers are watching.

Although I was sorely disappointed in his conduct, putting that deal together gave me some of my confidence back, and I realized that I could continue doing deals from the position of a lender with the use of promissory notes.

I began offering my fund raising services to companies in need of raising capital in exchange for promissory notes, which placed me into the position of lender. A promissory note, or what we would call a convertible note, can be exchanged for equity in their company. The great thing about this, I believe, is that I don't share the risk and the ups and downs of the business, especially if the business is already public.

If the business is not already public, I like for them to be on their way to going public soon, at least within a year. This way, I have the opportunity to convert my note to their stock that is trading on some stock exchange. A note places you in the position of a creditor. So in lieu of taking a salary, I prefer to take a note equal to that salary I would normally take for the services being rendered. That is all there is to it. That is my current-day formula, and how I go about structuring my deals to produce wealth.

This also helps the company by freeing up their cashflow to be used in other places. If you should choose to explore this methodology, you may have to supplement your income in other ways, but it pays off in the long run. Of course, as previously mentioned, I look at and scrutinize a company's management team, their board of directors, and their industry. I examine their potential customers, as well as their current customers. Finally, I do not draft my promissory/convertible note by myself. I use seasoned professionals to assist in constructing these agreements.Some might be confused and puzzled because of the risk I am taking by providing my services for free on the front end. "Solomon, you may or may not get paid if the company does not have the means or the ability to pay you." At this stage, I have enough wealth to mitigate those risks. But in the beginning years, yes, there was some risk involved, but I had confidence in my ability to gauge a potentially lucrative opportunity and it paid off. With one particular early deal, I was owed two hundred thousand dollars, which turned into a pay out of a little over a million dollars when all was said and done. The deal also provided great tax benefits, because it was a long-term investment rather than a short term investment.

Lastly, I live by a motto. You don't have to lie, cheat, or steal in business. You just have to do the work. There is no exception for doing the work.

For you, your path may look entirely different from mine, but I hope you can draw upon the words in this book to guide and light your path, to respect your own inner wisdom, your moral compass, your newfound money habits and skills, and most of all, to honor the gifts you bring to the world.

We are counting on you.